Bolt from the Blue

Also by Sarah Miles

A Right Royal Bastard
Serves Me Right

Bolt from the Blue

SARAH MILES

ORION

First published in Great Britain in 1996 by
Orion
An imprint of Orion Books Ltd
Orion House, 5 Upper St Martin's Lane, London WC2H 9EA

A CIP catalogue record for this book is available
from the British Library

ISBN 0 75280 207 0

Filmset by Selwood Systems, Midsomer Norton
Printed in Great Britain by
Butler & Tanner Ltd, Frome and London

For the one and only Tomcat

Author's Note

My father was an atheist.

'Death is the end, Pusscat, and that's that – nothing out there but oblivion.' He was my hero so I too was an atheist and lived my life accordingly. In 1974, I was on location making a film of Mishima's novel *The Sailor Who Fell From Grace with the Sea*, when all that was to change because I received my first Bolt from the Blue.

Walking home at dusk to my cottage on the Dartmouth estuary I experienced a series of revelations, and heard a voice whispering in my head. Later, back home, the whisper told me to light a candle. I put up a great deal of resistance, but the voice – little did I know the same voice was to haunt me for over seven years – commanded me with such quiet authority that I found myself obeying. After I lit the candle the same voice demanded that I sit in a chair over on the other side of the room and control the flame. It was mine to tame, it said.

The flame did indeed seem to be within my control, for it shrank and grew according to my wishes. Was this imagination, illusion, hallucination, make-believe? I was not on any drugs nor had I drunk alcohol. After a few minutes of this silly game of candle control, the intruder, the voice, had picked up on my doubt, for it told me to gather up my energy into a fine line and *will* the candle out.

I knew the candle would go out because of the mass of energy everywhere about me, the same mass I had experienced pulsating into my feet as I walked home that everning. I had no doubts whatsoever: putting the candle out would be a doddle, and so it was. As it went out the voice told me to remain in silence, forbidding me to share this happening with a living soul, thus making the burden at times almost too heavy to bear. I went into a three-year spiritual catharsis, forced to wipe clean my life-tapes, repattern the whole of my father's atheist philosophy and start again from scratch, relying only on silence for comfort.

Life. What is a life? Is it a gift? A lesson? A curse? A blessing? A punishment? Is it a miracle? Karma? Nothing more than random chance? Or are we all part of some overall master plan, having our strings pulled by that great puppeteer in the sky? 'Having our legs pulled more like!' cry the humanists. I am aware that the great minds have chewed over that one for centuries, indeed the aeons of our evolution – many more aeons than we have so far been able to prove, and therein lies the answer. For I believe we all carry the knowledge of everything we ever were and everything we ever will be. This sacred knowledge is neatly locked away in the Pandora's box of our sub-consciousness.

Surely the question is not 'What is life?' but what is my *aim* in this life? Is it to become a great windbag of information or a creature of enlightenment? I don't believe there are any short cuts, for the only way of experiencing those first flickerings of enlightenment is simply to attend to whatever seeps through from our subconscious into our conscious mind when we sit in silence.

The candle going out (and I believe *anyone* can put the candle out at the right moment of openness) was the reason I decided to chart my journey through three volumes of memoirs, starting with the light of childhood in the first volume *A Right Royal Bastard*, into the darkness of my second volume *Serves Me Right*, where ambition, materialism and needs of the flesh take hold, through into the third volume *Bolt from the Blue*, where, after the candle episode, I was able to recall detailed memories right back to six months after birth. After my catharsis gradually I pushed through the darkness into the light. A different light to the intuition and unblinkered blessings of childhood, for I had to go through hell and damnation to try to grasp all over again the knack of living in the moment.

I now see all religions as different colours of the same rainbow, beaming down from one original truth – a truth discovered in silence. I still have a long journey to go before finding enlightenment, but if along the way I can introduce just one person to the undiscovered adventures to be had through sitting in silence and seeking what lies *within*, let alone the possibility of embracing silence as a friend, even master, rather than hearing only the babble of the information age, then this trilogy of memoirs has been worth it, and the candle incident will have served its purpose.

As long as I march on never lowering my values when I'm broke; as long as I continue putting life and the living of it *before* my career; as long as I cause as little harm as possible, I don't feel God – or whoever it is – will be too impatient with me.

So to answer my original question – what is life? To me life is an art form, therefore to live life as compassionately, courageously and wisely as possible is the highest form of art there is.

S. M.
Chithurst, June 1996

Back to Earth

I was arriving home once more. Home in England, the best place on earth. The more I travelled the world the more I realised that England was truly Shakespeare's precious stone set in the silver sea – a silver sea of integrity, or so I had thought, blinded as I was by home sickness. Was I merely a hopeless romantic or was it still possible, in the autumn of 1972, to detect remnants of integrity's flotsam and jetsam floating on England's high seas?

What a relief! Not only were my feet secure once more on the best soil on earth but I was to be reunited with the best man on earth, my husband, Robert Bolt, who was bunged so full of integrity that surely, one day, some of it might rub off onto me. Any minute now I would be safely entwined within those Dutch-barge arms of his.

Wonderful, isn't it, the power of love? When no love awaits you at the airport gates, those tired suitcases look irredeemably drab, crawling snail-like around their carousel. But if a loved one awaits, the suitcases come bobbing merrily down. That day at Heathrow, waiting with Tom, called Tomcat, our five-year-old son, his hand gripped tightly in mine, the suitcases came jigging along, perky as pie.

As I helped the porter pile up our trolley (for some unfathomable reason, movie stars get help without asking for it), Tomcat began leaping up and down. 'Is this England, Mummy?'

'Yes, Tomcat, we're home – look, there's Daddy!' Clear of Customs, we watched Robert push his way forward from the crowd and climb over the barrier in a most harassed fashion, whereupon someone dressed in brief authority firmly escorted him back whence he had come. What was up? Our reunion, which should have been pure heaven, with Tomcat digging his excitement deep into the palm of my hand, was already marred by mystery. I ploughed on regardless,

1

determined to reach Robert's outstretched arms, my safe haven, for they were all the home I needed.

'Darling!' But as the three of us hugged in those first few seconds and I felt the ache of the past two months miraculously lighten, Robert brutally cut it short. He pushed me back. 'Quick, follow me!' Flashing lights were suddenly everywhere.

That day it was impossible to dodge the media at Heathrow. They swarmed at us with the greatest lack of sensitivity – even for them. My Knight in Shining Armour protected us as gracefully as was possible under the circumstances.

'I hadn't reckoned on this, Robert – I'm sorry.'

He gave me a look. 'You'd better start reckoning because they're not going away – just like David Whiting.'

Right on cue one of them pushed his way forward. 'Is it true? David Whiting was murdered?' he asked.

'Suicide,' corrected Robert. Murder was never proved.

'Perhaps Miss Miles would care to answer?' Robert pulled me to the other side protectively, but the reporter followed.

Ironically I was less concerned than Robert over this line of questioning but, then, I had the strength of knowing I was innocent. I wasn't ashamed to speak out. 'I have no idea whether it was murder or suicide.'

'Come on, Miss Miles, you must have *some* idea.'

'None whatsoever.' The truth sounded good, even making me *feel* good for a moment.

'D'you think your marriage can last?'

Robert pushed him aside with uncharacteristic vehemence. I'd only witnessed Robert's temper once before, but now it was rising dangerously near the brim. 'Bugger off! I won't be telling you again!' Robert resembled Betty, his Staffordshire bull terrier pup, as he squared up to challenge the wretched hack.

'I suppose you'll be moving out of that beautiful Mill House of yours?' How *dare* he? But I was to be stunned a second time because Robert biffed him one. The only other time I had seen Robert raise his fists was the day he had protected himself from a David Whiting onslaught. That had been when David finally left our home after three years of overstaying his welcome.

How could a stranger overstay his welcome for three whole years?

David was the West Coast showbusiness correspondent for *Time* magazine and had come to stay under the pretext of doing a cover story on us. He never left. Each time we threw him out he attempted suicide. To blackmail us in this fashion was unforgivable, but we found ourselves surrendering to his wishes, which were to be back in our home again because he had no family of his own – or so he claimed.

Three years previously David had been my lover briefly. Only Robert knew of that fleeting affair, although many were aware of David's dangerous obsession with me. After he had made three no-nonsense suicide attempts, Robert and I, not wanting to take responsibility for his death, decided that he should become my business manager. Soon thereafter he secured for me a plum role in the film version of the best-selling novel, *The Man Who Loved Cat Dancing*, opposite Burt Reynolds. As I recorded in *Serves Me Right*, while I was filming in Hila Bend, Arizona, I found David Whiting dead on my bathroom floor in our motel, with Tomcat playing only a few feet away. Twenty years later the gruesome memory still lingers. There were three verdicts: suicide; murder; suicide. I was indirectly accused by the media of foul play.

Only those who have been mauled by media intrusion could know what I went through. The shock of finding a friend dead on my bathroom floor – especially a friend whom I had dutifully prevented from committing suicide on three previous occasions, and with that same friend having been Tomcat's close buddy for three years – was quite enough without the media adding false accusations.

Nonetheless there *are* questions that need answers. Why did David choose to kill himself – if he did, for the mystery still lingers – on *my* bathroom floor in the public glare of location filming? Had it been his desire to make Robert a public cuckold? I don't believe so because David hugely admired Robert, worshipped him even. No, I think there *was* foul play that night in Hila Bend.

As it happened, seven years later I was given information that would certainly have cleared my name, but Robert was against acting upon it. 'Do you really want to drag the whole sordid affair through the courts again just because a few people still suspect you of murder?' No doubt he was right but, then, he wasn't the one who had been accused of murder. Still, my conscience is clear so what does it matter?

Purring silently along the A3 to Guildford, homeward-bound in his open maroon Rolls-Royce, Robert perused me. 'You've aged con-

3

siderably.' Never one to pull his punches, was Robert. 'May David rot in hell. He couldn't have you, so he destroyed you.'

I studied my husband's classic profile. Fine dark hair, full brow, enormous, slightly bulging periwinkle eyes and noble aquiline nose. His mouth embarrassed him for he found it too small, but to me it was perfect. A determined chin and a surprisingly delicate neck sat slightly out of place above his strong barrel of a chest, all so beautifully familiar. Would our love survive?

The Knight's Tale

Robert Bolt was born on 15 August 1924 in Sale, Manchester. He was the second son of Ralph and Leah Bolt. Leah, maiden name Binion, was a junior school mistress from Lancashire with a more Bohemian, academic background than Ralph, even though her father had been born in the workhouse. Like John Miles, my father, Leah had plenty of Welsh ancestors to spice up her blood. When she met Ralph at a tennis-club party their differences were blotted out by their individual intelligence and immediate mutual attraction. Thus their courting began.

Ralph was the fourth son of John Bolt, a dreamer who upped sticks and sailed the whole family to Canada in a madcap desire to become a farmer, a man of the earth. This turned out an abysmal failure, signalling the family's return to England where Grandfather Bolt started a furniture business. He ended up in a romantic old house in Derbyshire, which held fond early memories for Robert.

Ralph bonded with his elder brother, also called John, who must have been a colourful chap for he left an indelible mark upon Robert's early recollections. Indeed, Robert would talk more about Uncle John than anyone – except, of course, his father, Ralph, whom he revered. Robert would often recount Uncle John's words with great fondness. 'Pretty soon now I'll be at the Judgement Seat,' he'd say, 'and when I get there I'm going to demand an explanation!' On his deathbed, he beckoned the family closer and whispered, 'There'll be tons of scrap metal when this war is over. *Buy it!*' And promptly died. He was right, too. Those that bought became millionaires.

Ralph was a fine-boned, upright little fellow of great integrity and moral fibre. Like his father, he had an eye for furniture, and put this gift to good use by opening his own furniture shop in Sale, which supplied a modest but steady income.

An avid sailor, the name Bolt always delighted Robert. 'Bolt,' he would tell me proudly, 'is a West Country seafaring name. That's us. From sea captains to ships' carpenters.' Many of his relatives came from around Bolt Head Bay in Devon, where the name Bolt is common. With typical romantic fervour, he recognised the West Country as where his true roots lay, and once he was capable of earning his own living, like a homing pigeon he made for the West Country, never returning North.

Robert became a rebel. Possibly his brother, Sydney, through no fault of his own, was at the bottom of this. Sydney was a handsome lad but, more significantly, amply equipped with grey matter. He came home from school continually with top marks. He won a scholarship to his prep school as well as to Manchester Grammar School, whereas Robert, unable to keep up with Sydney's glittering track record, had to be paid for.

Sydney was four when Robert was born, and in Leah's eyes her baby son could do no wrong. Sydney recalls returning from school each day to find Leah billing and cooing over the cot. Was this squawking new arrival in their midst the reason why Sydney worked so hard and became such a brilliant student? Did Robert get into the habit of rebelling because he was never able to crawl out from beneath Sydney's academic shadow? Or was Robert's growing naughtiness more the result of his mother spoiling him rotten? Whatever the reason, at an early age Robert felt inferior to Sydney and was determined to go his own way.

The whole Sale set-up, the intellectual left-wing banter bouncing back and forth at the dinner table, the clever elder brothers and Robert's devotion to his dog Patch, all echoed my own childhood. I can just see Robert creating daily uproar – exactly as I did. Though our creativity was of a different kind, we had both been unable to access it, which gave us a shared bedrock of childhood frustration.

In 1931 Robert began at a private prep school in Sale, where he remained for two years before going on to Sale High School at the age of eight, where it seems he was determined not to learn a damn thing. It was during this period that he and his mother became at odds, for she was unable to have much effect upon Robert's naughty ways. When he got bored with merely making a nuisance of himself, he even took to stealing.

In 1938, aged thirteen, he arrived at the dreaded Manchester Grammar School where his elder brother's footsteps were still visible, shimmering with brilliance. During this period he wrote a one-off essay, almost a novel, which he gave Sydney to read. This tale of the knights of old impressed Sydney, not only for its neat construction but for the persistent effort that had been required to *finish it* – something hitherto unheard-of in Robert's restive nature. But Sydney's glimmering record continued to intimidate him as Sydney won an exhibition to Trinity College, Cambridge.

Manchester Grammar School held no such luck for Robert. He loathed the place and most of the teachers too, and at the age of sweet sixteen, with no hope of passing any exams, he packed it in before it could pack him in, and began work with an insurance firm, little realising how excruciatingly dull and soul-destroying it would turn out to be.

Then, one evening, walking home, Robert bumped into Mr Bunn, Sydney's old history teacher, who had been to the Bolts' home a few times. His first thought was to scarper, for he felt embarrassed and something of a failure at having to confront the one person he not only respected, but to whom Sydney had introduced him.

'What are you up to, Bolt?'

'I'm working in insurance.'

'Contented?'

'No.'

'May I accompany you home for a cup of tea?' Thus good old Mr Bunn took Robert under his wing and managed to persuade him that he was worth a great deal more than he was offered as an errand boy in an insurance office, and to go on a crash course in economics, English and history. How I wish I'd had a Mr Bunn at Roedean, for I would have gone to any lengths to learn if I had had just one teacher I could respect.

Robert worked himself to the bone. In fact it was the beginning of his workaholism, for he never really slowed down until his death in February 1995. Thanks to Mr Bunn's coaxing and coaching, plus a phenomenal capacity for hard work once his mind was made up, he won himself a place at Manchester University.

'In three months!' exclaimed a proud Mr Bunn. 'That's near to a miracle!' It was indeed.

In August 1943, at the tender age of eighteen, Robert was called up to fight for King and country and went into the RAF. Shortly after joining, Robert, by now a fervent Communist, met Anthony Quinton, an equally fervent Trotskyite, and so began their lifelong friendship. Tony's silky smooth upper-crust eloquence, erudite and razor sharp, was a good match for Robert's witty, blunt, economical and Bolt-upright repartee. No two people were blessed with more of a gift of the gab than Robert and Tony. I can see them now, up in their aeroplane, surrounded by enemy guns, arguing over Robert's heroes, Shakespeare, Ben Jonson and the like.

Demobbed in 1946, Robert returned to Manchester University to finish his degree in history. Sydney, having served in India, arrived home with a stunning-looking female – a senior commander in the Indian army, no less, by the name of Jaya Chandran. Robert said that it was plain to see that the pair of them were devoted to one another, and they have been ever since. They produced two exceptionally bright boys: Paul, a civil servant, and Ranjit Bolt, who has recently made a name for himself translating classic French and Greek plays into rhyming couplets, which have enjoyed success at the National Theatre, the Royal Shakespeare Theatre and in the West End.

Back at university, fellow student Jo Roberts greatly took Robert's fancy; it seemed to be mutual and they began to go steady. So it was that Leah and Ralph could finally heave a sigh of relief, for both their offspring were leaving the nest to start building nests of their own.

Letting Go

I woke up one morning, roughly a month after arriving home at the Old Mill, and got out of bed to open the shutters. Lo and behold – the whole view as far as the eye could see was flooded. Gone was the glorious lawn sloping down to the ancient pair of cedars of Lebanon beside the river Wey and instead I saw a complete backdrop of watery mass.

Fred, the ancient gander with an oblong lump on his head, wasn't squawking, which was most unusual. The lump, which gave Fred the air of a Chinese mandarin, was the result of the local butcher having smashed him over the skull three Christmases in a row but failing to kill him. Finally the butcher doffed his cap to Fred and let him off the hook. Wily old Fred always slept on his island in the middle of the river where Mr Fox couldn't nab him.

Why was Fred not serenading us from his island? Where was his island – or the river, come to that? I rushed to the other side of the house and peered through the bathroom window to see if the stableyard was dry. Those Georgians knew how to build, for the house, the Old Mill and the stableyard were all clustered together on a little knoll. Then I saw my horses, ponies and yearlings, stranded on the edge of what had once been a moat.

As I stood there, watching the animals huddling together, I realised I was stranded too. The Old Mill had been my castle for almost seven years. Could Robert and I keep our balance? Could we stay afloat in the flood? Could we retain trust and loyalty against the tide of negative energy coming in from all sides? I doubted it.

Strained silences, broken by the noise of gatecrashing *paparazzi* grew impossible to ignore. We both agreed our love was still there, but something dark was blocking what had been pure and fluid. I couldn't help chuckling at the irony of it: to lose all I had created over the past seven years simply for one night of marijuana-induced lust in a clothes cupboard at the Sherry Netherlands Hotel, New York, seemed banal beyond belief. How short-sighted I had been but, then, how could I have known that one night in a cupboard would send David Whiting to the point of madness? I certainly wasn't *that* spectacular!

The sordid saga never abated. No peace to be had either at home with friends and family or in the village. Curtains curling inwards, culled whispers, tight smiles and knotted brows querying or, worse, challenging my every move. Was it nothing more than pathetic paranoia I was placing on the pavements with every tread? No, for they were there – the locals, the public, the *paparazzi*, the papers. A strong marriage could have survived it, but ours was going through a frail patch and in dire need of privacy and nourishment. Outside I felt stranded, inside trapped by my own sins.

Nothing good can come from a woman's breaking her marriage vows. For truly evolved men I'd say the same, but how many are there of those? More realistic, surely, for the woman to aspire toward unconditional love than bully man for his baser male instincts. Besides, for me the magic lay in the *difference* between the sexes.

I knew the horses weren't in danger as I watched Robert splashing through the flood to secure their safety, but men have to do their 'thing' and Robert was certainly some man! He believed in fidelity and aspired to link up with the more refined part of his hunter nature to achieve it. Yet I had made him a *public* cuckold. Only after I'd broken the marriage vows did I realise how essential they were, craftily designed to uphold the most precious of life's jewels: continuity. I know now that the best of all is mutual fidelity and, failing that, the ability to love without needing to possess. Is not love infinitely grander than mere possession?

In a way I had practised a form of unconditional love during my *amour* with Laurence Olivier. It is of my selfless love for him that I find myself least ashamed. I had always been there for him, yet to break up his marriage with Joan Plowright had never been my plan. Though there were times when I longed to stuff him into my kangaroo pouch and lope away into a selfish sunset – a private dream, but never a plan.

Strange how I had forfeited my secret *grand amour* with Olivier for marriage vows with Robert, which I later went and broke. I knew Robert still loved me dearly, for he wanted us to try again, yet external pressure plus self-doubt had eroded our will to fight on. My head was, indeed, bloody and bowed.

Robert returned from the flood, severing my reverie.

'All the animals are safe.'

'Let's get the boat out.'

Despite everything we had terrific fun that day, messing about in the flood playing St Francis of Assisi together. We rowed across the meadows to make sure our neighbours were safe. They kept free-range chickens and were far from any road. Wet to the bone, floundering about in the water saving poultry, ducks and what-have-you certainly helped to keep less constructive thoughts at bay.

Later, drying ourselves by the fireside with all the animals warm, safe and sound, we looked at each other with a complete and overwhelming sadness, the depths of which I shall never forget. I spoke up quickly, thinking he wanted rid of me. 'I think it's best if we have time apart.'

He shook his head, dumbfounded. 'Fucking press – they've won.'

But was it only the press?

'I'll be the one to leave. Shall I take Tomcat with me or what?'

Oh! I shall never forget the way his forget-me-not eyes filled with longing. His silence sent me on. 'I'll do whatever you want, Robert, since I'm the guilty party.'

He scratched his chin. 'Tomcat ... should be with his mother, I suppose...'

'Yes, probably.' How ignorant I was! Where was I find the strength, let alone the selfless dedication, to bring up my child *without* a partner – it had been hard enough *with* one. We decided that I should take Gladys, my Skye terrier, and Robert would keep Arthur, our Old English sheepdog as well as Betty.

As the flood subsided my emotional body calmed down sufficiently for me to see a way forward. I had been offered a good deal of money to play Sabina in Thornton Wilder's *The Skin of Our Teeth* at the Arlington Towers Theatre, Chicago. My brother Christopher was to direct and went out to start pre-production while I began to tidy up the sad remnants of a failed and lost life, the good life I had stupidly destroyed.

One drizzling autumn afternoon before I left the Old Mill for good, Sarah Gough, called Goffie, my dresser from the time I played Mary Queen of Scots in Robert's hit play *Vivat! Vivat Regina!* was helping me to pack up my life. Thank God, Goffie had agreed to come to Chicago with me. She had such a stalwart, cheerful nature, just what the doctor ordered – even though we were opposites: she was a redhead, slightly wider of girth and certainly taller than me as well as a decade younger. We were clearing out my bureau in the drawing room. 'What are these?' She held up a small bundle. Olivier's lost love letters flashed through my mind and I recalled David Whiting stealing them. Never hang onto secret love letters: they get into the wrong hands. When I retrieved them I burned the lot.

The letters Goffie passed to me were to David Whiting from his mother. What were they doing in my bureau? Why was I never curious enough to snoop, even through my own drawers? 'Listen to this.' Goffie began reading: 'You still can be President, as long as you still believe. So come home, my dearest one, it's time to groom you for destiny.' I was stunned. I had no inkling David harboured any such ambition but, then, I suppose one doesn't go nattering with every Tom, Dick or Harry about becoming President of the United States. But more amazing still, David had always said he had no family – though a wife surfaced later!

'With a mother like that no wonder he was barking,' mumbled Goffie under her breath, holding up a single grey sock. I took it. Dead David's sock.

She noticed my troubled look. 'Let's burn everything of his, and then let him go.' A shiver galloped down my spine convincing me that a brand-new chapter of my life lay ahead of me and that this graceful, privileged existence was already drifting into the past.

California Dreaming

City of Cinema, bleeding blue sky.
Police siren squabbling with coyote cry.
Proud Pacific in sunset solution –
Paradise puckered up with pollution

'Gotta get myself a darker tan, man. I really gotta get myself a darker tan.' Such was the ultimate ambition of those around me. I, alas, had to sniff out other ambitions for I was allergic to the sun – something I hadn't fully thought through before moving to sunny California.

In the beginning, life in Malibu was as good as you could get, though a trifle noisy, perhaps, sandwiched as it was between the Pacific Coast Highway and the Pacific Ocean. I even forgave the tacky little detached house we had temporarily rented, with hideous flying geese stuck upon its cottage-cheese stucco frontage because its back door was right on the edge of that seductive ocean. The roar of the traffic coupled with the pounding waves seemed to wash away any constructive thoughts. The good news was that the racket conveniently washed away all negative thoughts too, not that I had many of those as my mind was a complete blank. My life, now free of its major players, all the heavyweight archetypes such as husband, lover, father, mother, brothers and sister, made most welcome the sensation of having undergone a successful lobotomy. Besides, I still had the most major player of all, my son. It was a time to count my blessings.

I was staggered at how quickly Robert had faded away, and with no pain whatsoever. With hindsight I must question whether the fading was a natural process, or a subconscious suppressing, yet at the time I felt nothing but the euphoria of laid-back freedom and anonymity. I had been a so-called name for well over a decade – the burden made it seem like a century. In England I had always found myself an embarrassed movie star, but out here I was able to breathe at last, rejoice in

13

being one of the herd, a mere tiddler in an ocean of LA sharks. Though here on the Pacific's west coast there were more sperm whales than sharks. How joyous it was to spy them migrating past our window twice a year, to and from their mating grounds off the Mexican coast.

I had been doing some mating of my own. The new man in my life was Bruce Davison, an unusually fine young American actor, a few years younger than me, with tousled blond hair and classical English features. We had worked together a few months previously in *The Skin of Our Teeth*, in Chicago, and his sensitive, daring acting, his cool, laid-back manner – a quality you only find in a certain type of American male – I found most calming. He was funny, played a tactile guitar, puffed on joints and made me feel like a million dollars. What more does a young girl want? (Not so young anymore, either.) Robert Bolt, perhaps...

Bruce had a relaxing effect on Tomcat too, and even Gladys found him soothing. The three of us had just returned from Italy and Spain, where I was meant to have been shooting Robert's script of D. H. Lawrence's novel *The Plumed Serpent*, directed by my brother Chris, with Oliver Reed, Stacy Keach and the Italian actor, Giuliano Gemma. It was a good script and the role of Kate, the heroine, gave me a fine opportunity to show another side of my craft.

Shooting was delayed *ad infinitum* so we hung around the poolside of an instantly forgettable hotel achieving absolutely nothing except perhaps the first stages of skin cancer. (Little did I know that I'd be returning to Spain the following year to make a Spanish film, *Pepita Jiminez*, with director Rafael Moreno Alba. The producer ran out of money, failed to pay his team, ended up in prison so the film was blacklisted – shame, I wasn't too bad in that one!) Finally Robert sent an exceedingly tough letter to Mario Ghio, the producer, giving him an ultimatum. He might have had the rights to the book, but Chris and I owned Robert's screenplay. All was to no avail, and one morning Chris rang telling us, most apologetically, to abandon ship.

With filming cancelled, we stopped off *en route* to Malibu at the stunning little paradise – in those days – of Puerto Vallarta, Mexico. After we had dumped the luggage in our antiquated *pension*, I rushed out to the ocean and flung myself in. I love to swim out for miles, must be to do with my name. After roughly half a mile, I came up to get my bearings and found myself surrounded by a perfect semi-circle of whopping great fins. I cursed myself. Were these shark-infested waters? Lacking, as I did, the slightest clue, I deserved to be eaten alive.

All I could do was try not to panic. I put all my concentration into keeping still, gently treading water as fearlessly as possible. I maintain that fear in the potential victim plays a much bigger part in encouraging sharks to attack than hunger, therefore staying calm and surrendering *should* quieten them. I wanted to wave towards the beach where I could just make out Tomcat and Bruce. Could they see the great fins surrounding me? Their wet, slimy texture shone silky pink, temporarily snatching the sunset from the horizon. I wondered how long I would have to tread water in my false state of calm, when I saw a fisherman rowing his wooden boat in my direction. He must have spotted the fins because he was headed straight for me – bless him! 'Mira! Mira!' he kept repeating, while pointing to the fins.

'What are they?' The concern with which he continued to point made me wonder if they were sharks, after all.

'Mira! Mira!' is all he would say as he hauled me up the side of his boat.

The great fins had belonged to giant manta rays. At times these quaint and alien-looking fish can get nasty, but they are not considered shark-dangerous, although a shoal in a bad mood could certainly do some damage. I might have been unlucky with *The Plumed Serpent*, but not with my manta rays.

Before David Whiting's death I had been asked to play St Joan at the Music Center in downtown LA. Afterwards the Center's board of directors (Katharine Hepburn and George Cukor, among others) decided I was no longer fit to play St Joan: perhaps they didn't want a whore playing a saint!

Bobbie Friar, who ran the Music Center was appalled, and stood firm on my behalf. 'If she goes, I go.' It is a rare and wonderful day when someone sticks up for me.

'OK,' replied Katharine Hepburn, seeing that Bobbie meant it. 'Then get her a squeaky clean Dauphin – a real boy-next-door type of guy.'

At nineteen I had played St Joan at Worthing rep and got some great reviews. Backstage on opening night was the first and only time my father showed the tiniest speck of enthusiasm towards my chosen career of acting – probably because he had wanted me to be a tennis player. 'By Jove, Pusscat, perhaps you *can* act after all!' Father's long-awaited acknowledgement of my ability rang in my ears for over a decade – it had to, for he never again mentioned my acting. I realised I had to have another crack at St Joan just to hear my father's praise once more, so I forked out two return tickets for my parents and worked diligently towards a St Joan to end all St Joans.

Squeaky clean Richard Thomas came hot-foot from playing John Boy in the smash-hit series *The Waltons* to give us his Dauphin. Isn't it great how we actors get ourselves cast? We hardly ever get the part on merit, simply from being the best person for the job. It's usually who you know, nepotism, arse-licking or politics. So John Boy ended up playing the Dauphin, a role that deserved a John Hurt or a younger Walter Matthau, just to clean up Sarah Miles.

In a sabbatical from running his prestigious Long Wharf Theater, Arvin Brown was brought down to direct it. Although he was kind, sensitive and talented, he was unable to bring together the finer tuning necessary for *St Joan*, which is probably Bernard Shaw's most difficult play. I usually know the first day of rehearsals if a project has legs or if it's sinking – not difficult for someone with a lot of sinking practice!

The *LA Times* reviewed *St Joan*, and I quote: 'This is not one of Shakespeare's better plays.'

Bill Haber, a handsome young man, came regularly to the stage door with red roses. He was starting up a new theatrical agency and wanted me to join. Flattered by his attention, I ended up finding myself suitably wooed to take that daring leap into the unknown. His new agency was CAA – Creative Artists Agency. I was one of their first clients, and the reason I left shortly thereafter was because they seemed more keen on recruiting new clients than nurturing those they already had. That, like most of my career moves, turned out to be another abysmal error because Bill Haber's partner was Mike Ovitz who became, and still is, the most powerful agent in all Hollywood.

Strange that my parents never came, what with the free tickets and all. Sad, too, because I think my father would have appreciated my new interpretation for I had matured considerably since good old Worthing days. I feel St Joan very close to my heart and salute what she stood for. The hubris, the altruistic, self-sacrificing, self-destructive fearlessness of the woman resonates somewhere deep within me, probably because Robert continually warned me about courage being so closely linked to stupidity. I must be stupid for I'd love to get a crack at playing St

Joan just one last time but, knowing my luck, I'll have to wait a long, long time – and St Joan would hardly be taken seriously were she to ride to war on her Zimmer frame.

Perhaps my parents were still smarting from the David Whiting incident, and because they believed the printed word, didn't want to be linked in public with a suspected murderess. Mother wrote complaining that she still couldn't go shopping at home, in Ingatestone, the village of my childhood: apparently the whispered innuendos were beginning to get both her and Father down. Yet it had been almost a year. Why do the English so *love* a scandal? Although many people in LA would ask the odd question on the subject, there was none of that prurient British smallmindedness.

Everything was cooler in the heat. Or had I blotted out the pain to such a degree that I was no longer noticing people's reaction to me or my infamy? Hard to notice anything too negative lying on the beach (in the shade, of course), puffing on the occasional spliff of Maui Wowee between Brucy's guitar serenades and swimming all day long.

I feel passionately about moderation in all things, but as I have never fallen victim to any habit, moderation is perhaps less of an impossibility for me than it is for others. Nevertheless, if it is not harmless, marijuana is at least less harmful than any other mood-altering drug, but only when used sparingly. Being stoned is a useless state, whereas being high can lead one to new boundaries of receptivity. Those who say marijuana is a dangerous first step towards hard drugs should either stop demonstrating their ignorance or put their money where their mouth is and make cigarettes and alcohol illegal, too.

Right through history until 1928, hemp was legal in America. It is probably the most useful and versatile crop of all. Before 1928 it was used for rope, many different textiles, clothing, *and* for its amazing effectiveness in caring for all kinds of pain by giving calm and con-tentment – that is until 1928, when competition became tough for the pharmaceutical companies. Yet it was the powerful campaign of the paper manufacturers that finally had hemp made illegal. The Ford Motor Company wanted to run the newly invented automobile on hemp. This would have been a wise move, as hemp is self-perpetuating, cheap, clean and, unlike oil, organically pure and pro-life. The powers that be chose oil. Will we ever learn?

My sweet Goffie, my *aide-de-camp*, my partner in crime, was as blind as a bat. This created hilarious moments, like the day in the ocean when we got caught up with an army of Portuguese men-o'-war. 'Which way to shore?' screamed Goffie. So blind was she that there were no specs or contact lenses on the face of the earth to counteract her one-off pair of peepers. It didn't matter too much in everyday beach life, but a non-driving *aide-de-camp* in LA is completely useless.

'I believe you *could* learn to drive, Goffie.'

Goffie remained adamant. 'No, Sarah, no and no again.'

'But it's easy—'

'No, Sarah. No! No! No! I'll walk. You know how much I love walking.'

'Where will you walk *to*?'

'The shops.'

'But, Goffie, the shops are seven miles away!' And so I began tentatively to tease out Goffie's driving potential. I hoped it was better than her riding. Two years before, she had wanted to come for a ride with me at the Old Mill. Half-way across the common, Daisy (my own unridable wonder horse) took off with her and threw her into her favourite dumping ground, the gravel pit. I was in two minds about whom to save first. I loved my Daisy May and there she was, reins around her fetlocks, galloping riderless towards the A3 and about to cause another hideous accident. I looked back at Goffie. She was still as could be. Was she dead?

I galloped after Daisy, caught her, tied both horses securely to a tree and then threw myself into the centre of the A3 where a van was forced to stop or run me over. 'It's an emergency – I need an ambulance!'

For quite a while Goffie remained in hospital with a fractured skull and broken ribs. She lost her love of horses, also her sense of smell. From that day to this she hasn't been able to smell a thing. Every time she goes to smell a rose, or anything come to that, she must inwardly curse me. It's a wonder we're still friends.

One fine bland blue day (yet another), I placed Goffie's hands on the wheel as we purred through downtown LA on my way to play St Joan. Suddenly a rude, angry megaphone boomed at me, forcing me to stop on the hard shoulder of the freeway. Two macho, futuristic-looking cops with guns and handcuffs gave me no option but to get out of the car.

'Stand here! Feet astride. Hands on the hood!' I did as he told me and he frisked me. 'D'you know your speed?' He leaned in to take a look at Goffie.

'I'm so sorry, sir – I mean, superintendent – no, I mean, officer – but—'

'Where are you from?' he asked, mimicking my accent, quite well, actually.

He'd given me a loop-hole through which to plunge. 'I come from England, my friend Goffie too.'

Goffie leant out the window, waving and smiling her great sunflower smile. 'Hello. Don't I get to be handcuffed too?'

Quick to spot that they hadn't seen the joke, Goffie ploughed on. 'We're so sorry. At home it's a seventy m.p.h. speed limit. If she was speeding it's because I made her late for curtain-up.'

'Curtain-up where?' He didn't believe her. Good. Money in the bank. 'This is Sarah Miles and she's late for the show. Please let us go.'

Both policemen stood there studying me from head to foot. 'Oh yeah. And what part d'you play?'

I stood up, straight yet humble. 'St Joan—'

They shared a dubious look, until one little spark of recognition flew between them. 'Oh, yeah! I know who you are! You made that movie in Arizona with Burt Reynolds?' They looked at each other as if igniting a *National Inquirer* headline.

'That guy – what's his name? – did he commit suicide?'

'It's still a mystery. Please don't let me be late for curtain-up!'

'Just slow down, St Joan. Keep it to fifty next time.' And so, with endless gratitude, I ingratiated my way back into Muriel, my ochre Volkswagen Beetle, and off we beetled, slow and straight as a die.

I was caught for speeding three more times and St Joan always came to my rescue, proving her to be the saint that she is. One particular occasion was a trifle hairy. Goffie was driving. (Yes, I finally got Goffie behind the wheel!) We were becoming pretty nonchalant about the fearsome sound of megaphones booming through the canyons – as long as I was driving.

'Pull over!'

I'd never witnessed a completely ashen Goffie before.

'We're not wearing L-plates!'

'Hide the stash!' I stuffed a small bag of marijuana up into her knickers. I was in trousers so I had no choice.

'Great! Get me done for both!'

'I'll do the talking this time,' I said, with a masterful air.

'Then we've had it. Oh, God!' a defeatist Goffie slumped.

'Get out with your hands above your head – both of you!'

My acting was so superb I actually *became* ill. 'Officer, I fainted on the freeway and nearly crashed. So my noble friend here who cannot drive was given no alternative.' I nearly had him. 'Where's the nearest hospital?' I gave a subtle portrayal of the Lady of the Camellias while he scrutinised my license. 'It must be overwork.' I waited for the usual next line – what work?

'Which hospital?' This had me flummoxed.

'That's why we're so grateful you stopped us. Please show us the way – we're from England, you see.'

'Holidays?' I was sitting on the verge by now, unable to stand with my hands on the car because I was so dizzy.

Goffie piped up with the by now winning cue line. 'This is Sarah Miles and she's playing St Joan at the Music Center.'

'I don't care if she's Shirley Temple. You're driving without an L-plate or a licence.' He started making out the ticket, so I had to gather my wits.

'What would you have done in our shoes, officer?' They looked at each other before realising the alternatives.

'OK. Get back in the car.' This being a test, I subtly guided Goffie away from the passenger seat. She gave me a look, but once we were settled he put his face through my window. 'Wise move – too ill to drive.'

They directed us to a hospital miles away, so Goffie had her say. 'No. Home's a lot closer.' The now terrified Goffie pressed the windscreen wipers, headlights, horn, air-conditioning, radio and brakes in her rush to be homeward-bound. 'I'm never driving again as long as I live!' She never has, either.

I liked Julie Christie's non-showbizzy image. She lived just up the beach and would regularly waft by, her beauty never marred by hair in curlers. It was always in curlers. I've always had a huge admiration for the mysterious ability to manipulate hair into rollers. How nonsensical life was, for there I was, forever dreaming mine straight. Ironical to think that David Lean had wanted me for Lara in *Dr Zhivago*, but because a certain Robert Bolt thought of me as a North Country slut (then he had never met me in real life, only on the screen in *The Servant* and *Term of Trial* playing North Country sluts) he refused even to meet me. Still, Julie was always more glamorous and did a much better job, I'm sure.

I looked up from my shady sand bed of bliss to spy Tomcat playing with a posse of privileged brown Californian beach bums. He was in seventh heaven, no doubt about it. His asthma had done a bunk, leaving him healthy and glowing. He had started at an enchanting primary school in a secluded Malibu canyon. Never before had Tomcat liked dressing for school, but for him Carden School was paradise.

I went off into a trance, wondering if my life would have been different if I, too, had gone to a school like Carden. Warm sand caressed my face.

'Ma!' Tomcat looked tall, standing above me, silhouetted against the sun. I moved myself over to block the sun with his body.

'Hi, Tomcat – want a game of hopscotch?'

'No! I wanna talk!' Bruce got the message, as always, and went for a walk.

'What's up? Spit it out.'

'It's my winkie.'

'What about your winkie?'

'It's different from all the other boys'!'

'That's because yours is natural—'

'No, it isn't, Ma. It's funny.'

'Depends from whose point of view—'

'From mine, Ma!' he fumed, punching himself in the chest with painful affirmation.

'They've had theirs done—'

'I want mine done too!'

'You want to be circumcised?'

He backed off a little, then realised he had to stay cool, man, cool. 'Yeah ... How's it done, Ma?'

'I'm not entirely sure. The surgeon would remove this bit round the rim, I think.' His nakedness might have made demonstration easy, but his eyes were far from easy as I gently nipped a clump of skin. 'About this much.'

'Is that all? So what's the big deal?'

'Exactly! So why change it?' I had to admit that the more his beach-bum pals gathered, the more it grew nakedly apparent that we were surrounded by a sea of circumcision.

'Are you listening to me, Ma?' I wasn't. I was wondering how to take it from there. Oh, the fickle folly of fashion! I was being asked to take responsibility for pointless butchery when, in my limited experience, those who are uncircumcised are tons better off, for surely it's common sense that the more *acreage* of erotic potential at one's disposal the better? How could he bear to be part of such a barbaric ritual?

'Come on, Ma, let's go for it.'

Since he continued to badger me for three months with his odious request, I decided to pick through the dilemma with Robert, for it had been a mutual decision not to tamper. At that time, I found our conversations awkward and rife with clichés, due perhaps to the armour we both donned to protect us against more hurt.

'Robert, Tomcat wants to be circumcised,'

'But he—'

'Tell him in your own words.' I put Tomcat on the phone and that was that. I should have known that the two of us warning him of the hazards of circumcision would be sufficient to spark off a renewed determination on his part.

Eventually Robert caved in, 'Find a good surgeon, for God's sake!' and rang off.

I put some time and effort into finding a sympathetic, first-class surgeon, but when the dreaded day was finally nigh, and I asked, 'Ready for hospital?' Tomcat looked strangely blank, then freaked.

'No way, man!' Was it fear or had he forgotten? Perhaps he had simply gone off the idea once he knew he had our permission. I believe the whole exercise, like so many others, was his way of testing me and my love. He never complained about his winkie again, so I suppose he's happy with what God gave him – I know I would be if I were him.

I designed my own dream home a little further up the Pacific Coast Highway, just beyond the Malibu Colony, where all the heavyweight movie stars lived, on Old Malibu Road. What I liked about Old Malibu Road was that only a few scattered homes were dotted along it. (A line of them now, alas). Even more important was the lack of noise: a small range of mountains protected it from the roar of the Highway.

I had definite ideas about this new house of mine. It was made entirely of wood with a huge balcony the length of the ocean frontage. Stained-glass windows, strategically placed, would echo the sunsets, moonrises and stars. In the centre was an effective open fire, with a great chimney rising up through the ceiling of the main living space, which was surrounded by a minstrels' gallery. Lying there in the main room upon cushions, surrounded by flames, glass, balcony, ocean, whales, horizon and finally the daily phantasmagoria of sunrises and sunsets, served as a luscious backdrop to our new life.

In the middle of my bathroom I installed a great Jacuzzi in which more stained glass tinted my body different colours according to whether the sun or moon was shining.

I furnished the house by having a ball on the celebrity tennis circuit, refusing to take it too seriously. (Can't think why we don't have one here.) My first year's winnings: a fridge, three tellies, deep freeze, washing machine, washing-up machine, spin dryer and God knows what else – pure fluke! Why don't I feel bad about that when I'm too high minded (or pompous!) to do commercials?

It didn't take long, however, for the laid-back Californian lifestyle to have a deleterious effect on Tom's manners and attention span. How could I cope with his incessant cheek and hyperactivity? He sat still only in front of the telly, from which there was no budging him for swimming, hopscotch, walks or games. Bruce got us a rubber dinghy, but Tomcat and his spoilt little circumcised gang demanded endless Kentucky Fried Chicken, candy and Coke – all to be consumed in front of the TV. It slowly dawned on me that I wasn't able to contain Tom's awesome stubbornness single-handed. Bruce was a great help, but he wasn't his father. Tomcat needed a strong hand, otherwise there would be anarchy.

With hindsight it's so easy to see the problems. A wayward son or daughter needs that quintessential balance of masculine and feminine from which security develops. To fall short, as I undoubtedly did, is frightening and bewildering. I kept putting off the day when I would have to deal with it. That would be after Tomcat's remaining year at Carden.

While he was still there, he was cast as Hansel, in the musical *Hansel and Gretel*. At first he said he couldn't do it but suddenly a mighty determination overcame the terror. Yet even this failed to fool his nervous system and an attack of athlete's foot to end all athlete's foot was the result. With both feet bandaged right up the ankles – not only making shoes impossible but his skinny legs look ridiculous – his desire to soldier on was painful to watch. Unbandaged, his feet resembled something from a horror movie: great scaly, pustulating lumps of raw flesh. Goffie was wonderful with him.

Many children of well-known parents feel under pressure but although I may be guilty of many parental errors, I can never recall putting Tom under pressure to succeed in showbusiness – or anything, come to that. Corny as it sounds, I just wanted us all to be happy. Perhaps I didn't push him hard enough. Judging from his final brilliant performance as Hansel it was plain to see that he was a born actor. Later I was thrilled to realise I hadn't just viewed him through the biased eyes of a proud mum, for parents, pupils and teachers alike all recognised it as Tomcat's day of triumph.

Goffie wasn't only wonderful with Tom. She was always wonderful.

One evening at the press party for the opening of *The Skin Of Our Teeth* I turned to see a journalist grilling Goffie. Dealing with the press was hard because they all wanted to dredge up dirt on the David Whiting tragedy or the split-up of my marriage, making it a tricky responsibility for her. Well into the habit of keeping a regular ear cocked, I could sense that although Goffie didn't need saving yet it was just around the corner. I got a glimpse of the elderly, over-painted muckraker, talons poised over her tape controls as she breathed over Goffie.

'Now tell me, Miss Gough—'

'No. You tell *me*. Tell me something nice,' retorted Goffie, giving as good as she got. She was learning fast, was Goffie.

'I hear through the grapevine that you and Sarah Miles are practising lesbians. Is this true?'

Goffie's face was a caricature of horror and disbelief. Time for intervention. I put the Valkyrie straight by whisking Goffie away. '*Practising*? We're *perfect*!'

Charlemagne and a Crescent Moon

I was full of *Great Expectations*, flying first class over the Atlantic – homeward-bound to film a remake of Dickens' classic story. How excited I always became when travelling home to England. Since I don't drink alcohol and sleep for most of the journey, I wouldn't normally have dreamt of travelling first class – unless someone else was paying. From my window I watched LA disappear into the smog. Had moving there been a mistake? Two-thirds of me yearned to return home for good, but the other third knew I couldn't until Gladys was dead, which meant staying put in LA for at least another year. Only Saddam Hussein would put a dying dog through quarantine kennels. I sat and wondered how transformed my life would have been without quarantine laws, for my dogs had certainly ruled and ruined my career – but what about my life?

A few weeks earlier I had taken Gladys to the vet because of an allergy: most of her back and tail had been bitten raw by Malibu sand fleas. At the same time I asked the vet to look at a nasty lump growing on her hind leg, upper thigh, and that's how I discovered Gladys had a malignant tumour.

'How long has she got?'

'At a rough guess, nine months to a year.' This news hit me hard because, apart from Addo, my Pyrenean mountain dog, Gladys was the most unique and special pet I'd ever owned. Skye terriers are known for their loyalty – Greyfriars Bobby was a Skye and had been awarded the freedom of the city of Edinburgh for spending nine years at his master's grave. (I believe he stayed there that long because the town came out and fed him!) Mary Queen of Scots kept two Skyes under her skirts – or so the story goes – and when she was beheaded both died of a broken heart shortly afterwards.

Gladys was a cantankerous Scottish bitch, loyal only to me, with the habit of biting or grinding everyone else on the ankle. Gladys and Tomcat had been arch enemies ever since the beginning. How they hated each other! Tomcat claims that when our rowing boat capsized when he and Gladys were aged one and two respectively, I had saved Gladys first. This was partly true because Tomcat could already swim, but Gladys had disappeared into the murky depths.

'We'll be landing at Heathrow shortly, please fasten your seat belts.' Goffie nudged me awake. Tomcat, fast asleep beside me, was going to stay with Robert in the Old Mill for the film's six weeks' duration. Having now finished at Carden School, the future didn't look too bright on the education front.

Picking up a *Daily Telegraph* left by my neighbour down the side of his seat, I noticed a painting on page three headed *Charlemagne*, of a proud, grey Arab stallion standing in the desert with an Arabian tent in the background. The picture filled me with a dark foreboding as well as tremendous hope, for the stallion stood either snorting at the oncoming storm or seeing it off. Either way he was daring it to do its worst. The text beneath read: 'Will *Charlemagne* return to America, or stay in England where he so rightfully belongs?'

'Goffie, look at this.'

'What a horse!' I'd never hankered before to own a painting but I was a goner with *Charlemagne* by John Ferneley, Senior, a nineteenth-century artist, the greatest horse painter after Stubbs. It was to be sold at Sotheby's the very next afternoon, which was deeply frustrating because I had costume fittings all day long, and therefore wouldn't be able to attend the auction. I had no alternative but to send Goffie.

'But Sarah, I can't!'

'Why ever not?'

'I haven't a clue what to do. It's unfair to ask me, it's too much of a responsibility.'

'What nonsense! All you have to do is to continue putting your hand up until everyone else has stopped. Nothing, surely, could be easier than that?' At the time I didn't know that you could get Sotheby's to bid for you.

'At what price do I stop?'

'You don't. You simply go on to the end—'

'But what if it reaches—?'

'That's *my* worry.' Although my purse wasn't well lined I was determined to acquire *Charlemagne*, whether it was a good investment or not. I managed to persuade Goffie in the end. She took an old friend from *Lady Caroline Lamb*, Syd Field's grandson Nick, who knew a little bit about bidding.

A tense, tired Robert stood at the airport barrier waiting to greet us. I found it strange that he was still living at the Old Mill when his heart remained firmly locked in the West Country. He had never really wanted to live in the Home Counties, but felt I'd have better access to London for working. Friends who had been down to the Old Mill since my departure said that a mist of glumness hovered over everything. Perhaps they were just being loyal.

Robert greeted me with fond courtesy. Was that how he felt or was he acting? Walking off hand in hand with his father to the Rolls, Tomcat looked back at me. How could my heart not ache at that moment for all things past?

'I'll see you at the weekend, darling – that's right, Robert?'

Robert turned. 'Bring Bruce, if you want.' Bruce was arriving a few days later.

'Is that all right?'

'Of course it is.'

The next evening at the Berkeley in my sumptuous suite overlooking Hyde Park, Goffie returned from her Sotheby's adventure. Beneath the apparent harassment I detected a flush of triumph. 'Once Nick nudged my attention towards the only other person bidding against me – an Arab sheik–'

'Bleedin' robes and all,' joined in Nick.

'– I wanted to pack it in, but we soldiered on regardless.'

'Brilliant both of you! Where *is Charlemagne*?'

'Don't you want to know how much he went for?'

'How much?'

'Sixteen thousand pounds.'

It was a lot of money for me. 'Cheap at the price.'

'Sotheby's will send him wherever you want him to go.'

I hadn't thought about where *Charlemagne* would go, but in the meantime he would look magnificent hanging in the hall of my parents' new home. Father and Mother had finally cracked and left Ingatestone. They had moved to one of the few remaining houses (the rest had been divided into flats) in Lewes Crescent, on Brighton seafront. Those Regency houses may have aesthetically glorious proportions, but I never felt cosy in them. I found an austere bleakness permeating every room.

Following my mother's elegant hips up five flights of stairs to my room sent my spirits plummeting.

'Here we are, darling. Like it?' The room was small, which she knew I preferred. As she went over to show me the view from my window, I detected a certain Machiavellian glint in the corner of her bright Wren-like green eyes. 'You see, darling, why I thought of you for this room?' There, behind the drawn curtains (to keep the sun off her precious antiques), she proudly revealed Roedean School. Those familiar with my first book of memoirs will understand the great bend in her humour. I had hated Roedean with a passion and finally achieved expulsion after three years – three very long years, I may add. Mother went on, 'A great warmth sweeps over me when I look back at those days.' I wanted to clock her one. 'Roedean must seem like Shangri-la after all the troubles you went through in Hila Bend.'

'Thank you, Ma.' I leant out of the window. 'I can almost touch the chapel from here.' She refused to react to my sarcasm.

Down a flight of stairs, she took me to the window in the main bedroom.

'Look.' I didn't feel inclined to look out of another window because no part of Brighton held any feelings of joy for me, but I did as I was told – always best with Mother. There was miles of shingle beach, Regency houses and a mass of traffic moving along the front. 'Your father's down there every evening – he loves it.'

At Barn Mead, our old family home, there had been wonderful walks along bridle-paths, through woods and down unspoilt lanes. I felt angry that Mother had chosen to live here where the walks for Father would be limited to slippery shingle, litter and a mass of holidaymakers swarming in front of endless salt-gnawed, dilapidated Regency houses.

'But why Brighton seafront?'

'There's no gossip and it's healthier here. You mark my words, he'll live to be a hundred with that sea air filling his lungs – and look!' She pointed ahead beyond the roof-tops.

28

'What am I supposed to be looking at?'

'I did it all for you – a chance to continue where you left off.' Did Mother really move to Brighton on my account – right next door to Laurence Olivier? I very much doubted it, though sometimes I *did* receive glimmerings of my mother's love for me.

I found Father alone in the gigantic drawing room, marching up and down sucking his one false tooth (he lost the original in battle during the First World War) and simply itching for his evening walk. 'Come on, Pusscat, let's be off!'

'Shall we go to Chanctonbury Ring in my hired car?' I'd always had a soft spot for Chanctonbury Ring ever since Olivier took me up there well over a decade earlier for a sexy picnic of smoked salmon and champagne.

'No. Follow me.' When it got going, Father's twinkle was more devilish than Mother's glint. 'I want to show you something.'

I walked ahead of him towards the sea. Waiting at the crossroads, I turned to find him pointing vigorously at me with his silver-knobbed cane, as he had done all my life. I loved that cane as much as Daddy's energy, which was undiminished inside his tiny frame.

'C'mon, Pusscat, this way. I have the key.' He retrieved a large key from his pocket as if it opened the door to paradise. 'It's a secret passage.' I felt it would spoil his fun if I told him that Roedean, too, had a secret passage through the chalk cliffs to the beach.

Father began tut-tutting at my LA lifestyle. Then, we came out of the secret passage into the light shimmering on the sea – blinding stuff! 'Why aren't you with your husband where you belong?'

'Please, Daddy, don't go on. I'm living with Bruce in LA now.'

'That little whipper-snapper.'

'Perhaps a whipper-snapper is what I'm needing right now.'

'Life isn't about what you *need*, life is about the need to *do your duty*!'

Together we crossed the miniature railway line, well loved by Brightonians. I watched Father's profile against the horizon as we slithered on the shingles towards the Palace pier. Was it because everything else about him was shrinking slightly that I had never noticed until now what a conk of a nose he had? I wondered what he would have looked like without his moustache. I'm not keen on moustaches, but Daddy's was most fitting and, besides, it had been there all my life propping up that stiff upper lip. A true Edwardian in every way as he marched along, wielding his silver cane. They don't make the likes of Father any more.

'Look over there, Pusscat – not at me!' Why was I so shocked when I turned? Am I a closet prude? For there, right above us on the shingle ridge, stood a man stark naked. It wasn't so much that he was the same age as Daddy, but more his attitude in demanding that we should, in some way, respond to his tired, lonely cluster. The sea breeze was exceptionally bullish that evening, and shrank what he had into a most woefully apologetic object. I was fascinated, not by his nakedness but by the mystery lying behind such a need to display all in this fashion.

'He'll get arrested!'

'It's all legal.' I couldn't believe it. 'Climb up a bit further?'

'You obviously know every inch of this beach.'

Father turned to face me. 'I know this damn beach, Pusscat, because there is no other!' Why Mother had chosen to place him in a nudist colony was beyond me. Again the injustice of it all churned me up inside. Could she have failed to find out that there was a nudist colony on her doorstep?

'Why you let yourself be dumped here like this I cannot fathom.'

'Too late – it was a *fait accompli*.' Father's need for peace of mind meant Mother getting her way over most things.

'Toot! Toot!' went the merry beach train as a posse of icy-blue elderly nudists scuttled out of nowhere and stood to attention.

'Perhaps they've made a deal with the Brighton tourist board.' I was unable to understand why they felt the need to flash veteran pride 'n' joy. Perhaps it will become clear to me when I'm in my sixties.

Daddy shook his head sadly. 'They've all missed out on their Moon River.'

All his life Father had been dedicated to doing his duty and, consequently, he too had missed out on his beloved banana boat. I remember him sitting in Barn Mead at his magnificent Bechstein grand, serenading us with his magic. 'Moon river, wider than a mile, I'm crossing you in style some day.'

Father was a true artist and finding himself with a nine-to-five job in the City didn't strike me as crossing his moon river in style. Now he had chosen to relinquish his little dream cottage, tucked away in some lonely wood in the middle of nowhere for a nudist colony and a vast Regency house on Brighton seafront. His previous words rang in my ears.

'Life isn't about what you *need*, life is about the need to *do your duty!*'
He was correct, but I didn't see it at the time. All I was interested in
was *right now*! Wanting everything *right now* is far removed from what
became my ultimate goal, which is to *live* in the *right now*. But, right
then, I had no inclination to learn from the wisdom of the umpteen
decades echoing between us. I only began to realise how right he was
once I'd been given proof of life after death. How was it that he, a
convinced atheist, believed in the need to do one's duty even though
the end for him was blank oblivion?

Great Expectations

In David Lean's *Great Expectations*, John Mills played Pip, Jean Simmons played the young Estella and Valerie Hobson played her grown-up. The slim chance of repeating such classy stuff almost prevented me from accepting. Michael York was to play Pip.

'Who will play the young Estella?' I asked the director, Jo Hardy.

'You can play her all the way through – it'll give you more of a challenge.' I knew that the film would be no more than a worthy attempt, even though Margaret Leighton was to play Miss Havisham.

I had always regarded Maggie Leighton as one of our finest actresses ever, and when we worked together on *Lady Caroline Lamb* we had become great friends. Her relationship with Michael Wilding was a joy to behold, particularly since both he and she had experienced such unhappiness and rejection in their previous marriages, Maggie to Laurence Harvey and Michael to Elizabeth Taylor. The trip to England would have been worth it just to hang around those two wise old birds for a while. Maggie Leighton bore a spooky resemblance to my mother: same English-rose type, same thoroughbred limbs, same hair, same features. But there all similarity ended. Maggie Leighton was *not* my mother! Mother! Locking horns with her again on Brighton seafront had made me understand how I'd missed the old bat. Seeing family and friends again was important to me because I hadn't been with them since David Whiting's death.

Shooting *Great Expectations* was an unusually pleasant experience, considering that something ghastly always seems to befall me in my somewhat ill-fated professional life. It's a good job I wasn't too inward-looking, in those days, otherwise I might have had to question why such out-of-the-ordinary events happened around my ever-so-ordinary attempts to live a normal life. For me to have gone six weeks without some devastating mishap was pretty unique.

Like most serious performers, I usually end up in a good wrestling match with someone at some point during a shoot, due to my obsession for perfection. Estella is meant to be a great beauty. Acting the subtler aspects of Estella's nature might help me to get my rocks off, but those deeper understandings mean nothing if the outer shell fails to convey *ravishing*. Looking ravishing can be tricky, especially for those like me who weren't born ravishing but have to create, then act out the illusion. The only problem with achieving this ravishing state is that audiences tend to sit back and regard *only that state* and not bother to notice the actor's characterisation etched beneath to as near perfection as he or she is able. With Estella I had to show a spoilt yet lonely young girl mature from innocence and youth into maturity and guile.

I was in Maggie Leighton's caravan on the set at Shepperton studios waiting for her to put the final touches to Miss Havisham for our important scene that afternoon. Maggie had felt a little odd over the past six weeks, and had been to see her specialist in Harley Street. She seemed in her usual calm good spirits.

'Did you get the test results?'

'Guess what, Smiles?' She always called me Smiles. 'My specialist confirmed today that I definitely *do* have it –'

'Have what?'

'Oh! Did I forget to tell you? It must have slipped through my slippery old mind.' She delivered her bombshell as if it meant nothing more than a stubborn curl refusing to sit on her forehead. 'Multiple sclerosis has now been confirmed.'

I wasn't sure what multiple sclerosis was. 'What does that mean?'

Sitting there, regarding her refined features in the mirror, she brought up a wonderfully unaffected gurgle of a belly laugh, which resonated through the depths of life experience. 'It attacks the nerves. Creeping paralysis is the result. I hope I die with as much dignity as Larry apparently did.' He did, too – I was there. When Larry Harvey was told he had stomach cancer and less than a year to live, he laughed just like Maggie and proceeded to have himself a ball with all his friends, travelling the globe and spending money like water.

Why did Maggie's smile seem almost triumphant? Creeping paralysis must be the cruellest joke of all.

'Will you cancel your play in the West End?'

'I'll play it in a wheelchair – die on the job if needs be. (She did!) No

33

one must know. They'll cast someone else if word gets out.' Maggie went to work that afternoon, acting her usual best; as if all was roses in her garden, and continued thus till the end of the shoot.

It was only at brief moments alone with Maggie and Michael at their home in Pont Street that the horror of what was coming truly hit home. Michael probably took it harder than Maggie: his love for her was what he lived for. He would occasionally comment on the utter cruelty of life, but Maggie, sensing a maudlin note intrude into their endless honeymoon, would remind Michael of the brighter side. 'Think, darling, we might never have bumped into each other.'

'Absolutely!' responded Michael, as lightly as he could. 'One doesn't bump into creeping paralysis every day of the week!' He would open his arms and hold her firm with a love that remained rock solid for the rest of her life. Her death put Michael on a wobbler, till one day he had a serious wobble while carrying in some logs. He wobbled right over, and joined her.

On my second to last day of shooting I had to gallop on horseback in the morning, then shoot in an archery competition in the afternoon. I was proud of my twenty-inch waist and determined to have all my costumes made tighter than my measurements dictated. Meeting deadlines is good self-discipline, but it made my cutter, Maria at Berman's, very nervous.

'Don't worry, Maria, I'm losing weight so fast that by the time we start shooting, it'll fit with some to spare.' And so it was that with a good corset, determination and a deep breath I could just squeeze myself into my goal of eighteen inches. Vanity, vanity – all is vanity!

Film producers always like the stars to do the dangerous stuff last – for insurance reasons – hence my neck injury as I bailed out of the saddle while riding my beloved Daisy on the last shooting day of *Lady Caroline Lamb*. On that occasion we had to wait almost a year to do the pick-up shots. This particular morning on *Great Expectations* I wasn't riding my own uncontrollable Daisy May, alas, but a well-schooled film horse.

I was dressed up as the ravishing Estella in a dove-grey riding habit; the sharp bones in my corset forced me to sit straight as a ramrod. In the scene I had to gallop around the meadows, show off and flirt with all the eager young beaux, including Pip. I hadn't eaten since the previous day, and my tummy rumbles were growing grumpier by the minute. I rushed into the canteen, too hungry to remove my riding habit, and helped myself to a plate piled high with mashed potatoes. Spiffing! My favourite! I slopped on masses of extra butter and HP sauce, then found a spare table and wolfed down the lot, chased with a pint of milk. I have a ludicrously unsophisticated palate, the kind that babies have. Pure heaven it was, licking the platter clean.

As I went to my dressing room to climb out of my riding habit and into my beautiful white archery outfit, I realised I'd got a wicked bout of tummy cramps.

'You should never eat in tight corsets.' Goffie was furious with me for not getting undone first.

'In those days they must have eaten their meals in corsets.'

'They were used to them, you're not.' Goffie was pulling the laces of my archery outfit this way and that, but it needed a miracle if the dress was to meet round the back. 'What *did* you have for lunch?' Fortunately my dresser came in and between them they huffed and puffed and wrenched me into my dress.

When we had finished the long establishing shot of Estella beating all her beaux by shooting the first bull's eye, Jo Hardy decided to come in for a medium close shot from the waist up. To take my mind off the cramps I went to check my make-up – I always did my own – then went onto my mark.

'Right. Action, Sarah!' As I pulled back the arrow way beyond my waist – showing off! – pain and dizziness overcame me and I lost consciousness.

I came to in an ambulance screeching through the Middlesex suburbs. Above me stood an elderly grey-haired man with appalling breath. I tried to duck the main blast, but couldn't any more than I could speak. I had been sedated and my lips were unwilling to shape a single word.

'Don't be alarmed,' he said. 'I've sedated you. It's appendicitis, I'm afraid.' I knew damn well I hadn't got appendicitis. Was I going to have a scar on my stomach for the removal of an appendix that was in tip-top condition?

I knew I had to be strong and not allow anyone to give me any more sedation until we'd talked this through. Then it dawned on me that appendicitis would guarantee an immediate settlement from the film insurers whereas a mass of mashed potatoes squelching around in my guts might not.

Later, back in my room via the X-ray department, a nurse came in to administer another injection. I refused to take it until the doctor was present. Fortunately, from everyone's point of view, the specialist appeared in the doorway – the one with the breath. He came over to my bed with a gait of studied compassion, combined with blinding ego. 'We've planned the operation for six thirty tomorrow morning, so we need to prepare you now.'

'Who is we?' He looked at me before clearing his throat. 'My team and I.'

'What about my team?'

'Your team?'

'Yes. My body and I?'

'Miss Miles, your appendix needs to be removed immediately.'

'Tomorrow morning isn't immediately. May I have the phone please?' He didn't like that, but asked the nurse for a phone all the same.

I rang Mother.

'If you're being told it's infected, Sarah, then you must listen.'

What she meant was that she didn't feel like rushing up to town because fighting my corner would entail fighting a wretched traffic jam – and who could blame her? In the end I had no choice, so I surrendered to the knife. I wonder how many others have had the same experience? Wouldn't an introduction at school to our body parts and how they function be more prudent than *amo, amas, amat*? I'm convinced a basic knowledge of and new targeting on health rather than illness is the only way to prevent ourselves being used and abused. Think how much money the Government would save.

As I bade my appendix farewell at six thirty the following morning, I remembered something. I pushed the great needle away.

'What now?' demanded the exasperated surgeon with the smelly breath.

'If you leave the minutest scar, I'll have your guts for garters.'

The needle plunged into my arm and under I went.

Climbing through my drugged stupor, dizziness and nausea, I saw before me a vague silhouette of Mother, dressed in pale grey and sporting a blue cloche hat. Was that really her, sitting swan-like, or simply a flickering fantasy at the far end of the bed?

My efforts to speak disturbed her, so she came closer and with one delicate gesture stopped my mouth before kissing me on the forehead. It was then that I realised it wasn't Mother at all but Maggie Leighton.

A couple of years after this I was asleep in a friend's house in LA, when I had an unusually vivid dream. It was the first of a new batch, almost 3D in texture, and its content was a rerun of that moment when I saw Maggie/Mother sitting at the end of my bed as I came round from the anaesthetic. In this dream/vision I could even recall her smell. As before, she bends over to stop my mouth before kissing me on the forehead, and as before I realise it isn't mother, after all, but Maggie. A call woke me next morning. It was Mother, calling to tell me that Maggie Leighton had died.

I found a jewel of a New Zealand nurse at the hospital called Jenny, who later returned with me to Malibu and became Tomcat's nanny. She knew where my appendix was and stole it for me. Holding the bottle up to the light I saw my healthy appendix floating around in a sea of chemical. 'As pink as a baby's bottom,' said a delighted Jenny. I kept the bottle for quite a few years, but eventually it disappeared, as everything does around me.

Lying in hospital is a dangerous occupation, because one becomes aware of unwelcomed life questions, all queuing to surface. Robert and Bruce both came to see me regularly, but their visits failed to help me find life answers with any earth-shattering clarity. What was really going on with me at that time? All I remember is a great numbness protected by the Miles stiff upper lip. But since I forbade those life questions to make an appearance I was, all in all, pretty merry.

When I was up and about once more I went to stay at the Old Mill for a few days before flying back to LA. I desperately needed to lay a few old ghosts to rest. Would returning to Robert and the Old Mill ever be a possibility? I felt in Robert's silent heart of hearts that he wanted us to reunite, but did I? Walking around the grounds, even seeing the little filly, Buttercup, that I had bred myself didn't change my mind; no, oddly enough, not at any time did I feel that a reunion held the remotest possibility – or so my *conscious* mind kept telling me.

I remember wandering with Bruce into the lower floor of the ancient barn.

'Why is that beautiful boat in here? Let's take it onto the river.'

I explained to Bruce that Robert, eager to return to his nautical Bolt roots, had decided to carve out a sailing boat with his own hands. All who came to see it marvelled at his hidden professional skills as a carpenter. That is, until it was nigh on completed and Tomcat waddled in, aged about four.

'What are you doing, Daddy?'

'Finishing off your sailing boat.'

'Where will you put it?'

'Why, on the river, of course.'

'But, Daddy, how will you get it out of the door?' Neither of us so-called grown-ups had thought this one out. The boat was bigger than the exit and we were forbidden to widen it because the Old Mill was a listed building.

Whenever I think of those seven idyllic years at the Old Mill, Bruce's incredulity at the sight of such a lovingly carved, elegant boat lying on its side, waiting to be taken out into the light for its maiden voyage up Moon River clings in my memory; the catalyst for all that followed – a symbol of Robert and all the beauty I had abandoned, or that had abandoned me.

The Knight's Tale Continues

Soon after Robert married his first wife Jo, they settled down in the Somerset village of Topsham, where he taught at the village school. Those were simple, honest days for Robert, but they couldn't last. The more successful he became, the more those innocent days at Topsham village school flamed like a beacon of peace. Yet when I put this to Jo she responded, 'Then why was he always in such a hurry to move on?' But that was Robert. Always in a hurry to move on. Always, always. It wasn't until we moved into Chithurst Manor, where I still live today, that Robert finally stopped running and said, 'I've come home.' Yet being a schoolmaster at Topsham village school was probably the next best thing to home for Robert.

He wrote a nativity play for the school, which was a triumph and gave him the confidence to continue with other ideas for plays, including radio plays. After teaching all day, he would return home to mark the homework before retiring to the back room to scribble all night. This punishing schedule began to take its toll on his marriage as well as on their two young children, Sally and Ben.

A Man For All Seasons was Robert's eighth play. He had sent it to an uncompromising but renowned agent, Peggy Ramsay. Although on some occasions her undiluted honesty could be devastating, she held the reputation of being the most selective and respected agent in London. 'If you want a nursemaid then you've come to the wrong place,' she said, and suggested Robert create a worthy radio play out of *A Man For All Seasons* first. With his monumental energy, Robert's next draft took him no time at all and was a terrific success – just what he needed to spur him on to greater things.

Around that time he answered an ad for an English teacher at Millfield School. Now this was a bizarre career move, to say the least, with

Robert coming from such a left-wing background. Millfield was a public school catering to the offspring of the rich and privileged, which often meant the victims of broken marriages. His time there, however, was unexpectedly enjoyable, for he was given the job of sailing master as well as teaching English. Though an extra task on his already over-burdened curriculum, it gave him enormous satisfaction. His enthusiasm was somewhat dampened when the headmaster asked him to teach religious instruction too. Robert protested – he had no idea of how to go about it. The headmaster ordered him to watch an RI class that he himself was giving, to see how simple it was. Robert learnt a hell of a lot that day, thanks to the headmaster's fury with one pupil who refused to concentrate. He came over and bashed the boy over the head with the Bible, shouting, 'How many times do I have to tell you? God is the spirit of infinite love!' Overworked or not, Robert brought home a heftier pay packet, which was much needed, for his second child, Benedict, had arrived, shortly to be followed by a third, Jo-Jo.

Robert must have been a rare English teacher because so many of his ex-pupils looked upon him as the greatest inspiration of their lives. Many made special pilgrimages to our home to share their gratitude with him. Even pupils who, like Robert, had been unable to learn anything from any other teacher responded to his enlightened teaching methods. (He even got me reading the classics, so juicy did he make them sound! I'd never read a book before I met him.)

In 1957 the colourful impresario Binkie Beaumont engaged Frith Banbury to direct Robert's first stage play, *A Flowering Cherry*, in the West End, starring Ralph Richardson and Celia Johnson. This was undoubtedly the major turning-point in his career. The play received great reviews and packed them in, so Robert decided it was time to take the frightening gamble and to become a full-time playwright. He gave in his notice at Millfield and the family moved to Richmond Green.

His next play was *The Tiger and the Horse*, with Michael and Vanessa Redgrave. Although it was not a huge hit it enjoyed a good, healthy run and Vanessa was always grateful to Robert, looking upon that play as her theatrical awakening. She once told me that it had given her the confidence she desperately needed at the time, and that the opportunity to act with her father, whom she adored, came as a gift from the gods.

Next, in 1962, came *Gentle Jack*. Every playwright has his favourite play and *Gentle Jack* was Robert's. It starred Dame Edith Evans and Kenneth Williams – a quainter pair of queenly thespians it would be hard to conjure up. How I wish I had been a fly on the wall during those rehearsals!

Was it any wonder that David Lean's large and pointed ears got wind of Robert's growing reputation? David, who was still riding high on the success of *The Bridge on the River Kwai*, had hit trouble during pre-production on his next project, *Lawrence of Arabia*. He was unimpressed with his commissioned script and surgery was required. It was quite a risk on his part to take on a young playwright with no screen-writing experience, especially since there was little time left before shooting started. David recalled: 'I was instantly seduced. All fears were eclipsed by Robert's enthusiasm – it was so catching.' In fact, David was deeply attracted to Robert's whole demeanour, finding his boundless energy as hypnotic as those great blue eyes. I'm not suggesting anything sexual here, for it *is* possible to be deeply attracted solely on a mental level. Their relationship was intense, and David looked upon Robert – as I'm sure Robert looked upon Tony Quinton – as his intellectual superior (when it suited him)! Whenever David got himself hemmed into the losing corner of an argument, he would play the role of innocent prep-schoolboy to the hilt, using his lack of a formal education with an uncompromising lack of remorse: 'You're the intellectual, you *should* know more than me. That's why I've employed you – to think!'

Under huge pressure, due to lack of time, Robert completed the first half of the script before being carted off to jail. In September 1961, having taken part in a demonstration organised by the Campaign for Nuclear Disarmament, Robert was arrested with John Osborne and Vanessa Redgrave. He and Bertrand Russell were sentenced to a month in prison, where Robert had counted on being able to continue writing the script for *Lawrence*. He had been unaware that anything created in Her Majesty's Prison would be automatically confiscated.

Robert refused to sign a document – which would have freed him – stating that he would not protest again. As a result Sam Spiegel went bananas, and flew over to confront him face to face. Robert laughed as he told how Spiegel frothed at the mouth with the fear that his huge investment with Columbia was about to thunder down the drain just so that Bolt could assuage his bloody conscience. Finally Robert had to give in to him and felt enormous embarrassment as he drove away from jail in Spiegel's Rolls-Royce.

One day Robert was being taken to his first experience of location shooting. Flying over the Middle East with Sam Spiegel in his private plane, feeling that the good life was more than living up to its reputation, he observed Spiegel looking down over Israel, Jerusalem and Jordan.

'What are you thinking, Sam?'

'I'm thinking those bloody Jews are everywhere,' he replied.

David gave Robert a walk-on part in *Lawrence*, just for fun. He's the one in the officer's mess, at the bar, puffing on his beloved pipe. Robert took to acting like a duck to water, but never felt the need to do it seriously. His determination that every actor must get the emphasis just right on every line left David with a hell of a task: 'Why not put all the dialogue down on tape for me so I can play it in my head before every scene?' Robert's tape of the whole screenplay was so polished and instructive that David insisted each actor come into his caravan and listen to it before shooting a new scene. Robert was afraid that this might patronise the actors but apparently it didn't.

One *Lawrence* story sums up David to a T. The actors were becoming irritable and exhausted, sore from the ruthless wind, sun and sand. Throughout the shoot David was the only one to be seen out there in all weathers, continually scolding the actors for being flimsy of spirit. When shooting finally came to an end he was taken to hospital to have his eyeballs briefly removed while pockets of sand that had accumulated during the long shoot were cleansed from his raw sockets. Never once did he complain about his oncoming blindness. 'Not because I was brave, but because I hadn't noticed.' That statement says it all.

David and Robert's complicated yet creative partnership and friendship lasted well into *Dr Zhivago*, four years later, and beyond into *Ryan's Daughter* five years after that. But, alas, as their relationship blossomed and flourished, Robert's marriage began to disintegrate. The common showbusiness tale.

Though Robert was never unfaithful in mind or body, he developed an uncompromising fidelity towards his work. His new lifestyle reflected his obsessive desire to achieve something worthwhile: he was bursting with ideas, and found the hours in the day far too short. Those who want to squeeze it all in usually do so to the detriment of their family.

In 1962, after Robert's treasured Staffordshire bull terrier Billy had killed a dog on Richmond Green, the family moved to a beautiful country house near Lymington, Hampshire, called Pylewell. Robert had always yearned to become Lord of the Manor, not because he hankered for a title – far from it – but because he fostered a certain image of himself as a country gentleman, a kind of Tolstoyan figure, walking through peaceful meadows with his stick, surrounded by dogs. Perhaps he picked up some of that Tolstoyan discontent too, forever yearning for the simple, quiet way in the midst of the excitements of city life, and longing for life's extravagances when country ways became too quiet. Oh, to be happy in the moment!

During their brief stay at Pylewell, Robert was so preoccupied with work that poor Jo grew more and more lonely, buried in the country-side. I have great sympathy for her because I, too, suffered through Robert's workaholism. He ended up paying a heavy price for failing to get juiced up by anything other than his blasted page number.

One crisp autumn day he looked up from his work to find that another unnecessary door had been erected in a place where no door ought to be. Finally he *had* to notice. 'What's going on, Jo?'

'What d'you mean?'

'Why so many doors and bookshelves?' It turned out that Jo, not receiving the care and attention she needed from Robert, had struck up an *amour* with the local carpenter, and who can blame her?

Robert could see no way forward. He left home and bought a flat on Chelsea Embankment while Jo went off with her carpenter. Robert's children, Sally, Ben and Jo-Jo, bought their mother a beautiful new home called Cuckoo Hill in Hampshire, with the proceeds of the *Man For All Seasons* trust, set up by their father. They are still together, living quietly in the countryside, and Jo is now a novelist.

The public's reaction to both *Lawrence* and *Zhivago* was tremendously enthusiastic, but neither David nor Robert ever received the critical acclaim their partnership deserved.

'Jealous, the lot of them!' grunted David, and I can only assume that he was right because what other reason could there have been for the critics to be so dismissive of such a high standard of work? They changed their tune in time, but why did it take so long? It remains a mystery to me.

Robert, never one to hesitate, began the screenplay of *A Man For All Seasons*, this time working with the great Hollywood director, Fred Zinneman, who was top of Robert's list. Robert was a great *High Noon* fan – who isn't? Theirs was an easy partnership and the entire shoot ran smooth as silk. They agreed on content, style, interpretation, actors, costume, everything. From the first day of shooting Fred knew he was on to a winner and so did Robert. That's where I came in.

Enter Steven and Exit

Steven Spielberg always felt guilty for taking me away from Bruce, even though he did no such thing. Our time was up, and Steven just happened to be in the right place at the right time. He lived in a charming wooded area of Laurel Canyon in a plain wooden bungalow; the dog that he had was a plain ordinary little mongrel, and the life that he lived was a plain ordinary life. You could easily have described him as a plain ordinary Jew from Phoenix, Arizona – until, that is, you took a closer look. I took a closer look, a much closer look, and the closer I looked the more I liked the simplicity of the whole set-up.

Steven had still to make the big time so I wasn't being drawn into the aura of the King of Hollywood because he wasn't even Prince Regent at that time. What interested me was his childlike lack of pretension, high intelligence laced with integrity, an untarnished curiosity coupled with an uncanny belief in destiny. He knew where he was going, all right, yet there was no boastfulness, no arrogance around his ego, merely the quiet wisdom that such knowledge imparts, together with the need to get on with it. The other great men I have known all had a touch of arrogance – Bertrand Russell, Olivier, Bolt and Lean – yet not even a glimpse of it did I detect in Spielberg.

Clever people are usually intellectual, and intellectuals find it hard to unblock themselves sufficiently to journey from the head to the heart, let alone to the third eye wherein reside intuition, visions and psychic phenomena. To focus one's energy in the heart or, indeed, in the third eye, involves leaving the intellect behind for a moment. Steven wasn't an intellectual and that, I believe, explains an experience he had as a boy. While he told me about his paranormal 'happening' there was not a hint of self-importance, merely a matter-of-factness tinged with a healthy embarrassment.

At the age of six or seven he had been walking home from school one day down a suburban street in Phoenix when the skies opened and the force of a revelationary experience sent him reeling to the earth. Looking up from where he lay, the skies opened even further, blessing Steven with a vision. He didn't feel blessed at the time, merely dumbstruck.

The fear of even the slightest inaccuracy deters me from attempting to describe his vision fully. Not believing then in all that rubbish – in those days I'd had no experience of the paranormal – I only half listened to his story. Let it suffice that his vision was a flash-forward that showed him as the King of Hollywood he became. A supernatural experience in itself is not important. What is important, though, is how it changes one's life. Steven's vision certainly changed him, so much so that he was off school for a while. When he was back in the land of the living and the catharsis had worn off, he said to his father, 'Dad, please may I have a movie camera for my birthday?' Being the sceptic I was, and still am, I asked his father, a lovely, gentle fellow too, one evening at a screening to verify the story. It *was* true. All of it.

I was deeply touched by Steven's childlike admiration of David Lean. He hero-worshipped him. True greatness is never mean-spirited for it recognises its own. Steven was always questioning me about David's directing methods and his eyes would light up like those of a child enjoying a favourite bedtime story.

I've been told many times that David Lean and Steven Spielberg became cinema giants because they were blessed with the knack of knowing what the public wanted. I disagree. Neither Steven nor David ever bothered to step outside themselves to search the public taste for inspiration, for they *were* that public through and through. They simply took it for granted that what they wanted to see, the public wanted to see too, and no one could ever take that identification away from either of them.

During my Spielberg era all his energy was going into his attempts to get *Close Encounters of the Third Kind* off the ground. We had the same agent in Guy McElwaine, but he wasn't optimistic about Steven's chances: *Close Encounters* was an expensive project to set up. So it would be fair to say that I was with Steven through his merely mortal period. In retrospect, I expect it did him good to understand those frustrations, familiar to most of us, of being stuck in limbo for a while.

Duel, a film for television, put him on the map because it turned out so special that it was given a proper cinema release. This was followed by *Sugarland Express*, a zappy, snappy, funny film with Goldie Hawn, also hailed as excellent. Although neither was a great box-office winner, they aptly demonstrated Steven's unique talent, and created a definite buzz around them.

He read a great number of scripts at that time, but only half-heartedly because of his commitment to *Close Encounters*. We rarely went out anywhere – he was no more gregarious than Bruce had been, which suited me just fine. Oddly enough, what I remember most was lying on his bed, with a mass of cushions propping us up, while Steven took charge of the night's entertainment. The standard of American TV was numbingly tacky, especially when compared with the high English standards I had left behind. We were still living in the primitive mid-seventies with no videos to bring home, and there was only *Saturday Night Live* and some educational programmes that were worth watching. Therefore, with the TV controls in one hand and me in the other, Steven would make his own home movies by switching from one channel to the next with immaculate timing.

Have you ever tried making your own movie by channel hopping? I have, and the results are usually pretty dire. But not so with Steven. He would spend about three minutes with the three different movies he had selected for the evening's entertainment and once he'd got the gist of the plot of each, he would edit a brilliant new plot, his fingers hovering over the controls like a vulture ready to pounce. It was during these occasions that I became aware of his sixth sense. He seemed to be able to time the snogging bits when he wanted snogging bits, action bits when he wanted action bits and so on. It was a truly eerie experience: how did he *know* that the miniseries on ABC would have a snogging scene precisely when he switched over?

'How d'you do it?'

'It's easy, just concentrate. Most Hollywood movies are written to the same formula.' I tried, but I guess I never got to know the formula.

I am a stickler for smells, having been cursed with a wretchedly sensitive nose, yet I cannot remember Steven smelling of anything. He never sweated either. Strange, that. It was as if he was pure and innocent both inside and out. He kept lots of miniature cars, engines, children's games and comic books littered about his floors, so I found myself regressing back to when I was little. Playing at mummies and daddies is exactly how it was and, in a way, Babes in the Wood too. We were fortunate enough to keep our loving cocooned and protected from the outside world. I would never know such a sweet and undemanding time as during my Spielberg era – until it came to an end.

One morning, Guy McElwaine put a new script through Spielberg's door. He read it with little enthusiasm. 'Piece of trash, but I think I can make something of it.'

He gave it to me to read, and I agreed wholeheartedly that it *was* a load of old rubbish. 'Unless you can make the shark a real character, as well as genuinely terrifying, don't touch it.'

Steven went quiet and thoughtful. 'Sharks ... the creatures humans fear most.' His eyes became glossy with hope. 'Might it be the key for getting *Close Encounters* off the ground?'

He tested out the idea of a killer shark eating people on Tomcat and, judging by Tom's reaction, sharks were hot!

As Steven took that mammoth intake of breath required for the commitment of giving birth to *Jaws* I, too, conceived a new life. (Wouldn't I just!) The shock shattered my equilibrium considerably, not because I was frightened that Steven might not welcome a baby, but because I knew damn well that *playing* mummies and daddies with Steven was a long way from actually *being* a mother again.

I didn't tell Steven I was pregnant, not at first, for I needed to go away to think about it. I had savoured the fantasy of plaiting the silky hair of a baby girl, but that spectacular sentimentality never warranted the serious commitment of motherhood.

Aware as I was of Steven's excellent father potential, I was also aware of the age difference between us. He was younger, and this frightened me. Was it because both Robert and Olivier had been so much older than I? True, Bruce had been six years younger, but then he never got me pregnant. Though I still felt a sense of loss, I carried no guilt from my last abortion, which I had had when I was sixteen, so guilt wasn't a factor. I found the decision devilish tricky to make. The overriding feeling was doubt that either of us was ready to put a little creature first.

I would have certainly aborted without telling Steven had I been 100 per cent sure of my own feelings. Inflicting an unnecessarily painful dilemma on him, when contraception had become the woman's responsibility, would have been downright selfish. So I suppose my need to witness Steven's feelings was further proof of my own uncertainty.

When I told him the news Steven became serious and thoughtful. Did I detect a flush of secret excitement – or was it horror?

'Do you want to keep it?'

I passed the question straight back. 'Do you want me to keep it?' The same flush of excitement – but this time his eyes indicated that he would have welcomed a child.

'That's an unfair question. I'm not pregnant, you are.'

Since no words were spoken regarding his wants, and because he made it absolutely clear that the ball was in my court, I took that to mean that he didn't want a baby. Or perhaps he felt that *I* didn't. His career was only just beginning, and for hugely ambitious men, the beginnings of their career tend to take up all their attention.

With the ball once again firmly in my court I suffered pure torment while trying to make up my mind, one minute doubt, the next certainty, on and on, toing and froing. Then a truth came at me. How dare I even contemplate giving motherhood another crack of the whip when I was already proving myself useless at disciplining the child I did have? No two ways about it, I had sufficiently proved that the role of mother was not my strong point. Yet we all are capable of change, therefore should I leap into an abortion just because I harboured a sense of failure at my inability to bring up Tomcat effectively?

On and on went the toing and froing until the final truth hit home. I found myself, against my better, sceptical nature, perfectly convinced that Steven's childhood vision had been genuine. And, that being the case, having to play the Queen of Hollywood one day to his King and give birth to the heir apparent was a million miles away from what my destiny was about. All of a sudden my choice was simple: join Spielberg's trip, or keep steady as I went on mine. I probably would have kept the baby if Steven was to remain merely Spielberg, but King of Hollywood? No. We were not meant to have children together.

Robert had made it clear that if a good school wasn't found in LA it would be in Tomcat's best interests if he returned to England for his education. He had found an excellent little school called Ibstock Place in Roehampton and his old friend Anne Queensberry, whom Tomcat had known all his life, had kindly offered to help out. I was still determined to find a suitable school in LA even though I felt I was fighting a losing battle.

Having done a great deal of research, I came to the conclusion that the local Santa Monica Montessori school would best suit him. How wrong I was! He came home one evening, fuming. 'Were you aware, Ma, of the one-way peep-holes in each classroom door?'

I was aware and he knew it.

'How would you like nosy-parkers spying on you?'

'If I were concentrating on the work in hand, I wouldn't notice.'

'Bullshit!'

We both knew that the peep-holes were only part of the problem. Tomcat hated the school. It was worrying for me because I was sure the Montessori method would have been just the ticket. I so wanted Tomcat to settle down because that way he could remain with me in LA. We were very close, probably dangerously so in many ways. I went to see some other schools, but they all made Montessori shine even brighter by comparison.

With no other school remotely suitable for the likes of such a one-off, I was tempted to try Krishnamurti's school in Ohi, northern California. Krishnamurti's idea was to teach from a place of love, from which the essential discipline would spring up naturally. People spoke highly of this method, so we gave it a try. The only snag was that the parent, or parents, had to remain at the school until the child felt sufficiently secure to bid them goodbye.

What an ideal setting for a school! Parkland as far as the eye could see with little wooden Noddy houses scattered hither and thither. Perfect!

'How about this Tomcat – homy, eh?'

Silence.

The other parents were weaned after a few days, but not us. A week went by and finally I was the only parent left, desperately waiting for Tomcat to give me permission to leave. He never did.

That week at Ohi should have been a privilege because Krishnamurti was there but, having yet to experience my own spiritual awakening, I stupidly paid little heed to the pearls of wisdom pouring forth on our meditation walk. Even so, I was fascinated by his exuberant chimpanzee gait, in contrast to the smiling eyes packed with melancholy. From what I could gather his sadness stemmed from a belief that his teachings never penetrated the non-believer (me!) only the semi-enlightened. For this reason alone, he thought he had failed.

'Your son isn't going to settle down here,' he admitted sadly.

'Why?'

Krishnamurti shrugged. 'He's too much of a rebel.'

After a mass of school-searching and an overdose of soul-searching, Robert and I both came to the decision that Ibstock Place was now the answer. How excruciatingly raw that first severing turned out to be. It is times like that when all the inadequacies and failures come belching back into the tastebuds. But worse still was seeing the agony of it all mirrored in Tomcat's eyes as we parted. The timing was appalling because the term began simultaneously with a TV special I couldn't afford to pass up. My career wasn't sufficiently robust at that time (any time!) to turn down good projects and, besides, I was broke. (I have since learnt my lesson of not placing career *before* life, but at the time all I knew was it had to be the right move otherwise my heart would have broken completely.)

It was a comfort, however, to know that he had settled down and was doing fine at boarding school. Robert took him back to the Old Mill at weekends, I went home for half-term and we were back together in LA during the holidays. No wonder Tomcat loved LA – we all love what is bad for us and his Ibstock manners rapidly dissolved into the pollution as he reverted back to a Kentucky-Fried-Chicken-and-candy-gorging TV beach bum within seconds (just like Steven and me!). If Gladys hadn't got her blasted malignant tumour, I would have been living in England again by then.

David Frost asked me to do a three-hour special, *Dynasty*, with his new company, Parradine. The screenplay was based on a James Michener novel of the first English settlers, which was then very popular. The character required a kind of Boston drawl, similar to Katharine Hepburn's. It was a tremendous challenge to be asked to play a leading lady with real character, especially as I was to play her young right through to old – a dame riddled with the brand of true grit that only those first settlers possessed. Harris Yulin played my husband with Stacy Keach as the wicked brother. They were great buddies in real life, which added an extra dimension to the shoot.

I had recently been practising my Deep South accent for a Public Broadcast Television drama called *Temple Drake*, based on William Faulkner's classic novel, *Sanctuary*. I played the character Temple Drake. Temple was a highly strung Southern belle, a cultured Scarlett O'Hara. I had the good fortune to act with Mary Alice, a black actress with a glorious voice, who turned into a God-blessed friend, for I was in dire need at that time of a woman friend I could trust.

Women have been suspicious of me all my life, for I fail to fit into any of the stereotypical female roles. I am not a feminist, more of an individualist I suppose. I am not a role model, or a leader, or a follower, and as such, other women don't know how to relate to me. So to meet someone who took me as I was and not as how the media – who don't know me from Eve – wished to perceive me was a real bonus.

Playing a classy dame in a classic drama was about as prestigious as LA acting got. On the big screen there were so few challenging female roles, and the one or two that came up each year, such as the one David Whiting grabbed for me in *Cat Dancing* would no longer come my way now that I was a black-listed scarlet woman – ironically, thanks also to David Whiting. The Lord giveth and the Lord taketh away! Another reason I didn't work too much was because I had made a vow at the beginning of my career never to act in violent films or films in which the actor responds to special effects. Little had I known then that they would soon become almost the only films to be made.

The *Dynasty* story spanned almost five decades, so as my character's children grew up, the actors changed. My latest 'son', a fine young man, had to play a particularly tricky scene with me, completely cold, on his first day on set, whereas I had the luxury of having played the mother for the past four weeks. This new son of mine (the actor had been a carpenter previously) asked me during the tea break if he could come home with me to get the scene as good as we could. I knew this request had nothing to do with seeing etchings – he was too serious-minded for that. Back at the beach-house we dissected the scene into sections to analyse its driving force and clarify the motive.

I'd met with enough excellence to recognise that this young man was not only serious-minded but driven. So hard did he work, that evening, that I realised he, too, like Spielberg, knew exactly where he was going. His name was Harrison Ford. His character had an ambitious minx of a sister. The girl they found to play her was perfect and also bore an uncanny resemblance to her screen mother – me!

Shortly thereafter I saw Bruce – we were still friends and have remained so – who told me how lonely Spielberg was, although this seemed unlikely to me since Steven was giving birth to *Jaws*. Nevertheless, this somehow led us on to the subject of what perfect lookalikes my 'daughter' and I were.

'I'm gonna arrange an evening for them to meet when Spielberg returns to town,' said Bruce, his heart always in the right place. I remember an initial pang of jealousy but, after confronting my feelings honestly, I could see that it was a good idea. I had found it hard to look Steven in the eye after the abortion. Not necessarily out of shame but out of a sense of hopelessness for, let's face it, an abortion isn't exactly the greatest aphrodisiac to lubricate a partnership's continuity. No, much as I'd always love him, there was no going back for me and Steven, which left a clear way forward for my 'daughter', Amy Irving. They got married and finally Amy gave Steven the son he so wanted – Max.

As far as I know, Steven has yet to abuse his power, or fall from grace.

Snapped Bolt

Tomcat was returning to Robert and Ibstock Place for the summer term. We chose to spend those last precious hours of the Easter hols at our favourite diversion, the fun-fair. Tomcat pulled at my sleeve with glee, pointing to the most horrific-looking ride I'd ever seen. 'Please, Ma! Let's go on that!' I turned to look into his eyes – the kind you can easily drown in.

My childhood daring for the more dangerous fun-fair rides, walls of death, big dippers, roller-coasters, you name it, had remained undiminished until that moment when I cracked.

'Getting old, Ma!' Tomcat hauled me around to face the terrifying monster, a cog-wheel with separate bullet rockets shooting out from spikes, all spinning in every direction.

'It would be no fun, that one, Tomcat.' *Was I* growing old?

'Cowardy cowardy custard!' He knew how to wind me up.

'OK. Let's get it over with!'

Once we started moving, sitting there side by side unbearably squashed in our steel mesh basket, it felt exactly like a torture chamber! It was the most brutal ride I had ever been on and I was a connoisseur, remember. Why, oh, why, does one do it? After about seventy seconds, at full speed, hugging each other with fright, our mesh door flung itself open exposing a gaping hole of death rushing at us with every spin.

My task was first to underplay the danger, second to pin Tomcat against the back of the mesh basket with all my body weight, my thigh as the barrier, and thirdly to bar the gaping exit with my right arm while holding on for grim death with the other. Hard though I tried to stay cool, Tomcat was no fool and fully aware our chances were slim. Fortunately we were both wiry. They claim that a woman never knows her true physical strength until she has to save her offspring from certain death. We hear of women lifting cars, trucks even. How I prayed that those stories were true.

'Will we make, Ma?' No longer could I drown in Tomcat's eyes, for in them had sprung a glassy wall of fear, in touching contrast to my earlier sight of his little face, which had emulated the bravery of his father's ... His father. Where was Robert? How I needed him then. I tried hollering for attention, but with all the fun of the fair raising a chorus of high-pitched terror, not even Pavarotti would have stood a hope in hell of being heard that day.

I was losing my grip with the sheer force of gravity. Tomcat was beginning to slip out from behind my scrunched-up thigh and there was nothing I could do about it. I saw the mass of sharp, torturous machinery, people, children that would be our mutual deathbed. Just to let go seemed so tempting. All just to stop. My bladder burst with the sheer terror of one certainty – I could only hold on a few seconds longer.

I saw Tomcat's greyish-green countenance lighten slightly. 'We're slowing down, Ma! We're slowing down!' Our torture chamber slowly came to a halt. Our testing time, for the moment anyway, was up. We would live to see another day. I told the guy in charge to close down the ride until the snapped bolt had been rewelded. He said he'd see to it. I hope he did. He didn't apologise, but we were past caring. Back home we bathed our dents and bruises amazed that nothing was broken, and, horrific though it had been, the nightmare served to bond us tighter than ever.

That snapped bolt had me thinking. However much I had cried out for Robert's strength in the mesh torture chamber, I knew our bolt would never be rewelded. No, we had snapped for good, just like Bruce and me, just like Olivier and me, just like Spielberg and me.

Only with hindsight was I able to understand that something power-ful had taken hold of my subconscious since the death of David Whiting. How else could I account for the fact that I wasn't *un*happy with this messy life of mine? I should have been. The truth was, I felt uncomfortable in showbiz having lost my sense of ambition as well as direction. Why couldn't I commit to anything or anyone? I should have been longing to, for surely I was a woman with a healthy need not only to disperse healthy talent but also to fulfil normal human needs – success, family and home? Why hadn't I taken advantage of the groundwork Mother had so thoughtfully prepared for me on Brighton seafront? I wondered how lonely Olivier had been over our years apart. Had he found another mistress or had those needs been made redundant due to a new understanding with Joanie? Christ knows, he deserved it – but that didn't prevent me from going weak at the knees whenever his name was mentioned. He must have heard about my separation from Robert, so if he wanted me back it was he who had to make the running.

LA has always been a catalyst for future fads, and I found the resurgence of 'new woman' a tasteless fad lacking in femininity. 'Hey, man, you wanna fuck?' The men were being chased and becoming chaste before my very eyes, but then I'm just an old-fashioned girl.

But not an old-fashioned girl regarding my son, it seemed, just another messy, selfish, modern mum, having her cake and eating it. Yet, was I? I felt some confidence in knowing that, with me returning home regularly, Tomcat was far better being educated in England. Robert had been a rare teacher. It seemed that he, unlike Krishnamurti, had the knack of getting through to the layman, the unenlightened. Better, surely, that our son be around him than around the scarlet woman of Hila Bend. I was still revelling in the tiddler's free anonymity in the oceans of LA and lacked sufficient guts to return, an unjustly condemned fish, to that ever so small English pond.

Having hated boarding school with a passion, I swore never to send any of my children to one. Now I had to live with the hypocrisy of having done just that. It was a mess, for not only did I miss Tomcat hugely, but I had failed in my role as a single mother. So there you have it. I hope there was some selflessness amid *some*, doubtless, selfishness.

Falling into Aloneness

In the late summer of 1975 I went home to England, to Dartmouth in the West Country for eight whole weeks – glorious! I had returned to film Mishima's haunting novel, *The Sailor Who Fell from Grace with the Sea*. Gladys seemed perfectly happy to stay with Jenny, who was now a permanent fixture. Though her tumour had expanded, the vet warned that removing it would undoubtedly hasten her end. Robert would bring Tomcat down to see me at the little cottage I had rented on the edge of the estuary, and even my parents were coming down to stay for a week. Things were looking good.

Ironically, *Sailor's* producer, Marty Poll, had also produced the *The Man Who Loved Cat Dancing*. Perhaps he, knowing my innocence, felt it unfair that I should be blacklisted, for it was the first proper film offer to come my way since I had been indirectly accused of murder.

The director, Lewis John Carlino, was to realise his lifelong ambition in making Mishima's philosophy comprehensible to a Western audience. Mishima's controversial way of thinking is most succinctly expressed in his *thin* book *Sun and Steel*. He claims that when an apple is severed through its centre at the moment of ripeness, exposing its core to the light, it experiences a moment of glory rather than dwindling uselessly within the darkness of the dying flesh. He claims that knowing when to die, at one's peak, is what life is all about. Mishima honed his body to perfection, and committed suicide in early middle age, his moment of ripeness. Even though the purity of his actions was all scuffed up with politics, philosophers who practise what they preach are as rare as gold dust.

The film was about a small gang of schoolboys who believe that the sailor, by retreating to live on shore and thus falling from grace with the sea, is thereby forsaking his destiny, his dream of capturing his

57

white shark. The boys interpret his action of deserting the ocean in exchange for helping a woman run her antique shop as certain disgrace to any true great white shark hunter. In their eyes his action proves he has passed his peak, and rather than allowing himself to dwindle away into nothingness on the shore, like the core within the apple, the boys believe he must have a moment of glory and then die. Kris Kristofferson was to play the doomed sailor and Jonathan Kahn my character's son who kills him.

Kris had also rented a cottage on the shore of the estuary. At the time he was married to Rita Coolidge, a singer with a velvet voice. She was a beautiful woman, but not too fond of either England or Kris's drinking habits. Shortly after *Sailor* he gave up the booze for good. I was glad when he did because I didn't like to see him continually falling short of his poetic best. Kris Kristofferson serenading me with his guitar and 'Bobbie McGee' or 'Take The Ribbon From Your Hair' surely must rate as one of the most romantic highlights of all time.

It was good to see dear Goffie again. Though still a trifle plump, she carried it with a new-found confidence and personal style. What never altered with Goffie was her great sunny force of character. She was now of an age when the man of her dreams should appear. Goffie would make a simply perfect wife and mother – who was going to be the lucky man?

Then – another romantic highlight – he appeared, the man of Goffie's dreams. Dougie Slocombe, my favourite lighting cameraman – we went back to *The Servant* together – had a gaffer (the gaffer carries the lights) called John Gott. Gottie was a large cockney East-Ender of the old school. Gottie carried the sunshine with him (as well as his lights) wherever he went, so when he and Goffie bumped (due to the size of the pair of them, it wasn't infrequent) the whole area lit up with their joy. They were perfectly matched – still are, twenty-one years and two children, Jenny and Sam, later.

Father and Mother arrived. They were on their way to Shag Rock, our holiday home in Cornwall. In the beginning it was blissful to be with them again, but after a time, Father's continual references to a reunion with Robert became annoying.

'There's no way I'd go back, Father.'

Mother gave him a look. 'Yes, do stop, John. Besides their divorce became final last week.'

Strangely enough, the fact that, after two years' separation, our divorce had become final affected me not a whisker, neither emotionally nor financially. When we parted, I asked for nothing except my original half of the Old Mill, which we had bought jointly. I felt it was fair for Robert to keep the profit the house fetched when he sold it. It might take two to tango, but I still felt I had let him down badly and therefore should pay a price.

A few days later Robert and Tomcat arrived. They were continuing onwards with my parents for the holiday in Cornwall. Since our break-up Robert and I had failed to use our time together constructively, for whenever we broached emotional issues, Robert, just like his name, bolted up. Was it indifference or was he still too fond of me to open up? Had he another woman he was hiding from me? If so, why hide her? Was he being brave or simply pleasant? It was always impossible to tell with Bolt, but we all had a good time, nonetheless.

There was a yoga pose (except I've never met a yoga master who could master it) that Father had been able to do all his life. No one else had ever been able to come close to it. He lay down with tummy flat to the floor, both arms straight out beside his ears, palms and fingers pressed to the floor. Then, with enormous concentration, pressing on his fingers and feet, he would gradually lift his chest, shoulders, stomach, thighs, arms and legs off the floor. His body rose slowly like a soufflé, thus creating a beautiful bow-shaped arc, meeting the ground only at feet and fingers.

I mentioned this trick of Daddy's to Kris, who remained adamant that it wasn't possible. So one evening in my cottage I asked Daddy if he would kindly demonstrate it for Kris.

'Don't you dare, John, it'll kill you!' Mother warned. Daddy was eighty now, and hadn't done the trick for a year or two, so no wonder she freaked. But with Kris standing there, goading him on, it was impossible to resist. Mother turned her head away. 'Cup of tea anyone?'

'No, a whisky to celebrate,' said Father, taking off his jacket, socks, shoes, then rolling up his sleeves. I crept round and stood in front of him to watch his face as he did it. Perhaps the secret of his strength lay in his eyes. As he mentally geared himself up, I realised I had been blessed with a great father; no coward soul he.

'Don't do it, John!' The long gearing-up period was accelerating the tension, exaggerating Mother's nervousness. After about two minutes his eyes pulsated with an immense determination, or was it simply will? Whatever it was, his old body began to rise, very, very slowly. He did it! Not for the usual minute, but forty seconds was ample enough for Kris to acknowledge the amazing feat.

'Well, I'll be darned!' Kris got down to have a go but, like the rest of us, could get nowhere.

Mother always blamed that evening for Father's stomach cancer, which made itself known the following year. I believe the idea of dying at one's peak had gone to his head. I recalled a conversation we had when Father had been irritated by the whole concept of Mishima's philosophy.

'How the hell d'you know when your peak has arrived?' he asked.

'When you miss your banana boat to sail you down Moon River.'

He dismissed my sentimentality with an impatient wave of his arm.

'Death is the end' was my father's philosophy and I never questioned it because it suited me fine. Besides, Father was my hero so his atheism must be right. I lived my life accordingly, with death as the goalpost, then oblivion. That is, until I made *Sailor*. During that shoot my life changed dramatically. So much so that today, twenty-three years later, I am still living according to the new rules that were forced upon me one evening as I walked home beside the estuary – but I'm leaping ahead of myself.

I had just seen the rushes of my previous day's work – the masturbation scene. That day was a day of firsts. The first time a woman had masturbated naked on screen, and the first time I had experienced the true meaning of loneliness. I had spent the previous day eaten up with terror at the thought of that scene. I yearned to make this virgin ground acceptable, true and erotic, for Mishima's sake, as well as to put my own devils to rest.

The reason I had accepted the role lay in Mishima's graceful poetic prose. He describes a woman's loneliness in coping with the loss of fulfilment with such dignified compassion that both the woman and the artist within me was duty-bound to attempt to echo the same, even though it was the most difficult professional agenda I had ever set myself.

Add to this my mother's admonitions: she believed the wicked old wives' tales that masturbation is evil, and leads to blindness and baldness. And there you have it. So with a youth spent in daily terror of sight and hair loss, I had a great desire to banish the taboo in whatever modest way I could. Masturbation can help release often dangerous pent-up energy; more important still, it causes harm to no one – and that's rare indeed. To help raise awareness and erase the taboo so consumed me that I failed to think through the actuality of performing it.

I was going to have to perform a public wank! With an all-male crew, Lew John Carlino included. How could *they* advise me, a woman, on the finer points of masturbation? I hadn't bargained for the ghoulish pit I'd naïvely dug for myself. How was I going to re-enact a woman's most intimate private world in front of a crew I'd known since *The Servant*?

How vividly I recall sitting at my dressing-table mirror (just as Mishima describes in his book), waiting to commit the cursed scene to celluloid. In the scene the son finds a loose notch of wood within his bedroom wall, and pulls it out to spy on his mother's private moments. Even as I sit here writing about it my fingers have gone cold as I recollect the dank tongue of terror lapping through the cracks in the floorboards, oozing saliva of ridicule between my thighs – even higher, into those profoundly private, sacred areas.

I had never experienced such full-hearted enthusiasm and relief as greeted me that night after the rushes were over and the lights went up. Apparently I had pulled it off. I had no wish to linger: the need to return quickly to my little cottage, and cook myself a simple meal before turning in for the night, was more pressing. I hadn't slept much for two nights due to crippling fear of having to walk the high wire, and I was exhausted and starving.

A good evening's rushes is only half the film actor's lot, the rest lies in the power of the editor's scissors. *I* might have pulled off that masturbation scene, but only if the editor had allowed the truth of the scene to be sung and not, as is so often the case, to be left abandoned on the cutting-room floor. To some actors the editor is saviour, to others, their ruination. I'd have to wait and see. Yet walking home alone, for the first time in my career, I felt a slight twinge of – dare I say? – mission accomplished.

That's when it happened. My first Bolt from the Blue. Walking home alone through the Dartmouth dusk, I experienced a weird, all-consuming energy begin to swirl its way into my bones. It was an

61

alien, cosmic ache coming up through the earth, a gloriously loving omnipresence pumping into my limbs. As that strength thumped through my body, spiralling up and out into the Dartmouth evening, linking me to all things – or so I felt, I felt fleetingly the overwhelming luxury of living life precisely in the moment. This almost orgasmic abundance of loving strength, although painfully heavy, was at the same time making me too light to walk. This new feeling of omni-potence was in total contrast to the gaunt loneliness I had experienced during the masturbation scene. It was as if a God-forsaken *loneliness* had been eclipsed by a God-blessed *aloneness*. At that time I was completely unaware that any kind of spiritual phenomenon was taking place – I was totally uninterested in spirituality, believing it all to be hokum. I'd never read books on it or mixed in spiritual circles.

A powerful whisper from the deep enclaves of my brain told me to be alone. The whisper interrupted me. *Mind* not *brain*. It went on to explain that the brain was purely an earthly computer whereas the mind was part of the soul, linked to our collective higher natures, the part of us where our godliness resides – just as in our lower depths live our darkest demons. What was this voice on about? It was all new to me. Drugs weren't part of the phenomenon – I'd hardly taken any except marijuana occasionally, and never when working as I was con-vinced that, if I did, my timing, which is the actor's main tool, would go straight out of the window.

I was reminded of the time, some years before, when I was making *Ryan's Daughter* with Robert Mitchum. He had been amazed that I had never experienced LSD and during a week off shooting gave me a sugar lump, which, he said, contained the drug. As I sucked it, I received my first inkling of how all realms of nature are interwoven, a mysterious energy pulsating through every living thing, be it a wave, a leaf, a stone, a star, a fish or a pig. Later Mitchum confessed there had been *no* LSD in that sugar lump. I was dumbfounded then but now the mystery had been solved. Mitchum had been telling the truth and what I had experienced at his home on the Dingle estuary in County Kerry, but minus new mystery voice, I was experiencing again on the Dartmouth estuary. Did these strange phenomena only happen beside water? The mystery voice gave me a guided tour, demonstrating how I was joined to everything and everything was interconnected, not only to me but to the whole universe. I could tell the voice spoke true because I felt as if I was a single strand of a gigantic cosmic cobweb floating above the estuary up, up, into eternity. The old cliché of all is one and one is all. But, then, clichés aren't usually clichés for no reason.

Staggering slowly homeward I struggled to regain some degree of equilibrium. Wherever the voice was coming from, it was pretty persistent. I tried shaking my head, even holding my nose and blowing, but to no avail. Oddly, it didn't frighten me so much as annoy me. I just wanted to be rid of it once and for all, for my main concern was to fill my ravenous belly. I hoped that hunger pangs would turn out to be the culprit.

At home in my cottage with the estuary lapping below my sitting-room window, I was devastated to discover that the mysterious whisper had bleedin' well followed me home, and was still echoing the same command, to be alone.

'I *am* alone, Bossy Boots!' I heard myself say out loud. Oh dear! Talking to yourself is the first sign of madness. Mother would always reprimand me when I was little for talking to the trees, warning me that only witches talk to trees.

It would be hard for an actor to make a whisper so unflinchingly dictatorial.

'Leave me be!' I shouted, scampering into the bathroom hoping that a pee might relieve me of the voice. It didn't. The voice merely became more imperious and ordered me to light the candle.

'No,' I replied firmly. I was still starving. 'I'm going to light the stove and heat up some chicken casserole.' As I approached the stove to light it, I was again interrupted by the high-handed stranger telling me to light the candle. I was too damn tired to argue the toss for, hungry though I was, the voice in my mind was hungrier. I found myself obeying it and lighting the blasted candle. Having accomplished the voice's wishes, I went back into the kitchen. Old Bossy Boots called me back and commanded me to sit in an armchair at the opposite end of the small sitting room to where the candle was placed. Even as I sat I thought how odd it was that I was obeying. Once I was seated, the voice insisted that my will could control the flame.

Did I believe that I was controlling the flame just because the voice's rhythm was so seductive? Seemingly I *was* controlling the flame. I sniggered with disbelief as the flame seemed to grow smaller then taller with my will-power. I went icy cold. Could the candle flame *really* be obeying me as reverently as I was obeying the voice? It couldn't be so. Was it all imagination, fantasy, make-believe, illusion, delusion, hallucination – or lies? Only later did I come to know that any paranormal experience is in itself irrelevant. The only relevance is in how the experience changes you. At the time I wondered if it wasn't simply some monstrous cosmic joke, which went way above my head.

Was the candle flame somehow responding to my thought waves? There was no doubt that, from four yards across the room, the flame seemed to obey me. It grew smaller on command, then taller – but it couldn't have been doing that, could it? I'd had enough.

'I want *proof*, whoever you are,' I told the voice. 'Proof that it *isn't* my imagination!' The voice told me to gather my energy into a fine silky line and, with implacable doubtlessness, to *will* the candle out.

In my own time, I decided. There was nothing to gain by hurrying. Then, as that previous ache of loving strength returned in waves up through my feet, I gathered every scrap of it. The weirdest thing of all was that once this massive energy was gathered and tightly compressed into a fine silky line, there existed no doubt whatsoever because I already knew the candle would go out.

Out it went. A doddle, I thought. A piece of cake – until the mystery voice spoke again and told me that death is not the end, that birth to death is not a line but a circle of spirits spinning.

And so I *knew* it to be. That knowledge of reincarnation, for rightly or wrongly that's what I felt it to be, lumbered me with a huge burden to carry.

But right then all I could think of was that my mother had been right! I *was* a witch! What was this voice? The voice of Satan or of God? Satan it must have been because God wasn't in the habit of hanging around atheists. What power, I asked myself, could have put out that candle except the power of evil? I found myself crawling across the cottage floor, frantically searching behind curtains and praying for draughts. How ridiculous I looked to the me outside me. For that 'me' never prayed. Absolutely never.

Nothing was ever the same again because I went into a three-year retreat. I had to wipe my life-tape clean, repattern it and work out a new life philosophy. During this period my career as an actress, my motherly duties, my family and friends came second to my mystery voice, who never permitted me to share the experience with anyone.

Perhaps it was protecting me from the ridicule I could attract if my story was exposed.

Why have I chosen to share the story now, after well over two decades, knowing that it will be disbelieved? Because I have discovered only recently that one measly candle going out is nothing, for we are *all* capable of *everything* at the right moment of openness. Even scientists agree that we only use a minute proportion of our full 'mind' potential. The other reason I needed to get the whole damn saga off my chest was because – who knows? – it may lift the burden. Since the incident I have never for one moment considered myself in any way special, or 'chosen'. Quite the opposite, and that is the burden I am still carrying around: the eerie feeling of being cursed because my mystery voice just happened to choose the wrong gal.

PS I have never played at extinguishing candles since!

Purification by Water

Over the past two decades I have been guilty of evading the truth with the media. When journalists asked me about the three subsequent years in America, I told them I had been alone, living in silence with my dog Gladys. This is true, I was – most of the time! What I've never divulged was that I spent three years at the mercy of my voice – my man of mystery, or was it a woman? Or was it my inner voice, my higher (or lower!) self? Yet, having said that, I was as sure of its masculinity as I was of the wisdom in not sharing my secret with the media. Better, surely, to be the scarlet woman of Hila Bend than a mad witch possessed.

Christmas 1975 had me returning to LA and to Gladys. The pain of explaining to Robert my inability to have Tomcat with me for the holidays was matched only by the prospects of solitude throughout the Christmas season *and* on my birthday on New Year's Eve. I had never lived alone in thirty-two years, so that was shock enough without a mystery voice bullying me into silence.

I didn't go to a doctor, psychiatrist, spiritual healer or guru, for they all involved talking, and my mystery voice strongly disapproved of chatter. Chatter, he told me, got in the way of heart experiences. He forbade spiritual books for they, too, involved the intellect – a head trip, and he preferred me to remain in the heart. I was aching to share my candle experience with someone, but each time I thought about doing so, fingers, or *something*, pressed round my neck preventing me from breathing, so the secret remained a secret.

Here I was keeping secrets again, just like my secret affair with Olivier. Was I a *secret* junkie? Like any addict, I grew exceedingly canny, going to great lengths to leave no trace of my addiction. Was I addicted to the voice? A spiritual catharsis is probably as close as I'll get to describing the years that followed, but then I'm no expert, nor would I want to be – experiencing is all I'm interested in.

What I considered to be those three *lost* years were eventually to *find* me, for whatever knowledge came to me came fresh out of silence and true-life experience rather than second-hand from books and the experiences of others. I can grasp more clearly today what was happening on a metaphysical level, but who wants to read endless esoteric philosophical, spiritual hokum in detail?

The couple who rented my Malibu beach-house for the duration of my stay in England loved it so much that they wanted to stay on indefinitely. I heaved a quiet sigh of relief. The light was always too garish and the bashing of waves against the struts of the house had begun to drive me to distraction with its relentless, unchanging rhythm. How I wanted just one wave *not* to come in.

I went to stay with my old friend, Carolyn Pfeiffer, who had come to live in a sweet wooden house up Benedict Canyon. She was a rare creature, beautiful and enormously caring in whatever she chose to do. A high-powered job running her own PR business in London was probably to blame for her failure to find a man with whom to share her life, so she chose to have a child alone. The little girl, Lola, died a cot death at the age of two. The memories were too much for Carolyn so she packed up her life and returned home to America.

It was a godsend being asked to house-sit while Carolyn was off on location for it meant that Gladys and I could be alone among the sweet-smelling trees, dappled light and cicadas of the canyon without wanting just one wave *not* to come in. Blessed silence once more! Yet being surrounded by blown-up photos of Lola everywhere filled me with sadness because she used to play with Tomcat in the Old Mill days.

As Christmas Eve approached I became wretched. How was I to spend the Christmas season entirely on my tod? I was obviously mad, and because the voice was still telling me to be alone I decided to end it all. I had certainly passed my peak. As Mishima says, why hang around using up good air and food when you're not contributing to the general well-being of mankind? I had been cursed, and now that I had the knowledge of life after death I could die knowing that the end could only turn into a grand new adventure. I would be punished for my cowardice, but I was prepared to suffer anything rather than the icy hopelessness that was enveloping me. To halt the aching once and for all expanded into an all-encompassing need for everything to stop. Just stop.

Knowing that my neighbours would care for Gladys, I went down to Carolyn's bathroom, where I'd seen sleeping pills in the cupboard. I opened the bottle and slid some into my hand. As I reached over to fill the tumbler with water and swallow the lot, I heard the voice. It told me to look in the mirror.

The expression in my eyes caught me quite off guard for I was expecting the lifeless stare of a witch. Instead I was astounded by a pair of eyes almost innocent with their eager zest for life. I put the pills back and went up to my room to hide beneath the covers. I often wonder what would have happened if there had been no mirror near Carolyn's sleeping pills that day – or indeed no mystery voice.

Late on the night before Christmas Eve I filled two hot water bottles, took the covers off Carolyn's bed, placed them on mine and, fully clothed, got into bed. However hard I tried I couldn't get warm. The icy dread refused to go away. Frightened now, very frightened, I ran a bath, a very hot bath and stepped in. That was the first moment's warmth I'd had in days. Apart from getting out to feed Gladys and put her into the garden, I remained in that bath, topping up with hot water, for the whole of the Christmas season. Ten days of icy torment, simply topping up with hot water when required.

On another level I was undergoing enormous physical, mental and spiritual changes. It was as if the water was my mother's womb and I was metamorphosing into another being. Horrid it was. Completely horrendous. Then there were the feelings of betrayal – for why was the fear so all-consuming? Outrage, too, at why this should be happening to me. I reflected upon Spielberg's vision and felt envious. Envy and jealousy weren't familiar emotions and I didn't take kindly to their appearance.

Nevertheless Spielberg's vision was something concrete at least. 'King of Hollywood' – a goal to aim for, to act upon. What was one meant to aim for, or indeed act upon, from a candle going out? I could only interpret it as the darkening of the light, and that's what I was getting – in abundance! Shivering, I topped up with more hot water.

The whole host of visions, dreams and revelations that I experienced in my womb bath are only relevant in so far as how they changed me and what concrete evidence they produced.

On 28 December 1975 while still in my bath, I had a flashback of my whole life. Unbeknown to me at the time, I was regressing back to childhood, as far back as six months old. I was able to recall the cellar where we hid when the siren blew. I recalled the doodle-bugs coming over and hitting our house. I had believed that they were my friends, come to transport me back home beyond the sky of endless blue. The whine of the siren I mistook for the heart-warming noise of their rescue signal. Why did I want to be taken away when I was being perfectly well cared-for on earth?

Even further back I went, right back to my prison walls: the bars of my cot, the catnet over my pram and the diamond shapes of the lattice windows. I yearned to squeeze through these shapes, my prison bars, and swoosh back beyond the blue sky whence I had come. The reason I was trying so hard to escape was because out there somewhere I was being almost magnetically pulled to a place that I knew to be home.

I remembered my baby dresses, their colours and textures; swallowing a nappy-pin and being shaken upside-down like a rag doll; many of my mother's 1940s hats, scarves and suits; the ability to see the etheric round the trees, and many different colours or auras around certain people, and sometimes horrid, lifeless, bleak colours around others. Textures, colours, smells came blasting back. Too many memories to recount, yet time and again these recollections transformed into 3D on the opposite wall while I sat in that bath.

December 31st was my birthday – and I was still in the darn bath. I did get out to telephone Tomcat. Robert sounded too chirpy by half. Swigging champagne, so Tomcat said. And why not? Relieved they were happy, I decided to telephone Mother in Brighton.

That telephone call was probably the most important moment of all my paranormal experiences – and, indeed, of my life so far, because it proved I wasn't imprisoned in fantasy. If I hadn't dredged up those childhood memories from somewhere, I would never have written this trilogy of autobiography. I felt that because I had been given such an insight into my childhood, I had to commit those memories to paper. Not out of any self-importance, but out of the purity – innocence, even – from which I accessed them in the first place.

During our conversation it became clear that I was *not* off my head. Every memory I had recalled or seen on the opposite wall while in the bath was true. Every dress, every incident was accurate. Mother was astounded – and rightly. So was I! Some recollections even triggered off long-forgotten memories of her own. It turned into an expensive but enlightening telephone call for both of us. Father wondered when I was coming back home where I belonged.

On the evening of New Year's Eve, my voice demanded I climb the high hill behind my old home at Malibu – alone. To be on the very top, no less, when the midnight chimes struck. This concerned me because the previous year I had come face to face with a rattlesnake on that very same hill-top. He stood up right in front of me and delivered his death rattle. I remained glued to the spot. Fortunately Gladys hadn't caught up with me. At school, a few days previously, Tomcat had learnt that you must not move a muscle when confronted by the deadly rattlesnake. Tomcat's words of warning probably saved my life.

I hadn't reckoned on the voice, or whatever it was, strangling me when I refused the command. The attack was brutal, leaving me unable to breathe. I had no choice but to crawl out to the garden to take refuge in Gladys – my hairy little rock of Gibraltar. I was completely unaware, that New Year's Eve, of how quickly I would become accustomed to being strangled whenever I disobeyed my voice.

What made climbing the hill frightening was that my birthday fell around midnight, right on the turn of the year. Up till that night I had always disregarded my birthday, never having held or been to a New Year's Eve party. But climbing that hill I became uncomfortably aware of the auspicious heaviness enveloping me. We met no rattlesnake that night, and when we reached the top, Gladys and I alone, nothing happened. No fanfares, no cosmic encounters, no flashes or revelations. Nothing but a cold greyness all around, and no sea, horizon or sky for there was no light from either moon or stars.

As I looked out to where the sea should have been the voice told me I must learn to write, compose and sing, and deliver the message through a musical. That, for me, was the last straw, for being dyslexic I couldn't write, neither could I sing a single note and as for composing a tune – farcical! I dismissed the idiotic notion and began the downhill climb.

Safely back home again I drew another hot bath and quickly nestled under the surface. Then, as if on a movie screen, the taps faded into backdrop as a human hand exposed the royal signet ring. It proceeded to fill the wall in front of me. Suddenly the familiar hand in close-up swept a great bejewelled crown of gold aside disclosing Prince Charles. I interpreted the gesture to mean his renouncement of the throne, because he then appeared to me sitting at a plain wooden table surrounded by fine minds emanating integrity. Prince Charles could see the country's true needs because he had no powerlust muzzying up his vision, because he *was* power. A shiver went through me as I thought of the corny, clichéd King Arthur romantic fancy I was witnessing; yet didn't Aristotle say that democracy was the best form of government, failing a wise and just king?

Where had that vision come from? I had only met Prince Charles once, and even then briefly. At the time of that vision he was in his early twenties, unmarried, with spiritual attributes still unknown. Why did that vision remain all through the years, right up to today? Was that my true, one and only phantasmagoria?

The vision itself has remained the same through the decades, but my interpretation of it changes with current events. I wonder if I mistook Charles's renouncing gesture – did it indicate renouncement, or the crumbling of the monarchy? Could it be that that which has been crashed asunder Charles will rebuild in a new way?

I shook myself free of such nebulous fancies and filled up with more hot water. Then, on the wall before me, Prince Charles was replaced by the Duke of Wellington standing at my door, all in scarlet. Who was that greeting him? Lady Caroline Lamb? It could have been a scene from the movie. They embraced wholesomely before Caroline coyly allowed the Duke to lead her to bed. (In reality Olivier and I hadn't seen each other since Robert had made *Lady Caroline Lamb*.) In her bedchamber Caroline stroked the Duke's head in her lap. The texture of the dream (or whatever it was) expanded and deepened into a kind of 3D effect, while the original vivid colours faded into black and white, mostly grey.

As Caroline stroked the Duke of Wellington's head, a thickish, grey, whale-blubbery substance gradually began to seep from his scalp and the gap between scalp and skull widened. Caroline attempted to close the slowly widening gap but could not. She looked to see if the Duke was aware of the catastrophe taking place, but he just purred like a pussycat, mouth spread with a secret smile. Caroline chose to remain still, rather than alarm him. She took a deep breath and lovingly

71

continued to stroke his head while the mushy grey water trickled to the floor.

Although the dream, or whatever it was, ended quite suddenly, my body remained an army of freezing goosebumps accompanied by a dark dread. The familiar silver taps came back into view and, no fingers round my neck, I was able to fill up the bath with hot water, slowly soothing my chill with its warmth.

Re-Entrances

Two weeks later, on 14 January 1976, the doorbell rang. Blow me down with a feather! If it isn't the Duke of Wellington! I felt both dirty and sweaty, having just returned from a long walk with Gladys up the canyon.

'Hello, Sarah.'

'Hello. What are you doing here? How did you find me?'

'Didn't Sue Mengers [our mutual agent] phone to say I'd be ringing you?' I couldn't believe he was real until he kissed my cheek.

However blissed out I was at seeing him again, his air of frailty concerned me greatly, although he was putting up a superb bluff. He looked to the left and right of Yoakum Drive. No one was about.

'Aren't you going to ask me in?' So royal was his manner that I responded in kind by paving his way with a curtsy (just for fun).

He wandered round Carolyn's unpretentious wooden house – thankfully Fabrizio, her interior decorator, had yet to be given his head in my barren room, which held only a bed, almost on the floor, and a few scattered rugs and cushions.

'Bohemian little thing, eh?' From anyone else's lips that would've sounded downright patronising, but from Olivier it somehow slid nicely between all stools. I couldn't think clearly. Shock, I think it's called. He snooped into Carolyn's quarters. 'Makes Hasker Street seem quite posh.' Although Hasker Street, my sixties' Chelsea home, was another lifetime away, it held exotic memories of our secret trysts. The telephone rang. It was Sue Mengers.

'Hi, honey. Hope I did right giving Lord Olivier your whereabouts and phone number without calling you first. He wants to take you to a party tonight in his honour.' My beating heart sank. I needed a party in his lordship's honour like a hole in the head. I thought it indiscreet to divulge Olivier's close proximity.

'Thanks, Sue.' I hung up. 'How come you're here so soon?'

He tossed me a blatantly bedroom look. 'Another knockout before the bell?' How many times had Olivier been knocked out in his life? Too numerous to count. He came to peck me camply on the cheek, before whispering in my ear, 'How long ago was it – our last fuck?'

'You're the one obsessed with dates and times.'

He held my face for a moment, knowing something was up. Should I sit him down and tell him all? As I was about to, those familiar fingers pressed round my throat. Why couldn't I share the glorious knowledge that death is not the end with the one I loved above all?

'What is it? Are you in love with another?' Keeping all recent experiences to myself was unbearable. Yet those warning fingers might have had a point, for if I told Olivier, he would undoubtedly mock me and think I'd gone clean out of my bird. 'Beware, Dame Sarah, don't take a tumble from *Bohemian* into *drop-out*.'

This angered me, probably because it was too close for comfort. 'I *am* a drop-out – I'm smelly, and I don't want the chore of dolling up.'

He squared up to me. 'A whisky while you change?' He was ruthless. Always had been. I went into the bathroom to doll up.

Bathrooms allow for prolific thinking sessions, don't you find? Got me thinking that it would be best not to start another romance with Olivier. That was it: not even to start was the answer. If I was forbidden to share my candle going out, my visions, my psychic dreams, strange voices and fingers round my throat, then I wanted no intimacy whatsoever. For how can one be intimate with a bolster of secrecy rammed between? That in itself was answer enough. Everything *had* to be kept to myself.

I didn't remotely resemble a lord's lady as I re-entered the drawing room. There is only one thing worse than having to doll up for a party and that is having to doll up for a party *quickly*. As he came over and kissed me, the swiftness with which past embers flared up astonished me.

'Why do you insist on keeping all this under a bushel?' He was referring to my legs, I suppose. 'We haven't made love for almost seven years.' So much is sevens, don't you find?

My diaries never go into party detail but, then, with only four parties entered in them over a period of seven years, the answer is obvious: they hold no interest for me and that night was no exception. I'm able to remember Kirk Douglas, Dustin Hoffman, Ryan O'Neal, Natalie Wood, Robert Wagner, Gene Hackman, Tony Curtis, Burt Lancaster, Paul Newman, Jean Simmons, Ali MacGraw but, of course, there were many more.

Olivier had just finished filming John Schlesinger's *Marathon Man* with Dustin Hoffman. He gave me the impression that he was more cock-a-hoop at having survived the physical ordeal than with his performance, yet his twinkle convinced me that he had high hopes of the film's success.

The A group that night reminded me of schoolchildren, all hoping to get top marks from their headmaster and be noticed. But I found myself genuinely touched by their obvious sincerity. Some stood up to honour the great man by giving a little speech. Because Americans are so much more generous-spirited about success than we Brits, they looked upon Olivier as more than a great actor, more than a genius even, perhaps more of a god. Olivier – sorry, God – would gently rub my ankle under the table whenever their reverence went over the top.

Because movie stars need their sleep, the party broke up early, so Olivier let his driver go and asked himself in for a nightcap. He confessed he hadn't been sleeping well. After a few sips of his beloved whisky he glimpsed his watch, whereupon his hitherto chirpy countenance fell. 'I'm not able to give you what I once could.'

'Do you really believe love is linked to performance?'

'Perhaps not, but it helps. I wish I could just lie with you for a moment – it's the nights – I just—' I shushed him quietly and led him to bed ... just like Lady Caroline in my dream.

For the bed's sake it was fortunate we were both so skinny.

'We could use Carolyn's double bed if—'

'I'm happy here. So happy.' I was astounded by how perfectly we fitted into one another still. But, oh, how delicate he was! How frail – yet how beautiful! It never ceases to amaze me, the capacity of the human will. No doubt his body had shrunk, yet gradually his mighty spirit expanded his physical body outwards almost to the breadth of his Othello days. As I lay quietly on that familiar hairy grey chest, he gave voice to his vulnerability in a heartrendingly boyish whisper: 'Do I repel you?'

What attracts us to certain types and not others is as much of a mystery as woman's lack of sexual revulsion to man's old age.

'Does it seem that way?'

'Sorry. I'm a touch sensitive in mind and body.' Sensitive with good reason it transpired. Recently he'd had a prostate cancer removed, pneumonia, bloodclots leading to thrombosis in the leg followed by dermatomyositis.

'What's that?' He confided in a most matter-of-fact manner, as if it were the shopping list. Apparently it is a decidedly rare and painful disease that can kill. Only a handful of people in a million ever experience it. He had had to lie for sixteen weeks propped up in a certain position to avoid water getting into his lungs. 'See here. That's why I wouldn't hold your hand.' He put on the light to show me the greyish watery substance oozing from his fingertips.

The dream in which I had stroked his scalp came whooshing back, stunning me. Should I share it with him? Perhaps not. He didn't deserve to have his spirits crushed. My job had always been to keep those spirits high, so after licking clean each fingertip, I held him as tight as his sensitivity would permit.

The dawn inevitably cued in our farewells, and while waiting for the taxi I noted his youthful, bouncy demeanour was in stark contrast to the stooped creature who had arrived.

'Get that glorious body well oiled because I'll be returning in the summer, fit as a fiddle, to claim it.' Waving him off, I knew it would be so, for whatever goals Olivier set himself, he accomplished them.

In the interim I was committed to a heavy US tour, followed by a world tour promoting *The Sailor Who Fell from Grace with the Sea*, for which I had received, dispersed amid shockwaves, some knockout reviews.

The themes on which I chose to concentrate were the difference between pornography and erotica and the way in which the media continually couples violence with sex when the two are poles apart. For me erotica is in praise of physical love whereas pornography, sometimes linked with violence, debases it. These themes together with Mishima's philosophy of dying at one's peak, gave them all plenty to chew on.

It was a wonder I found it possible to leap from a life of silence and meditation to the bear-garden of publicity. I certainly wouldn't have had the courage if it hadn't been for the strange new strength I was finding in silence. Coming out of *Dynasty* as well as *Temple Drake*, with some terrific reviews, helped, no doubt. Was I on a roll?

I took Gladys, who despite her tumour, showed no signs of dying, around America with me. She had learnt how to curl up as small as a wood-louse in her box so she could accompany me in the aeroplane cabin, as well as how to steal all the talk-shows from me. Her trick was to drink all the water from my glass leaving it standing upright, while I was busy answering some tricky question.

I had spent a large part of my childhood teaching myself to walk fifty steps on my hands and I was damned if I was going to let all that sweat go down the plughole. So with courage plucked up, I walked on my hands onto *The David Frost Show* in New York. The audience loved it. Another talk-show host asked me to name two historical figures with whom I would choose to have dinner. I had recently studied Leni Riefenstahl's documentaries on Hitler, and as it was the use and abuse of power that fascinated me most, my answer was Jesus and Hitler. Well! You'd think I'd wanted Hitler's baby the way the letters of abuse came rushing in. Obviously none of my correspondents had heard the question.

At the Plaza Hotel I was honoured at some special do for having brought pearls back into fashion by wearing them in *Sailor*. I had always worn pearls and always would, but by way of thanks I was awarded a long string of beautiful natural pearls on behalf of the leaders of fashion. How kind Americans can be.

Gladys had gone back to Bruce in LA for my world tour because I was to finish it in England for the start of the summer holidays. I arrived in a June heat-wave, which turned into the famous drought of 1976, and felt lucky to be staying in the cool of the Dorchester Hotel while completing publicity. Having recently re-entered the past with Olivier, I spent a week at the Old Mill with Robert and Tomcat, eerily retreading the green English lawns that had once been home with Robert.

Robert was working on *State of Revolution*, to be staged at the National's Olivier Theatre. He had always been fascinated by Trotsky, Stalin and Lenin and told me he was having a great time putting his words into their mouths. It was an ambitious story of the birth of Communism.

Robert's love life was flourishing: he claimed that no fewer than three ladies were currently stealing his affection. He never had any difficulty with wooing: women adored him, needing to protect, nourish and pamper the lovable yet crazed creator. Although his blue eyes still affected me greatly, his chain-smoking and his obsessive, workaholic mentality troubled me more than ever. He, like Tomcat, seemed unable to be silent or to keep still. Why was he always on the run? It was as if some great monster was making a beeline for him from out there in the future somewhere and he was protecting himself from its advance with an overload of work, food, drink, cigarettes, pipes, music, TV or news – anything to block the monster's path.

Vanessa, my younger sister, had parted from her husband, Ceredig Davies, and was now living with an actor, Michael Osborne. As she cradled Luke, her firstborn, I was struck by her newly acquired serenity. I might have found her radiant but she, quite rightly, I suppose, found me exceedingly doolally, with a touch of the Blanche Dubois to boot. How I longed to share all with my sister – for isn't that what sisters are for? To share the candle going out, the fingers pressing round my throat, the voice, my secret inner life in turmoil. But I knew she would neither comprehend nor want to. Close as we were on many levels, there existed in our natures directly opposing factors that barred us from true intimacy. But I would never have wanted any other sister, and I hope we will grow closer together as the years pass.

The whole Miles mafia congregated together in our Cornish holiday home in early July. Nothing can be more ferocious than family, especially over a lengthy period; yet during those three unexpectedly idyllic weeks at Shag Rock, full of perfect weather as well as harmony among all family members, it would have been hard to have come up with a better backdrop to Tom's and my summer reunion. All was well between us.

Ripeness is All

The following summer, as promised, there, on the front porch of my enchanting new home, a clapboard cottage on Portola Drive, Benedict Canyon, stood a healthier Duke of Wellington than the one I'd met the previous year.

'Are you completely broke or what?' I was positively besotted with my new home and his remark left me a trifle crushed. It was one of the oldest clapboard houses in LA, and as it was also, possibly, the tiniest, I had constructed a real Red Indian tepee on my roof as a guest room. It faced a magnificent expanse of wild open canyon with mountains beyond, and not a single house as far as the eye could see.

To see Olivier sitting *à la* Big Chief Sitting Bull, puffing his pipe of peace, cross-legged in my tepee, smothered in sunset, was a sight worth preserving. I never took photographs of our times together – too tacky – but I regret not having that shot.

He was nicely perched on three meditation cushions, with two more under his skinny legs. He looked ludicrously like Gandhi, and I immediately flashed back to Hasker Street when he had grabbed the white towel and auditioned for David Lean's and Robert's upcoming film *Gandhi*. That evening he was practising his American accent for the film *The Betsy*, which he was still shooting. He insisted I hear his lines for the next day's scenes. His accent, as usual, lacked accuracy. He suddenly stopped mid-sentence so I cued him in, thinking he had dried.

'It isn't the lines, it's my mess of a life.'

'Life is a messy business.'

'You mean yours and mine?'

'Everybody's.'

My thoughts shot back to when we were shooting *Term of Trial* in

Ireland, just before we became lovers. He had leaned over the table in the restaurant where we were dining and bade me clink glasses. He had stated a simple fact, devoid of any bragging, that he was going to be the first lord of the theatre. It was at a time when his career was at its lowest ebb, with no such honour anywhere in sight. The dream might have come true, but it hadn't brought the roses he had expected to trail over life's picket fence.

'I christened you Dame Sarah because I thought you were going to turn into one of the truly greats. You had it all.' He looked at me. 'What went wrong?'

'Putting one's career *above* living one's life makes the tumble that follows inevitable – your piteous private life being a perfect example.'

'Perhaps, but stepping back from ambition hasn't brought you deliverance either, has it?' I sat very still. 'What are you afraid of?'

It was the best cue I would have for unburdening my inner turmoil, but those clutching fingers made their usual entrance so I changed the subject.

Later we went for dinner at his hotel, the Bel Air. I was aghast: he would never have permitted such a risky rendezvous during our previous time together.

'What can they do? Confiscate my title?' During dinner we spied Sandy and David Lean at a nearby table. Although David looked his usual dashing self, Sandy had transformed into a new and positively Meryl Streep persona. It was hard to accept that this was the same gauche child with whom David had absconded from Agra so long ago but, then I hadn't seen either of them for almost six years. They were definitely eyeing us as if they knew we were up to no good. I didn't want David gossiping about us with Bolt.

'You see how risky this was?'

'Only one thing to do. Go over and join them.'

Once we were seated, David plunged in with his plans to make a film of *Mutiny on the Bounty* with Robert writing the script. Their mutual Hollywood agent, Phil Kellogg, was to produce, with wicked old Dino de Laurentiis putting up the money. 'Robert and I will be off to Tahiti any time now.'

'Anything in it for me?' Olivier swooped in like a vulture – no shame. I wish I had the same courage.

David took a mouthful of wine. 'Let me think about it.'

I thought I'd stir things up a bit. 'Why have you two never worked together?'

'We did,' contradicted David, 'but I was editor in those days.'

'Thinks I act too much – eh, David?' quipped Lionel nervously. (Lionel, his old code-name, seemed redundant in this new life of ours, so we had dropped it.)

David turned the conversation to other things, but that I had been dining alone with Olivier textured the whole meal.

I wasn't sure why the episode had made me feel so uncomfortable. 'It'll get straight back to Robert.'

'Why should he care? He's having a good old fling around town.'

He was right, of course. What puzzled me was why *I* should care that *he* might care. 'If you're thinking of returning to Bolt I should take a deep breath and think again,' he said darkly. 'Going backwards never bears fruit.'

'What are we doing then?' That stumped him.

'Not bearing fruit, that's for sure – wonder if I can still do it?' His coarseness was turning me off.

'Where's my romantic gone?'

'You can only remain a romantic if you've got equipment to back it up.'

Later that night my battle-scarred old war-horse slowly but surely quivered with the possibility of victory ahead. He was as amazed as he was tickled pink. I was simply grateful for having him return to me, however briefly, at such a time.

He began to stroke me gently. Superb, it was, I remember. 'I haven't lost my touch, then?' There was no need to answer. What was it about Olivier that still burnt a hole in my heart, leaving me so full of the sweetest peace?

The next night I showed him a letter he had sent me earlier in the year. The heat of excitement I had experienced on receiving it had been so immense that my thumbs had literally burnt the page, leaving two clearly defined prints. He studied the letter for quite a while before putting his own, still suppurating, thumbs into the scorched marks.

'The difference between you and Vivien is that she was always *claiming* to be a witch and you *are* one!' Why, in God's name, should Vivien have chosen to boast about such a thing?

'Never call me witch again!'

He laughed uproariously. 'There's white as well as black witches, for Christ's sake!' The very word 'witch' made me shiver. But, then, I had been living out my private hell for two years so I was bound to overreact.

It was 4 July. My lawyer, Abe Somers, was giving a big bash and because I wanted as much of Olivier's spare time as possible, I rang up Abe to cancel. 'I gather Lord Olivier is a friend of yours.'

I was astonished. 'How d'you know?'

'Small town. Bring him along, gotta keep yer lawyer sweet.'

I relayed this to Olivier. There was no filming that day so he decided we had nothing to lose by going for a short while. 'Next time he sends you a bill, tell him he's been paid in kind.'

Off we set in Muriel on a scorching midsummer day with Olivier looking particularly elegant, right down to the fresh pink rose I'd scrumped from a neighbour. Abe lived in one of those vast, mock-Tudor mansions on Sunset Boulevard.

Drawing up in front of the house, surrounded by Rolls-Royces, Mercedes, you name them, with the parking valets dressed in maroon, poor little scruffy Muriel – each scar telling a good tale – felt a little out of place. In LA there are megastars, superstars, stars, starlets and parking valets. Because every superstar wants their car when they want it, they make it their business not only to know every parking valet by name, but to turn them into superstars too. Because I rarely went anywhere, I was unaware of any of this until that day. The approaching valet looked at Muriel with true disdain. I smiled one of my better smiles. 'Can you park my car, please?'

He looked in, saw, but didn't recognise, Olivier, glanced at me and then said regretfully, 'I'm afraid you'll have to park *that* round the back at the tradesmen's entrance.'

'But—'

Lionel interrupted me with a tweak on my knee. 'Come on, I've always had a penchant for tradesmen's entrances.'

We had been driving around LA for a few weeks and Olivier had never once mentioned my car's scruffiness; to him she was simply Muriel. I approved.

Once Muriel was neatly parked at the tradesmen's entrance we got terribly lost amid the maze of sculleries and kitchens at the back. Each time we asked for directions, we became even more lost.

'Reminds me of the engine room on the *Queen Mary*.' I felt acutely embarrassed on his behalf, but he wasn't the least bit perturbed.

'Who are you looking for?' inquired an all-in-white Mexican chef.

'For our host, Abe Somers.'

'You came in the wrong way. One moment, please.'

The look on Abe's face as he approached us in the bowels of his house made the whole occasion worthwhile. When I introduced him to Olivier, Abe didn't know where to put himself. 'My lord, it's a very great honour to have you in my home.'

'What fine kitchens you have.'

Abe wasn't sure how to take that so he ushered us briskly through to the main part of the mansion.

Watching the place swarming with LA types of all sorts, I knew that the kitchen maze would turn out to be our 4 July highlight. Lionel knew it, too, whispering in my ear, 'If someone wants to shake my hand please step in and explain on my behalf.' His fingers were still oozing and very painful.

Not a soul recognised Olivier, unless introductions were made, which came as a great relief. What I did notice was how, once he had been introduced, Larry was regarded as some kind of god even among non-showbiz people.

After about an hour, when both of us were yearning to make an exit, a tacky, valley-type female with a backcombed beehive made a beeline for Olivier. 'Oh, Lord! The great Lord Olivier in the flesh! I can't believe my eyes! Look.' Her long red talons were pressing into her overly roasted flesh. 'I'm having to pinch myself to make sure I'm not dreaming. May I shake you by the hand?'

'You can shake me by the cock, if you like,' replied Larry, in his brash *Betsy* drawl, allowing many guests to overhear. While I stood there nonplussed, she decided she'd better start laughing.

To put an end to her meaningless squawkings, I held up Olivier's purplish, seeping fingertips. 'They're a little sore.'

Whereupon the dame wiggled a little, fluttering her mascara-laden lashes with delight. 'Oh! You *weren't* kidding, then?' Her glance brushed his crotch as if she was about to kneel down and blow his lordship all the way back to the Bel Air Hotel! I wouldn't have put it past her. Larry's reaction was naked terror.

'I've booked a table at Ma Maison.' So efficient he was when it suited him, ill or no. 'Stop the car.' We were at the top of Mulholland Drive looking over the San Fernando Valley. Shaking his head in disbelief, he pointed to a vast sea of lights stretching right to the horizon with no countryside to be seen. 'In the olden days, before you were born, Clark Gable and Carole Lombard had a ranch down there – the only farm for miles. They asked me to bring casual clothes for my weekend in the country.' He put his arm around me. 'And they call it progress.' We had that in common. A genuine reverence for nature.

Half-way through a sumptuous Ma Maison speciality of the day, we were interrupted by the intoxicating presence of Rachel Roberts. She plonked herself boldly between us and began to lubricate her maudlin reminiscences with Larry's wine.

'I almost got a blow-job at a party just now,' he told her.

As she fixed on him with admiration, it seemed a good time to check out the truth of a tale that both Mitchum and Rex Harrison – her husband at the time – had separately recounted.

Mitchum was at some posh party, leaning against the fireplace with his toke and his whisky, minding his own business as usual, when he turns to find a dame he doesn't even know crawling towards him across the drawing-room carpet in a tight black dress. Arriving at his crotch she proceeds to snarl tiger-like before ripping open his flies with her teeth. Mitchum, so he claims, just stood there, still hanging loose and minding his own business as usual.

'Well, Rachel. True or false?' She looked not the least bit embarrassed.

'Don't! I almost ruined my new dental work tearing open the gates only to find the beast fast asleep!' She turned to Larry. 'How's your beast, nowadays?'

'Can't arouse him for love or money.'

Rachel looked at me and said, quite slyly I thought, 'Well, if Sarah can't rouse him, who can?'

I had known Rachel for many years as Rex Harrison and Robert were close friends. How wretched she had become since those balmy good old days when Robert and I had stayed with them at their delicious home in Portofino. Since their marriage had gone on the rocks the change in her had been dramatic. Devastating. Rumour had it that Rachel's bad patches could be pretty bad, and that evening she quickly degenerated into inebriated self-pitying mode. Her general theme was how she had misplaced her life somewhere along the way. 'Lost it for good, and, what's worse, if it returned I'd be too far gone to recognise it.' The staff were waiting patiently for us to leave, but we stayed on because Rachel didn't like the look of the long lonely night ahead. She took her own life shortly afterwards.

Back at Portola, in my old leather chair, Lionel kept staring into his nightcap of whisky.

'The nights play funny buggers. Poor Rachel. How I know that one!' He put down his whisky and stretched out his arms to me. 'Come six o'clock, rain or shine, I ache with the dread of oncoming night. It's been that way for years now. It never lets up – except when I'm with you.' He held me tight. 'When I'm with you, night still aches like the blazes but with awesome anticipation.'

Our nights were harmonising: I understood his needs better and better, and his stroking technique and my massage worked their special magic. Fascinated at my daily yoga, he would stand or kneel for hours in front of my cheval mirror, determined to master the many different poses. I would marvel at his skinny body, those now transparent thighs and calves that had once flown off ramparts with dare-devil bravura. I loved holding that sparrow's body in reverence of what it once had been and therefore still had to be, for it was still serving its master faithfully. That body aroused me then in a deeper, more venerable way than ever before. In fact, since my candle had gone out I had begun to feel a new depth in my capacity for loving, so not all had been lost.

The telephone rudely interrupted our ritual. It was none other than Michael Winner trying to wheedle me into participating in a remake of *The Big Sleep* with Mitchum.

'But—'

'I'll pay good money, make it all worthwhile—'

'But—'

'Come on, Miles. England in the summer, nice rented house, no expense spared. What more could you want?'

My strong resistance prevented Winner from scoring an immediate winner. 'I'll call you at the same time tomorrow.'

Larry didn't like the Mitchum bit. 'How many beaux do you have at this present time?'

'Only you, right now.'

'Are you seeing Mitch?'

'I've been *seeing* – seeing doesn't necessarily mean sleeping with –

Harris, Dave Swartz, Michael Brown, Mitch and Louis Malle—'

'Louis Malle, eh?' Olivier was surprised at that one. I had been seeing Louis a lot during that time; I liked the quietness in the man and admired his talent greatly. He was in the process of setting up *Pretty Baby*. His films have texture, thoughtfulness, integrity. His first film, *Black Moon*, haunted me quite thoroughly. Yes. Louis Malle's images linger.

Louis had invited me to a Beverly Hills showing of a documentary he had made on the starving in Calcutta. Not only will the film's uncompromising images remain with me for ever but also the audience's reaction to it. Later he and I wondered why so many had walked out and we both agreed it wasn't out of revulsion at the sore-ridden, stick-like bodies covered with flies, but a much more painful and complex realisation. In close-up the eyes of those starving Indians had a dignified, loving surrender that seemed to beam out from their vivid, luminous souls. We weren't romanticising for we targeted our attention deep in their eyes rather than on their bodies or the eye-catching horror of their surroundings. We agreed that the motive for that Beverly Hills exit had been an inability to look the truth full in the face. By comparison their own vacant and lustreless eyes were devoid of life. It is a fact: materialism suffocates the soul.

One time, when Tomcat was back for the holidays, Louis asked him to accompany us to a preview of the new Fellini film, *Casanova*, starring Donald Sutherland. It tickled me to observe our dates, Louis Malle and François Truffaut, each trying not to fall asleep before the other. As the film limped on they both repeatedly leaned forward to check if the other had succumbed. Most directors looked upon Fellini as the master so I suppose it would have shown a lack of respect for a disciple to fall asleep. Tomcat, who was about ten, sat hooting and slapping his thighs with glee at Sutherland (Casanova) masturbating in his wobbly golden carriage, with Malle and Truffaut sound asleep on either side. I sympathised for the film was a bummer. Fresh from their kip, Malle and Truffaut wanted to take us for a night on the town, but Tomcat, exhausted by all the masturbating, replied like some elderly roué, 'Personally I've absolutely had it!'

'Who's Michael Brown?' Larry asked. I had met Michael through Julie Christie and he had proved a pretty useful ally for those who remained

A night out on the town with Robert. By then we both knew we were doomed.
(*Pic Photos*)

As Sabina in Thornton Wilder's *The Skin of our Teeth* in Chicago. Bruce Davison sits in front of me holding a gun. (*Bill Arsenault*)

Bruce and Tomcat wearing masks in Malibu.

Interior Malibu fantasy home where the noise of the waves finally sent me potty.

With Tomcat, settling into sun and sea.

Playing Bernard Shaw's Saint Joan at the Los Angeles Music Center. The *LA Times* critic commented 'This is not one of Shakespeare's better plays.' (*Brian O'Dove*)

Sarah. (*Sergio Strizzi*)

Robert. (*Stephen Hyde*)

Playing both the young and
the mature Estella in *Great
Expectations* was a challenge.

Robert's parents,
Ralph and Leah Bolt.

Robert, aged two,
with his mother.

My parents near Shag Rock, our
Cornish holiday home, with Pooker,
their overweight chihuahua.

My new home in the silence of the Hollywood hills. That's me in my guest room, the tepee.

Sarah Gough (Goffie) meets her mate John Gott, and they live happily ever after.

unable to jive to the Hollywood rhythm. His mid-European intellect, laced with a rare irony, was a breath of fresh air. If you ever wanted the latest Hollywood gossip, Michael Brown's finger was firmly on the pulse, living as he did as Jack Nicholson's house guest.

Michael produced a documentary on the secret life of plants and asked Stevie Wonder to write the music. Stevie's handshake was a wonder all of its own: he held my hand for a good five seconds when we first met, keeping absolutely still. If we all did that perhaps we'd allow intuition to flow more freely, enabling us to link up on a more illuminating, deeper level than a mindless peck at the air at either cheek.

Stevie had a bit of difficulty visualising plants doing their *thing*, sprouting and evolving into their full glory, never having seen one. Michael asked me to act as Stevie's eyes and describe what the plants were up to in the screening room. Tricky business: he had been blind from birth so how could he relate to any plant description that he couldn't feel, hear, touch or smell? He made this perfectly clear in the rushes theatre. 'Save your poetic prose. I can relate to food and sex with no problem.' So that's what we stuck to. You try describing a Venus flytrap to a blind man, *clean*!

One day out of the blue Mitchum appeared (that's the way he always came) to persuade me to do *The Big Sleep*. I was both flattered and torn because, although I badly needed the money, I didn't want to leave Olivier alone in LA. Besides, I never saw the point in making an inferior version of an already successful classic. Best to let big sleeping dogs lie.

Larry and I were up in the tepee, watching the sun go down, as was his habit. That particular evening he seemed somewhat tetchy. The tetchiness had its seed in some remark of Ken Tynan's. He and Larry were in the midst of a bitter row over Larry's memoirs. Ken wanted to write them and was under the definite impression that they were promised to him. Larry had really got it in for Ken at that time – most of the time – and thought he had been viciously disloyal over certain private matters. Those two were capable of scoring and bitching like a pair of frustrated queens.

'Judging by your love letters, you should write your own,' I told him. He stopped twitching to think this through. 'Do you really think so?' 'As long as you're ruthlessly honest with yourself.'

We went on an outing to Malibu to see my old home on Old Malibu Road.

'Why in God's name did you sell up?' I shrugged. 'Shame. It'll be worth millions in a twinkling.'

(How right he was! It sold in the late eighties for *five* million dollars).

I decided to do *The Big Sleep* – I had to, low on filthy lucre – which meant leaving Larry in LA. He looked at me through his Heathcliff lashes. Why did this seventy-year-old have such an effect on me?

'What *do* you want?' he asked, stroking my arm. I remained silent because I needed too much right then. He needed a lot, too, and in his weak and vulnerable moments he wanted us never to end. 'I want to marry you,' he said. How easy it would have been then, in his bitterly lonely and tormented state, to have him fall – albeit a slightly overripe fruit – plop, into my lap.

To the Manor Born – But When?

It was the first day of August 1977, and I was back home in my England again, in all its summer glory. Robert, who had got an excellent price for the Old Mill, had bought a stunning fourteenth-century manor near Totnes in Devon. He was thrilled with his new home and invited me down to stay. Tomcat looked healthy and hellish grown up shooting about on his motocross bike. As I went through the heavy oak door and entered the great hall, with its arrow slits still intact, I expelled a gasp of disbelief.

A year earlier a certain Kebrina Kincade had asked if she could come to my home and regress me for a book she was writing. I was curious: not only was it free, but the voice didn't kick up a fuss. I agreed. All I had to do was answer her questions without pausing for thought. 'Just like a bullet from a gun, honey.' She spoke into a tape, dated it and off we went – fast. I shall spare you details as to where I went on this bullet-speed regression, but it's important to know that I wasn't taking any of it, or her, seriously. She regressed me back to medieval times when I was living in a tower with my mother and we were both wearing wimples. On the wall of the tower there was a mural of the resurrection of Christ and an obelisk stained into the stone with pinks, oranges, sandy browns and ochres. I described it in great detail on the tape, which I still have.

And now, staring me in the face above the ancient fireplace was the very same resurrection of Christ I had described on my regression tape. Same Christ, same obelisk, same composition, same colours exactly. Coincidence? Synchronicity?

Robert took me out to christen the tennis court. He looked very, very tired. He was still driving himself too hard and even his tennis had an air of desperation. He wasn't so much *playing* the game as determinedly *working* at it, pushing himself as hard as if he were writing. What was it all for?

89

15 August was Robert's birthday and we all spent it quietly at the manor. Birthdays punctuate where one is in life. Where were we? Robert knew where he was with his work, but his life was in a mess. Mine was no better. He was finishing his script of *Augustus John* before starting work on *The Bounty* with David Lean.

'I wish we could write it here.'

A pipe-dream, if ever there was one. David was a tax exile. 'How long will you be away?'

'Knowing David, for ever.' Puffing nervously away at the filter.

I wondered if the Old Manor was haunted. It was built around a quadrangle, and on three occasions I swore I heard the soft thud of feminine footsteps wafting round the inner cloisters. The innocence of some rooms in the house took me back to the nursery rhymes and lattice windows of childhood. I found the days there with Robert difficult to digest, filled as they were with a conflicting mixture of feelings. Neither of us was sure where we stood in each other's affections, and both were too timid to find out. I was carrying the burden of many secrets – the voice, the strangling, the candle going out, Olivier. Simply stifled with secrets. Both of us were suffocating beneath their dead weight.

I was far from happy with *The Big Sleep* and regretted making such a silly film, but more than that I regretted leaving Olivier behind in LA. Every morning he rang at seven fifteen, regular as clockwork. He was crying out for me to return during my two weeks off, but Winner wouldn't release me. When I told Larry this, he refused to take no for an answer, and forced me to go and explain his desperation in person to Lew Grade. His request made me realise just how acutely lonely he was. Had he no friend anywhere who could be with him? The whole notion of going to see Lew Grade was ludicrous: he was a businessman and wouldn't give a fart for lovers' needs. But Olivier just wouldn't let up. 'OK, what shall I tell him?'

'Lord Olivier beseeches you to release Sarah Miles for ten days.'

I laughed like a drain. 'He won't—'

'Do as I ask – please!'

Lew Grade has always been good to me, like his brother Leslie, my first agent. But I knew what he would say before I even entered his office. 'On the call sheet I'm not working for two weeks, so I would like permission to return to LA for ten days.'

'Why?'

'Compassionate leave, sir.' He wasn't having any of it, so I did what Larry bid me. 'Lord Olivier beseeches you, Lew.' He looked up at me. 'He's seriously frail.'

'He has a wife, hasn't he?' I knew I shouldn't have done this.

'Yes. But she's stuck in a play.'

'You know I can't release you, Sarah – not even for the king of Spain.' And that was that. Was Lew shrinking or were his cigars getting fatter?

Back in London during a party given by one of Robert's girlfriends, Tomcat came over to me and ever-so-gently broke the news that Elvis had just died. It was a poignant moment, for we both shared a great love for Elvis.

Robert took me to his play, *State of Revolution*, at the Olivier Theatre. Being in dire need of cheering up, and knowing it would be far from a laugh a minute, I was slightly reluctant. Having lived with Robert for seven years, I'd had Lenin, Stalin and Trotsky coming out of my ears. But as the story unwound, I was moved despite myself. Three phenomenal men living in extraordinary times cannot help but rivet, especially with Bolt behind them. He knew what truths to place in actors' mouths, and that night the actors mouthed them most honourably.

Dinner afterwards was a sad affair, stifled with *perhaps*es, *maybe*s and *might have been*s. He was off to Bora Bora the following day.

'Still, I'll be nearer to LA – I can just pop across.'

Tomcat had begun to play up at his new prep school at Dartington. This concerned me because I had still failed to come up with a school that was remotely suitable in LA. After much thought we decided that learning the Tahitian culture, enjoying the freedom of life in sun and water and getting to know his body's physical limits was much more life-enhancing than pining away at unsuitable schools. (Tom thought so, too!) No doubt my lack of respect for the education system had a strong part to play in this decision, although Robert claimed to feel the same way, strongly believing that we only ever learn when we want to, as reflected in his own childhood. Tomcat was still many years away from GCE so things weren't too serious.

'I'll help him in the evenings.' I doubted that Robert would feel inclined to do that after a day of bombardment from David Lean but we agreed that Tomcat would return with me to LA for a while and then go off to the South Seas with Julie Laird, a good friend.

Robert came back to the house I had rented in Victoria Road, Kensington, for a nightcap. Farewells are never easy, especially in Robert's agitated state. Upstairs he bade Tomcat goodbye as if he was in an egg and spoon race, delicately rushing. He devoured his last fag from a pack freshly opened in the interval at the Olivier Theatre, and marched up and down my living room swigging whisky galore. 'I don't want to go! I don't want to go!'

His and David Lean's relationship was pretty similar to Olivier's with Tynan. Schoolboys, the lot of them, consumed with attraction, respect, love, envy, hate and power.

'You'll have a whale of a time when you get there.'

He looked at me strangely. 'David said he saw you alone with Olivier at the Bel Air Hotel?' His tone was a trifle accusatory. 'Is this true?' I nodded. 'Does Wren [my mother] also speak true?'

'What has she been saying?'

'She told me down in Cornwall last year that you and Larry were lovers for years before we met.' How could Mother have divulged such an important secret? He read my utter astonishment. 'She didn't mean to, it slipped out.' Made me wonder how often things had just slipped out. 'Are you lovers all over again?'

Why was it hard to look him in the eye? 'Fragile as a butterfly.'

He puffed on his first fag of a fresh pack, smiling thoughtfully. 'Florence Nightingale at it again.' He polished off his whisky, kissed me goodbye, then, as an afterthought, added, 'Don't kill him, for Christ's sake!'

Watching him hail a taxi I realised I had never asked Robert about his private life. I knew he had mistresses, but I felt it was none of my business. Does lack of interest mean no love left? I was aware he had just finished a fairly robust affair with Felicity Kendal, and why not? As he stepped into the taxi, turning to wave me goodbye, I thought what an incredibly proud man he was. His Achilles heel – his pride.

Michael Winner gave a party for the cast of *The Big Sleep* – a fairly impressive cast for those impressed by such things. I didn't want to go.

'We've gotta go, it's only manners.' I laughed at that. Mitch didn't have any manners and typically failed to show up all evening – bastard!

A few nights later Mitch took me to dinner at the Savoy. He is the most perceptive of creatures, not so much an actor more a human being with his sixth sense still intact. That night he was in a bad mood. His moods ruled his life, or perhaps it was the mixture of drugs and alcohol that ruled the moods. Whichever way round it was, he was still, just like my brother Chuzzer, the most seductive creature on earth when the winds were favourable – but that night stormy weather was brewing. Maybe he knew that *The Big Sleep*, just as Olivier knew with *The Betsy*, was really a great big yawn. Yet Mitch was having the biggest sleep of all – and he knew it, too – dozing off in every frame.

We had been close, on and off, since I had been in LA. He used to drop round whenever he felt like it. I suppose that's the worst (or best) part of my nature, the ability to take people as I find them, without needing to change or possess them; a quality to which men are naturally attracted because I won't be giving them any ultimatums. I never wanted to destroy any family, nor have I. And that, m'lud, is all I have in defence of – what may seem on the surface – a somewhat loose lifestyle.

Yet the irony is that morally I'm fearfully strict, never indulging in fleeting one-nighters. My lovemaking rituals were as far removed from the expression *having sex* as it was possible to be. And I believe that that is why those who loved me kept loving me. It's not a brag, it's quite simply down to loving, *not* performance!

Once on holiday in Mexico with Mitch, somewhere in the remote, fly-ridden interior where he stood less chance of being recognised, we stepped into a potent-smelling bar during the siesta hour to take respite from the flies. He discovered that a messy, stubbly beard and an ill-fitting sombrero created a look that the Mexicans rarely identified with Mitchum the movie star. It was that damn walk which usually gave the game away.

So there we were, in that overly ripe bar in the middle of nowhere, minding our own business as usual, when a shot rang out across our bows, ricocheting on the far wall of the room. I ducked under the table.

'Don't worry, it's nothin' – a blank, probably.' I peered up at him sitting there minding his own business, just hauling on his toke as usual. That was the moment at which I realised he would drop down dead one day, sitting there, minding his own business, just hauling on his toke as usual.

'Why do these *unbelievable* happenings unfold around you without you ever lifting a finger?' I asked him.

He pulled me up. 'Because I'm around you, woman.' He had a point, I suppose. 'Not true. In these parts‹ believe me, it happens all the time. They're in a time warp, still trying to keep up with Wyatt Earp. How else is a man to get his rocks off in this God-forsaken hell-hole?'

Then, as if we had trespassed into a Mitchum movie, three men in sombreros stood, like fighting cocks fresh for battle, in the centre of the room, all carrying guns in holsters.

'Are those real guns?'

Mitch gave a tired shrug. 'Maybe, maybe not. They're full of shit, the lot of them.' He finished his drink and pulled out a wodge of Mexican money.

'Are you scarpering?

'If you want to stay here and give credence to those ass-holes be my guest.' He pinned me with those hypnotic green eyes. 'I can think of better ways of spending my time.'

Another funny Mitch event occurred in March 1976, while I was still living at Yoakum Drive. Eileen Atkins came over for tea. She was giving her Duchess of Malfi in the Music Center where I had played Saint Joan. We hadn't seen each other since *Vivat! Vivat! Regina!* when she played Elizabeth the First to my Mary Queen of Scots, so it was both unexpected and excellent to see her again. I was always astounded at how sexy Eileen was, though why I was so astounded had me completely foxed.

While she and I perched precariously on the floor cushions of my scant bedroom, Mitchum stepped unexpectedly through the garden windows. He made a habit of stepping through my windows whenever he felt like it, knowing I was nearly always to be found alone writing. Neither Queen Elizabeth the First nor the Duchess of Malfi could believe their eyes! Mitch didn't bat an eyelid, simply lit up a fresh joint to pass around – just minding his own business as usual.

French Farce

Olivier had been horribly lonesome in LA, shooting those last weeks of *The Betsy* but, thankfully, he was released early, so planned to spend that God-given extra time with me at Victoria Road, where *The Big Sleep* was still sleeping on. He arrived exhausted from the flight at exactly the appointed time, at 10 p.m. on the August Bank Holiday. What a stickler he was for punctuality!

My American agent, Robert Littman, was the epitome of the dapper Englishman, even down to the daily carnation or rose fresh in his buttonhole – such a refreshing sight to behold around Hollywood's sameness. He had arranged some time back to come to stay and any inconvenience – plenty because I hadn't known Larry would be there – entailed in this visit was nothing compared to the good deal he got me on *The Big Sleep* – the splendid house in Victoria Road notwithstanding.

Littman had gone off to Paris for a few days and arrived back in England just after that August Bank Holiday. He was quiet as a mouse, as he had his own key to the basement where he slept so we were well separated for privacy. But on his return home from Tramp one evening, he got a shock.

'Pissed and fiendishly peckish, I crept upstairs to the fridge to find a chap in nothing but underpants tinkering with the same idea – the bastard had beaten me to it! Obviously great minds *do* think alike, because there, in the glare of the fridge light, turning to gain elbow room for the important business of drumstick-gnawing, was a most familiar stance. As his profile turned to catch the light, I realised I was about to share a bit of nocturnal fridge-raiding with the First Lord of the Theatre!

Early that same dawn Olivier woke me up.

'What's up?'

'There's a man downstairs.'

'Oh, God! Littman!'

He looked down incredulously at his underpants. 'What must he have thought – a naked old fogey dressed thus, raiding the fridge!' He wasn't taking it at all lightly. Oh dear, oh dear! 'You should've warned me.'

'How was I to know you wanted midnight feasts after a huge meal?'

He suddenly saw the funny side. To give Olivier his due, as strength dwindled, humour expanded. He began to hum, 'Picking a chicken with me.'

'In the olden days you wouldn't have been humming.'

'Come off it! In the olden days your paranoia was much worse.'

That was true, actually.

It was a jolly time we had in Victoria Road, short but, oh, so very, very sweet – convenient, too, because the plan had been always for Tomcat to spend that week with my parents in Brighton. One night, however, remains locked in the cold light of many a dawn. A small moment but stubbornly clinging all the same. I was lying there in wonderment at how beautiful Larry looked upon the pillow, lashes still surprisingly lustrous in profile. Some heads look odd, incongruous even in their sleeping mode, but not Olivier's. He lay there magnificently sculptured, yet with the right touch of femininity so suitable for his swansdown backdrop.

Yet due to the angle of his head that early dawn, I couldn't tell if he was still breathing. I went quite cold, as cold as he felt. My mind began to race with imagined newspaper headlines temporarily eclipsing all. 'Why did Lord Olivier choose to embark upon the *Big Sleep* in Victoria Road?' Neither he, surely, nor Joanie needed that kind of humiliation. Did I, perhaps? Or was David Whiting enough punishment for one lifetime?

I panicked and called E.C. (my new aide-de-camp like Goffie). She would, of course, now know everything but, then, Olivier had been there every day, and no fool she. Besides, if not E.C., soon the whole world, surely. Being E.C. (pronounced Easy) she calmly felt Larry's pulse. At that moment Larry turned and looked at her as if she was the first thing he had ever seen. E.C. smiled and discreetly left.

'Where am I?' I held him tight; I was so relieved; he kissed me ever so gently. 'It's all your fault.'

'*My* fault?'

He nuzzled me, the way he always did when revving up for action – incorrigible!

'One death's enough for one night – and next time take me with you.'

'You're not frightened of death, are you?'

'Of your death just now, yes. My own, no.' It was true: since the candle all fear of death had gone, yet a lingering, painful dying process wasn't too witty a prospect. 'Are you?'

'Not if I'm with you.' I wasn't sure what I could do about that one, for something told me I wouldn't be present at his death. The sadness of that thought affected me more than any other. Funny, that.

One sunny evening, still in Kensington, Larry and I were downstairs, taking it easy and dressed accordingly, when the doorbell rang. I indicated we ignore it, but Larry had the devil in him and seized upon the ringing to dive headlong into his Feydeau-farce routine. He gestured to me to open the door while he camply swirled his scanty silk dressing gown and disappeared behind the drawing-room door.

How relieved I was to find my eldest brother, Christopher, standing on the doorstep rubbing his hands together as he had done all through his life. He lived quite close by in Selwood Place, which was most convenient as his daughter, Sophie, and Tomcat were extremely close at that time. 'Can I come in?' I stood aside and he went straight into the drawing room. A sensitive soul, he knew something was up, and Larry, a sensitive soul too, must have sniffed oncoming humiliation. Far better to own up with dignity than to be caught crouching behind the door, surely. I was well prepared for his entrance – how often had I longed to share my secret with Chris? – but drew back.

Out strolled Olivier, cock of the walk. Chris's face was a masterpiece, his smile frozen in respectful enthusiasm. He rubbed his hands together a little bit more, just to show the pair of us that he didn't think anything of it, in the true Wykehamist fashion. Manners *do* makyth man, after all. I could tell immediately that Larry liked him – mind you, it was hard not to for Chris is an enormously likeable fellow.

'Hello, sir. We met in Paris back in 1962.'

Larry looked at me wickedly. 'Around the time of our first fuck.'

Chris went straight on as if he hadn't heard – maybe he hadn't or maybe he knew he was being tested. 'I was living on rue Lepic, sir, studying at IDHEC at the time' (the film school of the day).

'Did you know we were at it back then?'

'No, sir. But, then, I don't know now, either.'

Olivier flopped onto the sofa with relief and we all had a jolly good natter.

The cat was now most certainly out of that proverbial bag. Mother, Robert, Chris, Littman, E.C. – Old Uncle Tom Cobbleigh and all. On pointing this out to His Nibs he simply shrugged it off, grinning as if he were proud of it.

It delighted Olivier to have me returning with him to Brighton. We were able to see each other a great deal over the weeks that followed, either at my parents' home or at Larry's. I marvelled at mother's psychic powers, her having planned my return to Olivier! She invited him to dinner.

'My poached salmon's playing up lately – your father hates it over-cooked.' She was nervous as can be, preparing the meal, and as usual forbade me to help as she bustled in and out of the dining room.

'Let me lay the table.'

'No. You put everything in the wrong place.' Larry had said as much – fusspots, the pair of them.

The drawing room was dangerous territory: Father was in it. Both parents, no different from everyone else's, mistook my new com-mitment to karma and reincarnation for pottiness.

'You're just frightened, that's all. I can see it in your eyes. Frightened, frightened, frightened. That's why you need this reincarnation lark.'

'On the contrary, it turns death into a *love* matter, not a *fear* matter.'

And off we went. Daddy was just getting into his stride, his face blossoming into a flush, eyes sparkling with renewed passion when we heard Mother climbing those insanely endless stairs. 'For God's sake, you two, when will you make your minds up to differ?'

Larry arrived at half past seven on the dot. While taking off his coat in the hall he looked up and saw my majestic painting of Charlemagne.

'Impressive. Who is he?' I told him proudly.

The meal passed pleasantly and I could tell that Olivier felt very much at home with my parents. It warmed my heart because it meant he would be welcome any time I was at home in England.

Father's stomach pains had gathered momentum since he had performed his unique press-up trick three years earlier for Kris Kristofferson in Dartmouth. Nevertheless I thought I'd puff up his pride with a demonstration. I lay down flat on the carpet. 'Then he raises himself upwards into a perfect bow.'

Larry was astonished. 'Don't believe it – not possible!'

'That's what everyone thinks before they see him do it.'

Mother became alarmed. 'It almost killed him last time. Never again – d'you hear me, John?'

But Father didn't perform. I was concerned, for it was the first time he had failed to rise to the challenge. I knew then that his 'trick' days were over for good. Why had I never thought of taking a photo of Daddy doing his party piece?

Commiserating about mutual fragility over coffee and brandy, Olivier and Father had the great wheeze of making a bet. Whoever died first would give the other £100. Daddy seemed confident, Mother far from keen.

'Sounds macabre to me.'

'You're my witness, Wren,' Olivier warned my mother. 'Otherwise I'll never get it.'

'Joan had better hear it too,' said Father.

They all looked at me sadly, with Larry the saddest.

'My private life's a fuck-up—'

'Shush! He'll send you to your room!' Father's hatred of swearing was fearsome. In the olden days it had been forbidden.

'It's important you know how much I love Sarah. I want nothing more than to be with her for the rest of my days.' I was amazed to hear all this. 'Joanie made me realise the scandal would be too much for the children to bear.' I hadn't asked Olivier to leave Joanie, I never would have, it's simply not my style. There was nowhere the evening could go after that. I felt hurt, badly hurt that Olivier had told me and my parents together. Also, I wasn't sure that I believed in his confession to Joanie. We all swiftly moved on to goodnights.

I loved my visits to Olivier's Malt House near Steyning, for there he was at his best. He would tend his enchanting cottage garden with such love – reverence, even. He caught me smiling.

'You watch! I'll soon have it better than Notley.' At Notley Manor in Oxfordshire was where Larry's heart still lingered, for it was there that he had become a seriously committed gardener, never to have the same opportunity again, till now.

I was shocked one afternoon to see Joanie coming across the garden to greet me. He had not warned me that she was expected – nor, I was sure, had he said anything to her about us, unless her acting was truly superb. I wanted to beat it, right through the vegetable garden and onto the South Downs.

'Hello and welcome.' She was most civil and outgoing towards me, but I felt the whole strain of *does she know or doesn't she?* so over-whelming that I asked if I could have a swim. Olivier joined me after a few lengths, cowering slightly, I thought.

'Why lie to me when I gave you no cause?'

'She *does* know, I promise.' It was becoming squalid.

'Just remember, we're drawing dangerously close to being sordid, something I never wanted for us. And also remember – I never pressured you into anything, ever.' He waved me away, giving me a sly Irene Handl-ish look, before grabbing his nose to jump.

The loathing of intrigue fell upon me with such waves of nausea that I didn't believe I would find the strength to get out. No way could I sit and have tea and crumpets with Joanie. The nightmare gathered momentum and I found myself with a severe attack of breath loss – a plain, ordinary panic attack, utterly dissimilar to the strangling sensation I got from the voice. (With hindsight it was beneficial to feel the difference between the two.) Next I remember the embarrassment of having members of the Olivier family standing over me while I strained to get my breath back. I felt a proper Charlie, I can tell you.

One afternoon Larry rang to ask me to dinner at the Royal Crescent with Joanie and Franco Zeffirelli. Mother nudged me to accept, so I did. It turned out a more pleasant evening than I had expected. Above Joanie hung a stunningly lit portrait of her as St Joan. Above Larry hung a stunningly vivid portrait of him as Richard the Third – unlit.

'Larry's light has gone out,' I blundered.

Joanie didn't look up from sipping her soup. 'Aye. Larry's light went out a long time ago.'

As our last week slipped by he became visibly more frail. I was due back in LA.

'Stay here in England. Your father needs you and he isn't going to live too long.' Was he speaking for himself, or for Daddy?

'Yet you made the bet anyway.'

'Of course! He's a competitive bastard – needs a fight to keep fighting.'

The following summer, during Wimbledon fortnight 1978, I noticed that Father had deteriorated. He asked me to invite Olivier round so he could pay off his debt. His cancer had spread and the end was undoubtedly drawing nigh. Thoughts of the inevitable didn't frighten me, but the fact that he wouldn't talk about it did. The nearest he got was with references to John Wayne, for he believed that if John Wayne could have a new stomach then so could he. (At seventy Wayne was over a decade younger when his new stomach hit the headlines.) Father had the operation anyway.

As I opened the door to Olivier I wondered fleetingly if his turn wasn't far off. He pointed to *Charlemagne* as he slowly climbed the stairs. 'Don't ever sell that painting – nor take it to America.' Sweetheart! He so wanted me home for good. Concern for that back slowly hauling itself up the three steep flights of stairs prompted me to push gently at its centre. 'Ah! It's a real knack that – pushing well.' I always would, too, for as long as I was needed, yet I knew I couldn't stay with Joanie just up the road.

As I entered Daddy's bedroom I felt him glower at me from his bed. His glowering had become quite familiar during that period because I had wanted him to recognise the face of death. (Nowadays, I would never be so insistent but, back then, the candle experience was still influencing me to convert others. Quite ghastly!)

Olivier broke the ice. 'Fine bed.' Daddy had a smashing four-poster.

'Hmm. Good of you to come round.' He was having great difficulty wrestling with his pride. 'You're about to be a hundred pounds the richer.'

'You may be jumping the gun, John. Miracles *can* happen.'

Daddy turned to me impatiently. 'Pusscat, fetch my trousers over here.' I obeyed. Larry stepped from foot to foot. 'Larry, please sit down.'

'If I sit down, John, I'll never get up again.' Daddy laughed with complete recognition of his own plight while counting out a hundred smackers. He handed over the bundle.

'I used to travel to London daily, you know, and I watched your National Theatre taking shape.'

This pleased Olivier a lot. 'Oh, yes?'

'I was tempted to forget our little bet but, after weighing everything up, I decided that having to fork out a hundred quid for my own death was far preferable than the weight of your heavy load.'

'What load is that, John?'

'Going to *your* death with that hideous National Theatre on your conscience.' This floored the pair of us. True it might be, but Father had no right to blurt it out so shamelessly. I went over and kissed him.

'Just start counting all those beastly carbuncles you've pooped out all over the planet!' (Father had designed steelworks world-wide.)

'Come, Larry, we'll go now.' He liked that idea a lot.

That day when Olivier left he questioned me.

'Is the National Theatre hideous?'

Awful to be put on the spot like that. 'Let's say I'll give it the benefit of the doubt till the dust settles.'

'Coward!' As he drove off, I realised what diplomacy is: continual cowardice and telling porkers.

Having a Go

Since my return to LA I had been experiencing a whole new batch of visions, psychic dreams and revelations, not all pleasant, and numerous tussles with the voice, which became curiously strident on the TWA flight back. Was it because we were flying nearer to its source, or was it just old Sarah being doolally? I was ordered to sing, dance, and write, alone, and put it into a musical – the same message I'd been given on my birthday on the mountain-top. All this was to culminate in a one-woman show called *SmileS*.

I had never written anything, except a few letters home from time to time. I'd been expelled from all my schools, finally leaving for good at fourteen, and had never put pen to paper in an exam. No wonder this particular command seemed impossible. I had no inkling of grammar and never having read, without difficulty, how the hell was I going to write? Musically, I was a catastrophe, having failed even to attempt the piano at Roedean, and my singing reputation was dire.

I had been Hal Prince's first choice for Sally Bowles in the musical *Cabaret*. The composer, Ed Cantor, and his music team flew over from New York to my parents' home to hear me sing the score (its first-ever airing) to the accompaniment of Father's Bechstein grand. I gave them my best shot, and after my unique rendering of 'Come to the Cabaret!', one of the team ripped his jacket on the cloakroom coat-hook, so impatient was he to be off. Father marched up and down the empty drawing room, sucking his loose front tooth. 'How *could* you bring them all the way from New York, Pusscat?'

All my life, my only dream had been to sing, and although I had been blessed with no talent whatsoever it never stopped me trying. I asked Chad Stuart, my ex-beach carpenter, to help me. Chad was from the sixties pop group Chad and Jeremy, who were going great guns before the Beatles came along and eclipsed them – but, then, the Beatles eclipsed everyone. Chad was sweet enough to go through the agony of accompanying in public this now infamous voice of mine thus demonstrating the British stiff-upper-lip kind of guy he was. Between us we came up with melodies and lyrics that even a tone-deaf milkman could whistle. So the next year scooted by, obeying the inner voice and getting *SmileS* slowly into shape.

Once Chad and I had got the songs as good as we could get them, I found it hard to refrain from reshuffling, editing and rewriting the bits of verse in between, never sure whether to emphasise the fool, enchantress, joker or child. We were due to open in San Francisco in February 1978 and I was scared shitless, but the voice became positively ruthless whenever I displayed the merest whiff of nerves.

Ken Tynan and his wife, Kathleen, kindly came over to see where I was with this damn musical and to give me some notes. I was shocked by Ken's sickly demeanour. His emphysema was visibly chronic and it was unbearable to witness him climbing my nine front steps. But without a wife as intelligent and sexy as Kathleen, his last years would have been a lot worse.

There were great passages of *SmileS* that Ken liked enormously, unless he was simply being polite. I decided not, for he was far too jaded to simulate enthusiasm. Later, over a drink, he asked me, 'Are you in touch with Olivier still?'

Why was it that whenever anyone spoke of our relationship it astounded me? I suppose because, in the olden days, we had always been congratulating ourselves on beating the Snoop system.

I looked deep into those nicotine-stained eyes of his but, dying or no, his trickiness ran deeper. 'What are you right now – worst enemy or best buddy?'

'Right now? Not the latter, I fear.'

'Is that because he won't let you write his biography?

'He'll make such a hash of it.'

'Surely he should be given first crack – it's his life, after all.'

Kathleen, having gracefully mastered the steep, narrow staircase, reappeared from the upstairs loo. Ken went on, 'Because you're giving us something new, an audience is essential to help you mould it into shape. That way you'll soon discover what does and does not work.' A wise piece of advice, no doubt, but trying out the show quietly, without drawing attention to it, would be nigh on impossible. He thought about this, before saying, 'Then you're fucked.'

Kathleen invited me to Ken's fiftieth birthday party, a simple meal for a few friends. I was incredibly touched by all the notes he had bothered to make. He suggested I emphasise the fool. 'You're a funny woman, don't be frightened by it.' Fear! Why did fear keep raising its ugly head? I felt Ken knew he hadn't got long and, from a certain meekness in his chain-smoking self destruction, I thought he'd decided to go gently into that good night. Was this the razor-sharp, power-crazed Iago from Olivier's Othello reign at the National? Ken Tynan died quite soon afterwards.

I remember sitting in my dressing room waiting to make my entrance on *The Johnny Carson Show*. I was about to sing a song that I had written and Chad had arranged. It was dedicated to my father and called, 'Every Day's a Birthday.' Chad was to accompany me on piano – his bravery knew no bounds! *The Johnny Carson Show* had the highest ratings of any talk-show in America, hence my terror. Why had I chosen such a baptism of fire? I had never sung in public before and decided that my fear was too great to hide, so I held up my shaking hand, spoke briefly of fear and of how we are all capable of singing, once we have conquered some of the fear, that is. Would I be able to conquer it? All in all, it wasn't as embarrassing as I had *feared* – just off the wall!

That night's little nest of horrors spawned two incidents. The first took place in New York the following day. I was looking in Tiffany's window when this sleek black dude next to me pipes up, 'Every day's a birthday.' Not only had he remembered some of the words of the chorus of my song but the melody too. I had to control myself from leaping into his arms and smothering him with kisses, so stunned with gratitude was I!

The second incident came in the form of a letter from a Warren Barigian, who turned out to be a fifty-year-old Armenian wizard from Hazlehurst in the San Fernando Valley. In his letter he claimed, 'There is nobody who *can't* sing. It's my job to hang a new octave on you in ten sessions – if you hang in there, that is. No singing or scales required.' Too tempting to turn down. He was only known in certain circles, and very quiet about those singers he *did* work on.

I was surprised to find a larger-than-life, fatter-than-Bolt, no-bullshit kind of a fellow. This Armenian ex-farmer had decided one day to dismount his tractor for good and dedicate the rest of his life to the vibration of the human sound. Through years of experimenting, and using as guinea pigs we poor fools with singing needs, he began to have some extraordinary results.

Here's an example of one of Warren's sessions.

'Sit in that chair, hon.' Having made me comfortable, he would sit opposite me, legs akimbo.

'Take some long, deep breaths.' If these weren't long or deep enough he would just wait until they were. Then, after what he considered to be a sufficiently serious intake of breath, he would ask me to hold it there. He would then ask me to hyperventilate. This is done by pushing down on the intake of air and grunting, thus compressing the inhaled breath for all it's worth as if trying to shit it out. At any given moment he would punch me hard in the solar plexus, knocking me for six as I imploded.

The first time I ventured into this knocked-out state, which usually lasted six to eight seconds, I saw an eighteenth-century gentleman, dressed entirely in black. He wore a top hat and cloak, the lining of which gave off a flash of silver that shimmered, as did the knob of his silver-topped cane. How well I remember that cane as he ran it along the black iron railings of a red-brick Georgian house.

Every time I went under – and everyone who experienced Warren's solar plexus punches admits to having entered some other zone – that silver and black image crept closer and closer. Whoever he was, he symbolised death to me, and his cane along the railings my death rattle – echoing my rattlesnake on the mountain. I could even hear the cane vibrating on my pillow at night. Is it any wonder that my reluctance to go under grew with every visit? Yet it wasn't death that frightened me but the terror of finding out who the man in black was. A conundrum I couldn't fathom.

On one occasion, after I had seen my by now familiar black-cloaked figure, approaching for ever closer, I returned to the here and now to find myself on Warren's study floor, curled up in the foetal position with the sensation of being strangled still vaguely present. Was I never to be safe from the voice or whatever it was? I felt the need to share all with Warren. It was an enormous relief, for not only did a heavy burden grow lighter but Warren believed every word. Later, when I mentioned

David Whiting's gruesome end, Warren grew more and more intrigued. 'Maybe it's all in David's hands, hon.'

Until that moment I had never linked David Whiting with the voice or with the fingers pressing round my neck. I felt the voice and the strangulation to be linked somehow, but if it was David Whiting, why did it take two years for him to make himself known? The odd thing was that I didn't want to know.

Warren knew I had been through more 'other time zones', as I had already taken more sessions than anyone else – a brave guinea pig indeed! He charged a high price for his bizarre services but, then, why not? He delivered. He wasn't a therapist; he spoke little because he was eager to experiment and get results, which were often phenomenal. I sometimes caught sight of heavy-duty singing stars leaving as I entered.

'The hefty down-payment,' he told me, 'is to stop 'em quitting after the first session.' I laughed, knowing just how barbaric and brutal Warren's octave-producing techniques were. 'Yet you take everything I throw at you.'

'That's because I want to sing.'

'That's why I have to deliver, hon.' He adamantly refused to give up and after the initial outlay for the first six sessions, I received free sessions *ad infinitum*! On we went, with Warren convinced I had a veritable goldmine hidden somewhere in my throat – bless him!

In the search for what he called my 'amazing potential'(!), Warren parcelled me off to some highly recommended practitioners of alternative medicine: he wanted my sinuses and swollen eyes cleared up. It was during these occasions that for the first time I brushed with the phenomenon that became the New Age movement: the dangly-crystalled sleeping giantess had always been with us and was reawakening. I made sure I kept out of her way. Eventually, he sent me to probably the only urine therapist in the world. I was loath to go but Warren was Warren, *and* he was paying! He wanted me also to take Tom, who was back for the holidays. It annoyed Warren to see me blaming myself for Tom's hyperactivity and chronic asthma, which had begun when he was two. Warren said, 'He's a holic, hon, he has an addictive nature', and explained that a chemical imbalance within the system, combined with inherited genes, create an inborn addiction. It is important to remember that Warren knew all this stuff over twenty years ago. 'Tom's addiction right now is to sugar but, hon, addicts are addicts, so he'll most probably move on.'

I asked him how one's own recycled waste matter could possibly prevent allergies.

'Taking back the melatonin and all hormones in their pure form from urine immunises you against your own allergies as well as stabilising the chemicals within the system.'

'All allergies?'

'All.'

And so it was that, every Wednesday, Tomcat and I would wait our turn to pee, sitting in the posh waiting room of the *très* posh urine-therapy clinic in the poshest end of Santa Monica. The clients came in all shapes and sizes. Some had asthma; all were fearfully well heeled.

When our turn was called, a crisp nurse discreetly handed over a silver bowl. 'Catch mid-flow only. Urinate roughly half, then catch enough to fill the bowl, then urinate away the remainder.' Once I'd accomplished this tricky task, Crispy Pants would escort me to the great white chief himself. The nurse would then hand him a syringe, and place the silver bowl before him. Plonk! My own pee injected back into my bum. Tomcat and I performed this absurd ritual twice a week for eight weeks.

At the end of eight weeks, I noticed Tomcat's asthma disappearing, his frenetic body language linked to his craving for sugar subsiding, and his concentration span quadrupling. On our last trip to the clinic, with Tomcat about to return to Tahiti and me soon to open in San Francisco, I decided to find out the cost of paying for ourselves the following holidays. I was horrified at the amounts of cash Warren had been forking out.

On my next visit, as the big white chief with poised syringe was about to clutch my bottom flesh, I gave it to him. 'Your charges are well out of line. I don't know how you sleep at night.'

'Look into my waiting room. If it was too cheap, no one would come. You've lived here long enough to know that, surely?' He had a point. 'If you don't like the prices, and I wouldn't blame you, then I advise you to start drinking it. Indians, such as Nehru, Gandhi and millions of others, have benefited hugely. It isn't an ancient wisdom for nothing.'

'I just couldn't.'

'Thank God! It's squeamish Westerners like you who keep me rich!'

'Do you drink it?'

'Of course.'

'How old are you?'

'Eighty next month, but don't tell a soul.' I'd have put the bugger at sixty.

Tomcat's decision *not* to start drinking his pee was final. 'I'll keep my asthma, thanks.'

I, on the other hand, gave the idea a lot of thought, which finally turned into a whirl. And from that day to this I've neither looked back nor understood what all the fuss is about. I'll whisper to the braver souls. 'Take mid-flow the first and last pee of the day. Three gulps is sufficient and each day you experience a different-tasting beer. It's only our brain, due to our Western conditioning, prejudging it disgusting. There's nothing to fear but fear itself. Results won't be immediate. After three weeks you'll start to feel the difference, and in three months, you'll be laughing.'

PS I hadn't heard from Warren in twelve years. He doesn't need to phone me, nor I him, for though we were never lovers, we are never far from each other's hearts. I must have been full of him while writing this last chapter because he has just phoned, completely out of the blue. He had rung merely to say hi and to ask after Robert's health. Always so engrossed in work he never knows what's happening in the world, so was unaware that Robert had danced off this mortal coil.

SmileS

Finally, in February 1978, mindlessly brave and full of pee – echoes of Robert's warnings that courage was closely linked to stupidity – SmileS had its limited opening in San Francisco. I had asked Carolyn Pfeiffer to be my producer – why not? It might have been her first time, but I knew she would be perfect and of course; she was. It was me who wasn't. Too much fear. Any woman, surely, who has no death fears and the guts to drink her pee, couldn't lack the balls like I did, could she?

The reviews could find no fault with the standard of my material and although the fear was present during my singing in San Francisco, it wasn't my singing, oddly enough, or my songs (many reviewers loved them), or indeed my writing (many praised my poetry) that was off, but my timing for doing such a piece in the first place. Twenty years too early. Hence, in San Francisco, two-thirds of the audience wanted to roast me alive, with the other third grateful for the blessing.

Mother came over for my opening night, which, considering Father was ill, I found deeply touching. She kept herself very much to herself, renting an apartment, taking home her ghastly cooked dinners.

'Please come out and eat with the gang, Ma.'

She'd smile gracefully. 'I've already bought my dinner.' Brother Chris came too. How brave and loyal they both were!

SmileS' theme was the endless mistakes we all make, generation after generation, never listening to our higher natures, plus an atheist movie star's *Bolt from the Blue*, culminating in the realisation that fame and riches don't matter a damn because death is not the end (corny nowadays, perhaps, but not back then). Chad on piano, with harp and drums; me in the middle, with Gladys, playing the fool. I didn't use the story of the candle going out (who'd have believed me?). It ended with Gladys and me climbing the Malibu mountain

110

and reaching the top at the turn of the year and waiting for the cosmic message.

One matinée Francis Ford Coppola turned up. I saw him sitting in the third row, a dark Byronic figure with a touch of Toulouse-Lautrec. At one point I saw him twitch his head slightly as the man behind him banged his seat and marched out after my masturbation scene (at it again!). Visually it represents such an economic, penetratingly eloquent symbol of aloneness. The scene was so subtly lit – merely shadows steeped in gentle music – so tightly choreographed that not even the Queen Mother would have been offended. During the scene Gladys walks in on a music cue. She was always on cue, with no one to prompt her backstage, malignant tumour and all. On her entrance she finds her mistress rising up to a gentle, swaying climax. Most of us animal lovers know in our hearts how hard it is, with or without a partner, to stay on a roll – let alone *come* – with those innocent yet all-knowing craters of wisdom staring into our souls. I bet a fair proportion of huffy seat-bangers scarpered because they weren't animal lovers, or else they were having problems stifling unloved memories lurking in their own closets. By the end of the show each night it was fascinating to realise that I had learned more about my audience than any of them had learned about me, yet it had been my truth up there on display.

Coppola sent a red rose backstage, with a sweet card asking me back to his pad. He might deliver some constructive tips, I thought. I was ravenous for some.

What a wow his pad turned out to be! It wasn't a house, but a unique space resembling both a Dutch barge and a space-ship – all brass, wood, white walls and electronic equipment the likes of which I'd never seen before.

He made me feel immediately at home. 'Would you care to come into my playroom?' Was he about to bounce me on his space-age water-bed? Not a bit of it. His playroom turned out to be another space-ship, a stunning miniature editing room linked to the main LA studio editing room.

'It's a hassle commuting to LA,' he explained, twiddling knobs dials and God knows what. Another playroom, another Spielberg, I thought. 'I'm *attempting* to edit *Apocalypse Now*,' looking skywards with pent-up fury, 'if the bastards ever leave me alone!' How swiftly that fury dissipated as he leant back in a king-size black-leather chair, regaining

111

knob control. The maleness of the ritual reminded me of the day when Robert took the controls of our black Lamborghini, for the first time – the one David Lean had given us. Men love guns and knobs enough to die for them – alas!

Apparently filming had come to an end yet still more shooting had to be done. He shrugged his shoulders as if to say that no one was going to hold his integrity to ransom. All I can remember of *Apocalypse Now* was being taken up a river, on and on, until at long last came my first glimpse of Brando – performing badly.

Olivier, recognising Brando similarities, had always yearned to be in a film with him. If their hugely contrasting acting styles had met on celluloid somewhere mid-Atlantic, we might all have learned some-thing – if only what *not* to do. They were both as capable of excruciating embarrassment as of shattering brilliance. Hooray for them, say I. Who wants everyone to be drearily lifelike and mediocre in the safety of the grey middle ground? Surely art is all about crafting the truth with style and daring?

Coppola gave me the blackest of black coffees. 'Now. Your show.' He took a sip. 'Your show will one day be a hit, but not yet.' He sipped some more coffee, thoughtfully. 'It's like a box of chocolates with too many hard centres.'

'I dislike soft centres—'

'What *you* dislike is irrelevant, it's what *we*, the audience, like that matters. Don't thrust your chocolate box of sharp-edged truths at us, just gently hand it to us with some soft centres too, nicely wrapped in pretty paper and tied up with a red ribbon.' I got the general drift. 'However great the talent, timing matters more, and your present concept is too brutally altruistic for the still sleeping seventies. A female Lenny Bruce shouldn't do tragedy.' No point in beating about the bush.

'In other words, I'm unfunny and in the wrong show too soon.' My face hung.

'Persevere. One day you'll mix the right chocolates for the right box at the right time.' I felt too hang-dog to hang around, so I made the right noises and he escorted me to the door. 'It'll all be completely worth it – you'll see.' I could see he meant it. 'You're a very funny woman. Use your humour, it'll always serve you well.'

Little did I know that I would soon need all the humour I could muster. Skirmishes had begun to occur at the stage door, until one night a guy physically attacked me, calling me dangerous, disgusting, obscene, even. From then on I had no option but for two stage hands to escort me to my hotel by the back way, avoiding the stage door completely. *SmileS* had been a triumph indeed.

Mother and I were at San Francisco airport waiting for her flight. There she was, always so beautifully elegant, breath smelling of violets, clean hair dancing with gold dust. She shook her head.

'Some moments will remain with me for ever.'

'Was it wrong, doing it in the first place?'

'No, not wrong – foolhardy perhaps.' I had always grabbed at mother's criticisms greedily. 'Chin up. It wasn't a flop and it wasn't a hit. It was something all of its own and, like the curate's egg, good in parts.'

'How bad was the rest of the egg?'

'Not bad, just too potent to digest – especially for the bland tastes of those plebeian, parochial San Franciscan audiences.'

'But, Ma, San Francisco is meant to be hip!'

'You could've fooled me. But be kinder on us audience next time.' As she was about to disappear from view, she said, 'But do it you must.'

The *SmileS* experience left a void. I doubted I'd ever find the guts to do it again. Had I learnt nothing about living, writing, dancing, singing, acting? Had I been doing nothing but air that old sinner Hubris? Had it simply been misinterpreted by one and all as the ultimate ego trip? Believe you me, it was no ego trip from where *I* was coming from. Yet where *was* I coming from?

Everything in my life has changed completely after the loneliness of my masturbation scene in *Sailor*. The candle going out, too – that was a horribly lonely experience. Now *SmileS*. If you were cursed with a great fear of crowds and performing, would you choose to perform a one-woman show – surely the loneliest of all art forms? My belief in God was being tested for sure, but why had I failed? If it was solely my strength being tested, it was a pretty stinky kind of a test – foul play, I'd say! With total honesty I would have to concede that during that period of my life a will other than my own was in control.

113

One Word, 'What'?

Horrors of horrors! On returning one day to my beloved little shack in LA I received a mighty shock – bright orange men measuring my lot and looking at what I had thought was my oak tree.

'What are you doing here?' I enquired, politely enough.

'The bulldozer's arriving any minute.' I felt like a little girl of nine as I stood in front of my tree in a pathetic attempt to save it from its executioner. How dare they chop down that same friend who had shared my daily meditations and prayers for over two years?

When I bought the house I was told that my land stretched the full three empty lots down, giving me a particularly spacious wild garden, the nearest I could find to the English countryside in sunny LA. Well, it turned out that I didn't own the land and, within no time at all, this grotesque cottage-cheese abomination shot up. Leaning out of my once sun-dappled window, I could touch its dark, unfriendly, stucco prickliness. My perfect little clapboard home was eclipsed for ever. It was a sign to move on.

It didn't really matter where I went because my life was changing its nature. I was spending more and more time in meditation, prayer, yoga. There were times when these daily adventures brought forth fruit, allowing me to glimpse virgin lands, tiptoe through uncharted waters, lose myself in undiscovered countries, transcend the here and now, revel in my new ability to cross dimensions. But this way of life doesn't pay the mortgage or, indeed, help one's career. I frequently had great urges to leave the tumult of showbusiness and the twentieth century behind me for good and all and become a non-religious nun. I recollect having had that same need as a ten-year-old when still at Roedean. Some dreams obviously don't change.

Then into my life stepped Harris Yulin, who had played my husband in *Dynasty*. Harris was a deeply respected actor/director, more at home directing than acting nowadays, who thought that my show had great potential and wanted to help me reshape it. What a brave man! I was none too keen to do it again, even though people who had seen it kept trying to persuade me to give it another bash.

Harris, born on Guy Fawkes night (in England my favourite night of the year), had been abandoned at a few weeks old on someone's doorstep. In a little basket he lay, like Moses in the bulrushes but with the rush of traffic instead, wearing nothing but a nappy, a woolly and a note that said, 'This baby is of Jewish origin.'

I felt comfortable with Harris for he was as far away from a showbiz type as it was possible to get. I would trust him with my life, as well as being hugely attracted to the mystery deep within him. I think it was all to do with his adoption, for he had spent many years trying to discover his roots. A serious man with a great love of the arts, especially the theatre to which he was as committed as Olivier, he only spoke when he had something interesting to say.

Was it any wonder that I found Harris so seductive in a country where talk, friendship, affection flow in and out with too much ease, and where loyalty amounts to a mere soundbite? More serious still was the spreading 'immorality disease.'I was witnessing Tinsel-town's already frail conscience disintegrating before my very eyes. The only rule in town was never point out to anyone their lack of it, which was disconcerting, to say the least. Just keep smiling all the way to the bank. (The disease has now crossed the Atlantic, alas.)

Harris had recently bought a romantic wooden 1920s clapboard house, similar to mine, down in Venice, nestling among luscious foliage in a forgotten backwater. For me it had the best of Benedict Canyon's shady trees combined with the seductive sun and sea of Malibu – no sound of waves to drive me potty!

During the seventies Venice Beach was in the vanguard of the body-building revolution, before it took over the whole of the Western world. We'd shoot up the Venice Boardwalk on our roller skates, marvelling at the rainbow-coloured Venetians – some of them supreme con-tortionists – doing their daily beach rituals. Transistors, headphones, roller skates and boards scuffing up the Boardwalk in time to the first primitive music, yet-to-be-called rap, ricocheting off ramshackle, sunblessed buildings.

Later, in the eighties, Venice got labelled with the 'fashionable funk' tag, and now, alas, people are afraid to walk the streets or even the Boardwalk alone, for the number of mindless random killings have severely shaken the place. But back in those days we never even bothered to lock the door.

I was in dire need of a healing period before taking my next version of *SmileS* to Chicago. Harris's large garden, overgrown and full of trees with a Jacuzzi, was just the ticket. It became my womb, and I was most grateful for it. Tomcat arrived for a holiday and, there being no room in the inn, he and his friend Geoffrey had a tent in the garden. Blissfully happy they were, too, shooting hither and thither on new roller skates.

One late after noon soon after Tomcat and Geoffrey had departed, Harris was off for his run. 'I'll get you some more tapes while I'm out.' As my lyrics always arrived in partnership with the melody and my mystery voice (if that's who it was) placed them unheralded in my brain, it was essential to have the recorder close at hand.

That same afternoon I was, as usual, scribbling when the familiar wall opposite me melted into 3D and a beige 1920s cloche hat followed by an elderly women spilt through. She sat looking out of a window in three-quarters profile. She and the window were equally familiar. As I was about to haul her from my mind's depths into my brain for recollection, Harris returned with the new tapes, sending the lady back through the wall of my subconscious. Though I was never to retrieve her again, she haunts me still. I sometimes bring her identity as far as the tip of my tongue, but then off she trots. Perhaps I'll finally meet her when I'm released from this cramped body of mine.

It would have been impossible to share my Venetian vision with Harris for, being irredeemably earthbound, he took all things supernatural with a large pinch of salt. Yet, oddly enough, it was he that I was next to share my secret with. Those familiar fingers didn't press round my neck the night I chose to share the candle tale – whether or not he believed is another matter. I put it down to a sign that I was permitted to write a poem about the candle tale for *SmileS* in Chicago.

Ridiculous, how gullible we are. Just because cocaine freak Freud linked inner voices with schizophrenia it became the conventional wisdom to assume that *all* voices in the head equalled madness. That

is a shame because *I* knew my voice had nothing to do with schizophrenia or madness (even if others thought it did), as was proved to
me that same afternoon.

I remained silent, continuing to scribble while Harris made some
coffee (he drank too much of it) and took it out to his garden study.
How I wished then that God, the mystery voice, whatever, would give
me *proof* of these paranormal happenings so that Harris would take
heed of the vastness of the whole and I could return to the land of the
normal and stay there. How hard it was to put these 'other world'
experiences into words, for I fail to describe with sufficient clarity the
division between the voice and the pressure round my neck; that
is because sometimes they were one and the same, at other times,
separate.

Soon after Harris's exit, the voice interrupted me and began to pull
me in the direction of the kitchen counter where my recorder was
placed. This annoyed me because I had a really good flow going with
my scribbling, and no lyrics or melody – the only reason for taping –
were anywhere in sight. I decided to continue writing and ignore it.
That was folly because those damned fingers began to close round my
neck – bully!

Next I found myself unwrapping one of the new tapes Harris had
just bought and placing it in the machine, still oblivious as to why
when I had nothing to record. Then, I was talking into it: 'You've
pulled me away from my work, whoever you are, so I demand you give
me a good explanation.' On and on I mumbled, pleading for proof that
the voice existed outside of me. I was wasting my time. I switched off
and just as I went back to sit down, whatever it was pulled me back to
the machine insisting that I play back the tape. So I did.

What struck me first was a noise like heavy aircraft over my voice. I was
sure there had been no such sound when I had been recording. I went
into Harris's study. 'Did you hear the sound of aircraft flying over?'

Harris looked at me. 'Not a dicky-bird.'

I went inside to play the tape again. This time, as I listened carefully
to my voice beneath the aircraft noise asking for proof, I heard someone
else utter one word, 'WHAT?' as if to say, 'What more proof do you
want? Wasn't the candle enough?' This voice, which was talking over
mine yet beneath the eerie aircraft din, was much lower, with a masculine timbre.

117

Who could ever believe that one little word would change my life? Don't you see? I knew I was sane but this tape gave me proof positive for all those doubting Toms. I scooted back, overjoyed, into Harris's study.

'Hear this!' He heard it once, he heard it twice, and it didn't end there, for Harris played it over and over, fascinated.

'This is not your voice because it's talking under you – yet it's definitely someone's.' He knew it was the tape he had just brought in to me and he was forced, against his better judgement, to admit that it was genuine. He laughed, picked me up and swirled me round. 'Poor baby, what a rotten time you've had!'

This incident made Harris keener than ever to put across my spiritual message.

'Why in the show are you so keen to share your mistakes?'

'In order to learn from them and become whole. Then maybe I'll stop reincarnating.'

'Why do you want to stop?'

'To rest in peace. Once I'm whole I need never return.'

'I would want to return.'

'You wouldn't once you'd sniffed the alternatives.'

He wasn't convinced. 'You can't kid people that death isn't frightening. The unknown is always frightening.'

'Until proof makes the unknown more familiar. With familiarity, it's possible to lift to the heart and die fearlessly.'

'Explain this "lift to the heart"?'

'It means lifting energy up from the groin where all our base emotions, greed, anger, fear—'

'How the hell do we lift this so-called energy of yours?'

'Practice. If you ever prayed, you'd experience it. It's called lifting to love.'

'Hard to put over in a show – unless you die every night, lovingly.' Beneath his sarcasm he was, none the less, seeing things differently, so we celebrated by going out for delicious local sushi. 'Take the tape to Warren and see what he thinks.'

After my work-out – Warren brutally woodpeckering my blocked energy with a genuine pneumatic drill before smoothing out the considerable pain with a terrifying industrial polisher – I played Warren the tape and his reaction mirrored Harris's.

(right) With Harris Yulin and Stacy Keach in *Dynasty*.

(below) With Robert Mitchum.

(main pic) Standing beside the Dartmouth estuary where my revelation took place.

Standing beneath the very same mural I described in my regression, a year before Robert had even seen the Old Manor.

Singing rehearsal for *SmileS* with poor Chad Stuart. He deserved golden earplugs for bravery. (*American Conservatory Theatre*)

Rehearsing *SmileS* with choreographer Onna White. (*American Conservatory Theatre*)

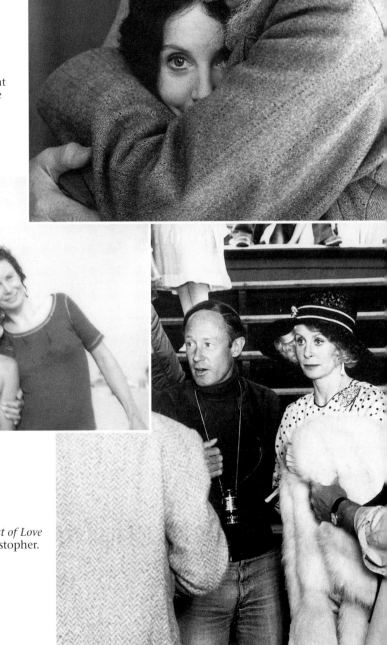

Being hugged by Sterling Haydon in *Venom*.

With Robert and Tomcat on Venice Beach, where Robert asked me to marry him and return to England. He had his stroke the day after he asked me.

On the set of *Priest of Love* with brother Christopher.

(above) Sussex House in Upper Mall, Hammersmith. (*Savills*)

(below) With Robert in Sussex House. (*Stephen Hyde*)

Gladys, a *grande dame* at fifteen years of age.

My friend Athene Seyler with
Peewit, Cuckoo's offspring.

Kense Rinpoche,
the Dalai Lama's teacher.

Our second wedding, outside St. Peter's, Hammersmith. Tom in the background.

White Mischief: About to shoot up, dressed as a Masai warrior, and protecting my face between shots due to my sun allergy.

Harem, and me as myself, taken by Robert and his favourite picture of me.

'No doubt it's genuine, hon. Do you recognise it?' I remained silent because I wasn't sure. 'Is it David?' I shrugged. 'Take it to Thelma Moss at UCLA.' Thelma was head of the parapsychology department there. Among other things she was researching auras through Kirlian photography. She kept the tape for tests and gave me a copy.

'It *is* another voice, no question.'

'What about the aircraft noise over it?'

'We cannot tell. Whatever the phenomenon, it regularly seems to interfere with natural frequencies, causing this peculiar whining sound. Quite a number of the tapes that go through this department have that same noise in the background.' Her verification was hugely comforting.

Tomcat joined Gladys, Harris and myself in Chicago for a week for *SmileS*. It was a modest venture, and took place in a tiny back-street theatre. Harris, now convinced of the voice as well as the candle, was keen to use the candle in the show, and I needed to experiment, to try out the tale from another angle, so the small space was perfect.

Gladys was brilliant (tumour and all) and Harris gave Tomcat a wonderful entrance because he had diligently learnt to play 'God Save the Queen' on the trumpet (a perfect choice for Chicago!). As he was the only one of us small enough to do so, he was also given the responsibility of crawling under the stage each night to pull down the light when my candle went out. He did it without a single mishap and I was might proud of him. Tomcat stole the show this time, just as Gladys had the last. Who was it who said, 'Never act with children and animals'?

With the second *SmileS* mission accomplished and many more lessons learnt (I've yet to try a third time) Tomcat, Gladys, Harris and I spent a holiday in a magnificent colonial clapboard house on the edge of a lake in Connecticut. Harris loved Connecticut and was trying to persuade me to come and live up there permanently with him, but I wasn't sure of anything at that time because my inner life was still taking priority.

One night, with Tomcat in bed asleep and the two of us reading in the sitting room, I looked up into the fireplace to find another 3D vision appearing out of the flames. It was Harris's mother, or so I thought, her soft brown hair pulled back, somewhat wispily, into a bun at the nape of her neck and wearing a high-collared lace blouse.

She was knitting and beside her was a baby. I described it to Harris and he became instantly suspicious.

'How can you be sure?'

'I'm only guessing it was your mother. I'm merely sharing what I saw—'

'What you *thought* you saw.'

'No. I *know* I saw it – I *thought* it was your mother.' I wasn't the least bit miffed, for these kind of differences kept me healthily grounded; I went up to bed with a hot cocoa leaving Harris downstairs reading.

The next recollection was the morning sun filtering through the thin white curtains and an ashen Harris frantically shaking me awake.

'What's up?'

'You ask your son.' Apparently Tomcat had woken up some time in the night and experienced his first vision, but all in black and silver. In the waking state, in 3D, the same woman had appeared in the window with the baby beside her. She, too, held knitting needles. But on her left stood the sinister presence of a man. He was the one who had frightened Tomcat.

'He was Harris's father, I'm sure of it.' We concluded that perhaps the father had abandoned Harris's mother, leaving her no option, back then, but to abandon her baby. No wonder poor Harris looked so shocked. It interested me that Tomcat's vision had the man in black and silver, very like the death man I saw repeatedly when Warren put me under.

Roughly three days later, at tea-time, I was washing up and Tomcat was behind me, sitting down in the pleasant homy kitchen, when suddenly the hairs on my spine stood up, turning me freezing cold. I spun round and found Tomcat transfixed by a ghost wafting slowly, dreamily, between the pair of us.

She was the same one I had seen in the fireplace, with the same hair drawn back in a low wispy bun. The bottom half of her body was filmy and faded away into no legs or feet. Neither of us had any reason to fear such a gentle apparition, so we simply gawped in awe as she wafted her way silently up the big kitchen, before disappearing into the deep freeze. Tomcat opened it and peered in. 'Perhaps she's peckish and feels like a pizza.' That Tomcat witnessed the apparition too was yet another robust confirmation of other worlds.

Lifting to the Heart

It was spring 1979, and courageous Robert was still stuck in Bora Bora, hammering out *Mutiny on the Bounty* with David Lean. Poor Robert! He had been out there for well over a year and was beginning to feel trapped on both land and sea. His letter highlighted his gathering disenchantment with great style and humour. It came as no surprise to me that he finally suffered a mild heart-attack, brought on, no doubt, by too much Boring Boring and David David – a lethal combination. David decided he wasn't prepared to take the rap for Robert dying in Bora Bora (no doctors out there of any worth) so he ordered him back to LA for some tests.

Robert wrote, inviting himself to Venice, so I warned Harris of his imminent arrival. I could never monitor Harris's true feelings: he guarded his vulnerable bastard's soul with a breastplate of steel. Ironically, I gradually began to query his mystery, the very part of his nature that had drawn me to him the first place. Was it a mystery in there, or a painful void? Why was I lacking the passion necessary for a true commitment? Was I so used to playing at unconditional loving with Olivier that I needed freedom at all times? Had Olivier eclipsed the capacity in me to love wholeheartedly, or was I mistaking a real, genuine, unpossessive, unconditional love for lack of real commitment and therefore branding it a lesser kind of love? Whatever, Harris and I never made it to the altar, but we have remained close friends ever since.

It was 10 April when Robert, just arrived in LA, asked if he could drive down to Venice and spend the day with us. He was so keen to get there that he had a mighty crash *en route* but scrambled out scratch-free. The hired car, though, was a write-off. He brushed the incident aside with his usual bravado, much more interested in filling his enormous belly with fresh sushi.

There was no doubt that that lunch-time brand new feelings, both unexpected and razor sharp, began sprouting in my tummy – almost prickly they were! I looked across at Tomcat and saw that he, too, seemed to have grown in stature, utterly contented at having Mummy and Daddy on either side of him. Robert, naturally, never missed a trick.

'It's smashing, eh, the three of us guzzling together once more.' Of that there was no doubt, and until that moment I wouldn't have dreamt that a reunion could be remotely on the cards.

Later that evening Robert, Gladys and I went for a stroll along the Venice Boardwalk. I was delighted to find Robert not smoking, for I'd never noticed before how sweet his natural smell was beneath all that foul tobacco.

'How long since your last puff?'

'Six weeks before my first heart-attack.' It figured.

As the setting sun slapped the walls pink and purple, Robert took my hand, just as he had in the olden days when we were courting. The same clasp, the same swinging arm, the same irresistible bounce in his step. As romantic nights go, it turned out to be one of the most memorable.

'Isn't it a bit daft, you and I living apart?' To remain out in LA – with Gladys my only excuse – suddenly did seem both daft and shameful. We both looked down at her, the most supremely stubborn, selfish, loyal, vicious, comical-looking dog of all time. Robert was responsible for her presence.

'Remember the day you brought her home for me under your jacket?'

'What's that mess all along her back?' I'd tried everything, but Gladys's flea allergy was stubborn as she was, like her malignant tumour which had failed to kill her for five years. 'Isn't she supposed to be dead by now?' I was just as flummoxed as he was. 'Imagine how grateful she'd be to come out of quarantine straight into the coolness of the Old Manor.' So Robert *had* bought the Old Manor for us to live in together; so many people had told me as much, but I hadn't believed them.

'She'd never make it through the six months' quarantine with her tumour.'

'Perhaps I'll never make it through without you.'

I looked at him. Beneath an outer coating of quiet desperation he had grown considerably older. But then the strain of working daily with David Lean was enough to shrivel anyone up. David had a knack of vampiring the very life-force from those around him, leaving his own countenance sparkling fresh as a newborn babe's.

We walked down to the shore as the slightly polluted and puffy moon rose up above the horizon. He put his arm around me. It felt nice. A niceness brimful of homely familiarity tinged with those newly sprouting prickles. I found myself turning gauche and somewhat confused as he kissed me tenderly. Indeed Robert's serenading grew as colourful as the Venice sunset. One by one the doubts began to clear, and as the sun was sinking below the horizon, he took hold of me and turned me round to face the moon.

'Come home and live with me at the Old Manor where you belong.' Of course, with hindsight, I can see how the voice had been manipulating me towards just that ever since the candle went out, but I couldn't at the time. My conscious brain had dismissed the idea of a reunion because it never seemed sufficiently tempting to put old wrongs right and try to make it work a second time.

Had I begun to experience a different kind of love? A love enriched by good and indeed tragic memories, both so nutritious for continuity. Love isn't merely a devoted mistress, or a great lover, for surely real love is all-embracing, interweaving *all* the textures of love's infinite capacity? Besides which, the world was going to the dogs, and in my eyes Robert Bolt stood for all the values that made continuing in it worthwhile.

'Yes, Robert, I will.'

'Good. That's settled, then.'

Two days later, 9 April, Robert fell ill at Michael and Shakira Caine's home where he was staying. They took him to Santa Monica Hospital for tests. His heart was in such terrible nick that a bypass operation was immediately decided upon. Ben, his oldest son and now a film director, flew out to LA to be with him, accompanied by Anne Queensbury. Apparently all went smoothly. The next day both Ben and I visited Robert in intensive care. He was high as a kite to find himself still alive and the operation successful. In fact he was so relieved that he wouldn't stop talking, not even to draw breath.

'Shush – you're blabbering.'

'You can't conceive how wonderful it is to have the fear of another heart-attack removed for good and all – you're bound to blabber when you've just been reborn!'

The next day Robert had a massive stroke from a bloodclot on the brain. When I went in to visit he could neither speak nor move. He lay there, his periwinkle blue eyes staring back at me in bewilderment. At first I thought it was a temporary setback, until the surgeon began crying on my shoulder. Why did his sorrow repel me?

'I've done thousands of successful bypasses – so why Robert Bolt?'

'Will he pull through?'

'Hard to say. He's completely paralysed at present.'

'Is there any hope?'

'Hard to know. Each stroke is different.' I didn't believe Robert was about to turn to the wall. No. He was a fighter if ever there was one.

Twelve years later, Robert sat bolt upright on Christmas morning. 'What's up? A goose walked over your grave?' Obviously shocked, he took quite a while to gather his thoughts. Finally he spoke with great care, clearly recalling what had taken place in intensive care after his triple by-pass operation. He had felt so euphoric that night, he said, after all his jabbering that he climbed out of bed and fell, smashing his head on the floor. 'That's when I got the stroke.'

No wonder I had been repelled by the surgeon's sobs. They had been false. How could they have left someone to fall out of bed in intensive care and then keep it a secret?

Coming into Robert's hospital room on a daily basis, those great eyes of his tormented me with a silent, tumultuous knowing. On the surface his bewilderment echoed my own, his tenderness echoed my own, yet the anger was mine alone – anger at the injustice of it all. But then I reminded myself that I had to look further than the here and now, for our actions, fate and destiny are being played out through so many dimensions and lifetimes, making this life only a small piece of the whole. But that was of little consolation at the time. Later, Robert described this as his goldfish period. He was the fish gone mad, mindlessly gawping, nose pressed against the glass at the people staring back at him from the other side of the goldfish bowl.

Robert made it clear by his eyes that he didn't want Tomcat to see him unable to move, with dozens of tubes hanging out of him. I wasn't happy about this, for children are much less squeamish than we credit them, and I was convinced that whatever Tomcat was imagining had happened to his father would be far more gruesome. But then indomitable hope came striding in, convincing me that Robert wouldn't be in his present state for long, so I let it be.

I bumped into David Lean breezing into the hospital one day, looking as spruce and sleek as ever. Having been party to his work schedule with Robert while Robert had been writing *Ryan's Daughter*, and observing Robert growing more exhausted before my eyes, a sudden rage engulfed me. How much did David really care? So damn hard to tell with Lean.

'Do you feel a little responsible?' I asked him.

'No more than you must feel, for he never got over you, never.' Touché! That put me succinctly in my place. I went home and wept.

After three months Robert was carted back to England. While he was still in LA Michael and Shakira Caine showed great kindness towards him. I was still regarded by his family and friends as the scarlet women, the dark influence that had ruined his life, who should be held partly responsible for the present tragedy. There was no way I could tell them of our pact, so our reconciliation on Venice Beach remained unsung. Was Robert letting me off the hook? Did I *want* to be let off the hook, or was I committed? One thing was certain: I had grown more and more aware of energy and I knew that I had taken huge steps forward, because I had finally managed that important life step: the lift to the heart. Once that step had been taken, the life force propelling me along began to be fuelled by love rather than fear. A luxurious feeling indeed, though keeping it *constant* would become the next test.

Coming and Going

Farewell LA! In March 1980, having packed up my American life, placed Gladys – tumour and all – in English quarantine kennels, I returned home to Tomcat and Robert. Without that damned tumour I might have been home six years earlier – bleedin' dogs!

To be fair, there were some Californian bonuses I would miss: freedom from infamy; my nightly unclouded moon; being able to turn right on a red light; and my neighbour Barry Bostwick's isolation tank. You go down three steps, open a door to a box-like submarine contraption, sink into water of blood temperature and float in darkened silence for as long as you wish as if you were back in the womb, making a complete mockery of time – the perfect solution for life in LA.

I'll never forget that first weekend, driving through the Sussex countryside on my way down to visit Mother, now a widow. I wept at the sheer beauty of all I had missed, and the tears tasted much sweeter knowing I would never leave again. The relief was staggering and a new lightness of being began to rise from the ashes of a long and painful homesickness.

What hit me most when I first stepped back onto British soil was how we were now looking to America for guidance, while America seemed hardly conscious of England's existence. We were rarely mentioned on the world news, and seemed merely an insignificant little country riddled with class, yet when I had left America had looked up to Britain. I was stunned at how misguided the British were in believing America to be a superior nation. It was as if someone elderly and worldly wise had decided to heed the advice of a teenager. Perhaps it should be compulsory for all of us to live in America for a while: that way we would recognise what's truly great about Britain.

At last a new and worthwhile shape was emerging from life's tangles. I had experienced a good deal of opposition from friends and family over my decision to return to Robert, whose wishes had eventually been made clear by both letter and telegram, and I quote: 'I love you tremendously. Come home to me.' It took several months for him to reach this decision – and quite rightly so. Why should he believe that my Venice Beach commitment had been that of a mature woman any more than he should expect a still young and vibrant woman to give up her life? Yet I never wavered for a moment.

In my meditation and prayers I had been repeating the marriage vows over and over to familiarise myself with the enormity of the task ahead. Marrying again was irrelevant, but the *commitment* had to be absolute: 'In sickness and in health till death us do part.' However heavy those vows were, I knew I was ready to honour them the second time around for I had finally realised that true salvation – by that I mean daily contentment – is only found through service to others.

I could have done without everyone else's doubts. Receiving no back-up, no one to believe in my commitment, was hellish lonely. But, then, they hadn't experienced a candle going out and all the other paranormal paraphernalia surrounding that dark period of growth.

'How does a candle going out change anything?' I hear you cry. It makes all the difference in the world. I know that other dimensions exist out there and therefore I want to progress the good in me – not out of fear but out of love.

While I was still in LA I was involved in healing a man with a brain tumour. I had been persuaded to take him on by his twin brother, who had a strong belief in my healing abilities since I had cured his headaches on many occasions.

'A headache isn't a malignant brain tumour.'

'You told me belief is all it takes.' I had begun healing seriously over the previous few years, though I kept quiet about it for fear of being misunderstood. I prefer 'absent' healing through photographs: I find it more effective if the personality is removed from the equation. I ask that the person receiving the healing is told nothing about me, or even that I am working on them, that way assuring that the power of my belief isn't marred by needless doubt or false hope.

When I received the photo, the tumour was too far advanced for there to be any hope of recovery – this was obvious from the greyness that hung around the man.

'Just try for us,' pleaded the twin, Steven. By now his brother was in hospital unable to eat, speak or walk and, due to my limited healing experience, I had intended only to try to ensure a peaceful safe passage and make it clear to Steven that there was nothing else I could do for his brother.

But daily phone bulletins from Steven told me of his brother's astonishing improvement, against all odds. I was baffled to say the least.

'It's a miracle! He walked up the corridor today!'

'Steven, it's no miracle, just a remission.'

The next day, 'He ate a huge meal today!'

Next day, 'He's asked the family in – he wants to talk again—'

'Stop!' I became nervous because I knew Steven was attaching too much to this quite freakish, but brief turn of events.

Towards the end of that curious interlude, which lasted a couple of weeks, Mother rang. Father, who had won the Military Cross for bravery in the First World War, had chosen to play soldier right up to the end and had died on Armistice Day in 1979. The shock, together with an absolute fury at not having being warned that he was close to death's door, eclipsed everything, including my absent healing on the tumour. Within two days the man was dead.

This episode put a halt to my healing for a long time. Moreover the pain and anger of not being called back to say goodbye to Daddy was so intense that I didn't return for his cremation. It was better by far that I said goodbye in my own way, in silence.

On that first weekend home, Mother, perfectly groomed and beautiful as ever, came to greet me. Standing beside her colossal front door, her house towering behind her, she epitomised lonely widowhood. Her frail yet determined stiff upper lip twisted into a courageous smile as I came up the steps into her outstretched arms.

What would happen to her now? Would she choose to join Daddy pretty swiftly, like all those examples of couples one sees on tombstones? Why did I find myself forgiving her for not informing me of Daddy's imminent departure?

'The last thing your father wanted was your crackpot loony notions of a life after death. I just wanted him to die in peace—'

'To die a peaceful atheist?'

'Precisely.'

Chris had previously told me that Daddy's death mask displayed great terror.

'But he didn't.'

'How do you know?'

'If not, why did Chris tell me the next old-timer to be put in his room at the nursing home refused to remain there due to the aftermath of Father's final freak-out?'

'A cup of tea?' It was no use. I would never penetrate her stubborn denial.

After tea: 'Are you sure you should spend the best years of your life looking after Robert?

'Yes.'

She knew I meant it. 'He may live for ever.'

'I hope he does.'

'You're mad – but it would make your father happy.'

'I'm not doing it for Father.' With clarity everything becomes so beautifully simple. Many people considered my actions mad – even the media. Are love, duty, compassion mad? Who is calling whom mad?

After Robert returned from LA, he had a spell in hospital, during which the left side of his body gradually reawakened. His will was really put to the test at Valerie Eaton Griffiths' Stroke Rehabilitation Centre, where he stayed for six months. Every day was a huge challenge as Robert faced the daunting task of learning to speak and walk all over again. At last his first word spoken – 'FUCKINGHELL!'

Every day was therapy, therapy, therapy. Roald Dahl had recently coped with his wife Patricia Neal's severe stroke and his experience was most helpful to Ben, Robert's son, and Jo, his partner, both of whom took off a year to care for him. Meeting Patricia Neal was also an inspiration to Robert. After a gruelling six months of rehabilitation, having gained some speech and with half of his body now functioning fairly well again, he passed out of the Centre with flying colours.

Fed up with the ferocious discipline of fight, fight, fight, Robert suggested that he fly down to the South of France for a holiday with Ben and Jo. His old friend Anne Queensberry owned a charming farmhouse near St Tropez, where we had all stayed over the years. On this occasion, unable to walk properly yet, Robert had to make do with the ground floor, and, of course, being Robert, he overdid it and suffered another quite severe heart-attack. An ambulance was called and he was rushed off to hospital.

On the third morning Ben and Jo went into his hospital room expecting to find him where they had left him the night before, with endless tubes sticking out from every orifice, only to find an empty bed. Ben went down the corridor to call a doctor and raise the alarm when Jo found him under the bed, fixing some part of his squeaky drip with a nail file. 'Drove me potty. Fixed now.'

My return to England to be with Robert occurred a few months after the St Tropez episode. Robert decided to sell the Old Manor in Devon, and had made what I believed to be a somewhat hasty decision, but all those around him thought he would never be able to negotiate the stairs again (little did they know!). He had settled into his new home in Doneraile Street, near the river at Fulham and was having his afternoon nap when I arrived. I lay down on the wrong side of the bed, the side of his stroke arm, without realising he couldn't hold me. He patted the other side and I leapt over, aching to be in his arms again. 'Sorry, it's just the one.'

Why do women weep with joy? I wish I could avoid such outward displays of emotion. On that first day I was drowning in the lagoon of seventh heaven.

His improvement since I had said goodbye to him – a vegetable more or less – in LA was extraordinary, and even the recent St Tropez heart-attack had failed to halt his galloping recovery. Perhaps it had been sent only as a warning to him to slow down and to have more compassion for his healing body.

I was so overjoyed to be with him again that it took me a few days to grasp that the natives were far from friendly. Robert was surrounded by a harem: some lived in, some were new friends, some were helpers who came in during the day, others were just there. I tried to be as warm and open as possible, but I got the distinct impression no one knew why I was there. Had Robert failed to communicate our plan of reconciliation? I was going to have to justify my presence if that was the case. How embarrassing! Should I gather them together for a conference? 'Excuse me, everyone, but Robert called me home from America to take care of him.' Not my style, I'm afraid. Surely Ben would have been told? He must have, for he and Jo had recently moved out of Doneraile Street and back into their old Kensington flat. Was my reluctance to talk to Ben due to his reluctance to talk to me? No one talking truths and no one laying their cards on the table – yet it was the same Ben who had shown such compassion and indeed had cared for his father through those first hard months of his stroke.

Looking back, I must have been mad to allow the Doneraile delusion to take hold of me as it did. Robert's moods fluctuated from hour to hour and gauging his true feelings became impossible. It was as if his logic, his intellect was giving out danger signals, telling him I would soon leave him, whereas his heart was yearning for our union. Most of us have two major lines running diagonally across the upper part of our palm. The top line is our head line, and the one beneath, our heart line. In Robert's case the two lines were moulded into one, meaning his head and heart were joined. This single line on both palms is fairly rare.

Had he forgotten Venice Beach? Why had he decided to under-estimate, to belittle, my love to such an extent? I didn't want to pile any of this negativity onto him, for I felt he should have nothing but light, but it proved a tall order. Every time I entered the kitchen, for example, I had to brace myself as conversations dried up. There were times when I just wanted to run away, yet any urge to pack my bags and leave was immediately taken care of by the familiar strangling sensation. (I realise this book would stand a much better chance without either the voice or the strangling but it would be untruthful, so here I am, caught between the devil and the deep blue sea.)

It was strange that no one was prepared to take me as they found me, but rather as their biased, media-influenced brains wished me to be. How could Robert, still an emotionally dysfunctional stroke victim, take me under his wing protectively when his so-called friends seemed to be ridiculing my newly found commitment?

The only good time was when we were tucked up in bed, even though he wasn't sure which side of the bed was best. Having me on his good side meant he had to forfeit the comforting necessity of a bedside table, yet his other side was dead. Embarrassed by his inability to have any frolics, it took a long while for Robert to readjust to the variety of frolics still to be had – one way or another. Those moments would have sufficed, if the final straw hadn't been about to break the camel's back.

I would bring up Robert's breakfast tray and sit at the foot of the bed

131

reading his mail to him while swiftly he scoffed down the lot. That doomed morning, I remember there being one handwritten letter, postmarked Hampshire.

'Oh. It's from Jo [his first wife]. Read it to me.' The sound of my voice reading that letter still reverberates in my ears. Let it suffice to say that the contents of the letter were sufficient to change the course of my life for many years to come. It was a lethal letter. It reminded me of how the whole world, me included, is rife with self-delusion. Everyone pointing the finger at others, unaware of the fingers pointing back at themselves.

Robert's still fragile emotional body couldn't cope. Once I'd finished reading the letter, his enormous frame exuded infantile moans of anguish as he fell backwards upon the pillows. He began rolling to and fro, groaning like an elephant in musk. Oddly enough I felt relieved – I'd never before heard such honest, heartfelt roars of doubt from Robert. Good! I was wrong. His intellect *hadn't* entirely robbed him of his pure animal instincts. Observing him flailing about from left to right on the pillows I knew there was nothing I could say. The only way to extinguish those roars would be with time and through action.

The roars gathered to an almighty crescendo. I phoned Ben and asked him to come over quickly. When he arrived I sent him to Robert, feeling that they should have time alone to talk it through. When I was finally invited upstairs Ben told me his father had said that calling me back from America had been a mistake. I looked at Robert for any glimpse of remorse and found not a glimmer which for me was proof positive that he hadn't yet regained his conscience, integrity, or trust in his immense capacity for love. Was it my fault that I lacked the ability to promote my commitment to Robert? No words are ever sufficient proof of anyone's commitment, for it's somehow false to brag of the depths of one's love. I believe one can only demonstrate devotion through daily action, and, as fate would have it, I was going to be denied that.

What a grand façade Robert had erected to bluff all comers of his recovery. Oh, that invincible pride of his! How often during my Doneraile period had I come into the bedroom to find him reading his book upside down! One day he would find out how misjudged I had been, but that day, I understood, was still a long way off. I had no doubts: my love for Robert was greater than ever and I felt sure his was for me, but there we were. I had to go elsewhere and tread water for a while.

Nothing remotely similar had happened to me before in my (so far) privileged love life. I had always been fortunate in that my men had always wanted me. To be thrown out was obviously a lesson I had had coming to me. I knew now a little of what Bruce and Harris had felt. Life is hard, is it not? I was well shaken up – too shaken to know what to do or where to go. I spent a long time packing my belongings, along with my smarting emotions. The voice – was it Whiting's? – told me that all would be well in the end. Had he transformed from a dark force into a white light, as his name suggests? Was he the Bolt from the Blue, or nothing whatsoever to do with the equation? I still believed it was the latter.

I entered Robert's room to say goodbye, and he never once looked me in the eye. How did I allow this parting and not fight for my rights? I wanted physically to force him to look at me, but for why? His decision was made and I had to abide by it. 'I love you, Robert, always remember that.' He looked at the ground, not moving. 'I would follow you to the edge of the earth – in my shift!' Mary Queen of Scots would never have left without a fight but, then, she was made of stouter stuff.

I left, quietly, without making a scene, and homeless and dogless, went to stay with a friend near Gladys's kennels. However, the kennels turned out so third-rate that I removed Gladys to better ones near Brighton, and went to live with Mother.

Released by Laughter

May 21 1980, Mother and I were off to Italy's famous Villa d'Este, Lake Lugano, because, just for a lark (I'm not proud!), I had accepted a teeny cameo role, that of a film star, in brother Christopher's new film *Priest of Love*. The screenplay charted the private life of D. H. Lawrence. Ian McKellen was to play D. H. and Janet Suzman, Freda. It was a good move because it created a healing episode, which helped to steady me up after Robert's recent rebuff. Ian and his boyfriend Sean Mathias were stimulating company and determined to give Mother a terrific time too. It was relaxing being directed by Chris, for he always managed to create a comfortable, warm atmosphere on set.

In 1981 I worked with Ian McKellen again, in the prestigious film *Walter*, which christened the first night's viewing on the new television station, Channel 4. The screenplay had been adapted by David Cook from his book about a mentally disabled but sweet guy called Walter, who has a soft spot for another loony in the bin called June (typecast again!). Stephen Frears, the director, caught sight of Tomcat (now a rock-a-billy with pierced ears, blond quiff, heavy chains and boots) and asked him if he'd like to be an extra. Tom leapt at the opportunity. Then the inevitable occurred.

'Ma. I'm gonna get my nose pierced.'

I had forbidden his tattoos and yet his arms were covered in them, so I tried a new tack. 'Go right ahead.'

He did a double-take. 'You mean I *can* have my nose pierced?' As time went by and his nose remained unsullied, I wished fervently that I had used that tactic with his tattoos. While in Tahiti, Tomcat traded his newly acquired tattooing skills in exchange for mangos.

Stephen Frears was determined that *Walter* would attract sufficient attention to give him the international movie breaks he deserved.

Strange, isn't it, how you can sense when someone's energy is geared for the big time? It certainly came for Stephen.

When I arrived home from that week on Lake Lugano, my nose was put severely out of joint, for I was greeted with stinging indifference as I crept into the drawing room with presents for Tomcat. He waved me aside without removing his eyes from the TV screen – he was glued to *Dallas*.

A few minutes later he turned to me, eyes bulging. 'J. R. has just been shot – have to wait for the next series to find out if he's dead.'

'It'll be a long wait.' Apparently just as many people can remember where they were on the evening that J. R. was shot as on the day of the assassination of J. F. Kennedy. The power of soap. I handed him his presents.

'Guess what, Ma?'

'What?'

'Dad's marrying Anne Queensberry.' Another damn Bolt from the Blue. This one zapped me right in the pit of my stomach. All was lost. Gladys was stuck in quarantine for no reason; I had returned home and my LA life – not to mention Harris – was irretrievable for no reason.

I'll never forget the look Tomcat gave me at that moment. I attempted to hide the effect of the news as he came over and gave me a kiss. He knew my dreams of getting the family back in order were dashed. Tomcat was only thirteen, but he knew it all. 'Why didn't Daddy choose you?'

'Because he apparently prefers Anne.'

'But he doesn't! I know he doesn't!' Tom was unhappy about it, and his unhappiness remained with him for a long, long time. 'Daddy loves you, Ma! *You*.'

Robert's team had decided he should now live in The Boltons and, being a sucker for posh addresses, he didn't complain. It felt profoundly odd to be sitting beside him on his new posh sofa at his wedding reception. 'Very smart, all of it.'

He waved my remark aside. 'Horridbull! Fucking hell!' He laughed like a drain. I tried to follow suit but failed to find the funny side. 'I'm so solly.' His look was that of a twelve-year-old caught scrumping Coxes from the posh folk's garden. 'Isn't it lovely?' He wanted me to praise that which only a moment ago he had been damning. 'Fuckin' hell! I just don't know...'

'That makes two of us.'

'What could I do?' Apparently Anne had taken full advantage of the leap year and proposed to him. I'd never heard of this tradition. No flies on Anne, obviously, for they were all on me. What a bolted-up family all those Bolts were! To think that they had kept the approaching wedding a secret from the rest of the world for over three months. Yet I felt no pangs of anger, jealousy or revenge, for in my deepest heart I knew everything in life happens as it should.

Anne had been very loyal to Robert over the years, always there whenever she was needed. As I began to understand the post-stroke Robert better, I realised that those who asked, got, and those who didn't got nothing. This tendency to put his own needs first didn't stem from selfish motives, but from the struggle he had to keep his head above his disability and breathe the essential air of normality. He *had* to pretend he knew what he was doing, even when he hadn't a clue. His brain had to be prompted into any situation beyond his immediate needs. Anne would be better equipped than I for the role of prompter. I loathed taking the reins of power because sadly it leads to the abuse of it.

I was still with Mother in Brighton with Gladys ensconced in one of the better quarantine kennels near by. My London bolt-hole, a tiny two-room flat in Mayfair, would be free for my return in two months' time. Until then I had to tread water with as much dignity as I could muster.

Olivier rang one morning in June and was surprised to hear my voice. He had been calling Mother quite regularly since Father died, which was thoughtful and touching – or did he have a soft spot for her?

'Why didn't you tell me you were coming home?' Since he'd made it perfectly plain that our relationship had threatened his marriage, I wondered where he found the cheek to ask me that.

'I didn't want to bother you—'

'Bother?' That he acted amazed, amazed me, but I let it go.

'How are the memoirs going?'

'It's a struggle.' I felt a little responsible for Olivier's decision to write them himself, and prayed that the end result would be worthy of him. 'Shall I pop over to dinner one night?'

'Yes, please.' And so it was that he came for dinner.

I had seen him from time to time in my Mayfair bolt-hole, but even so the change I noticed in him that night was considerable. He looked desperately unhappy. His eyes lacked any light, as if his soul had fled its vehicle. He caught me looking at him. 'Each time they put me into hospital I have a face lift.'

'Then you'd best not be ill again!'

As he blew me a kiss on leaving, I realised that, like Robert, I would love him till all the seas ran dry, or till all his pubic hair had been pulled up into a beard. Is it a sin to love two people equally? That's what loving's all about surely – simply love? Some confuse my devotion to older men as a father complex or fixation. Yet I'm fascinated by old women too. I would far rather be in their company, learning about their life experiences, than listening to the dreams of the young.

Olivier never understood the realms of experience he had to offer me *outside* the sheets. Alas, all he saw was how he had grown physically unworthy of me – just like Robert. Two grown men witless enough to remember me only for a romping good time between the sheets, when all our best times together were spent revelling in each other's company. The twentieth century has placed sex on such an idiotic pedestal!

I recalled Larry once explaining different types of women: those suited for the bedroom, the drawing room, the kitchen (I don't remember him mentioning those suited for the workforce!). They had lumbered me with the bedroom image, and their masculine pride in this respect had rendered me a loner.

Psychic Mama caught my thoughts. 'Sarah refuses to fight her corner, Larry. She allows her men to trample all over her—'

'Shush, Ma—'

'But it's true, Sarah. Your attitude is an embarrassment to feminism.' She poured Larry another glass of wine. 'If I'd been lucky enough to have been born in her era I would have stood up for my rights.' She would, too. Mother would have made a superb feminist and businesswoman.

'I know. I'm so very guilty. So very selfish.' Larry was at his worst on a guilt trip, so I climbed onto my high horse.

'Guilt is such a convenient substance, for it smothers all our sins, allowing them to run amok beneath when what they need is to be brought out into the light and examined.'

He thought about this. 'Oh Lord! My book's full of guilt ... and you may be right. I'd never seen it like that.'

'Sarah tells me you're not mentioning her in your book.'

'No, I daren't.' He took my hand. 'But I've given her permission to write about us – after I'm dead.'

'Since she never went to school, you're on safe ground there.'

During those six months of writing while I sat in prison daily with Gladys I decided to expose the ludicrously ineffectual farce of our quarantine laws. But, sadly, I found that editors didn't like anti-quarantine-kennel articles because of the public's rampant (through ignorance) fear of rabies. Now, almost two decades later, quarantine may be reassessed, so forgive me for making a few points:

(1) A *100 per cent* effective vaccine is available. In America it is compulsory for all dogs, so Gladys was vaccinated up to her eyeballs having had all the booster shots.

(2) Rabies is *only* passed on through *blood, saliva* or *excrement.*

(3) Each day the kennel maid would smile sweetly and let me into Gladys's concrete cell. When I was ready she let me out again.

  (a) Gladys's paw was bleeding and I left with *blood* on me.

  (b) I regularly stood in her *poo* because the kennel was so cramped.

  (c) Every day I got thoroughly kissed all over and then drove off with my son's black Labrador, Lizzy, kissing Gladys's *saliva, blood* and *poo* off me.

(4) *No checking took place. The kennels never tell you the facts of rabies. I was free as a bird with dog saliva, excrement and blood regularly on my person, clothing or shoes, which eliminated the whole purpose of quarantine in the first place.*

My case rests.

Gladys had come through her sentence! But I found this next period difficult, almost surreal, as I flailed about like a fish out of water in my sterile Mayfair bolt-hole – no life to be seen in Mayfair, even worse than Beverly Hills. What on earth was I doing there? Although I saw Tom almost every day, I lacked sufficient funds to move into a larger space where we could live together, which made me feel a failure. I am not good with money and dyslexia doesn't help: I had been given poor financial advice in LA and could not sell my Benedict Canyon home (too funky and decrepit for most people's taste), so I was relieved to be back with my old and trusted English accountancy firm.

Tomcat needed to catch up academically, and he was making heavy weather of his new school in Victoria. Ironically it was an American establishment and had come highly recommended. But I felt pangs of hypocrisy whenever I warned Tom of the dangers of no education, since I'd been so hopeless myself in the same system.

I was asked to open the 1980 Mind, Body and Spirit Exhibition at Olympia. This caused quite a hullabaloo because, naïvely, I listed all the alternative healing techniques (except urine therapy!) that had taken LA by storm. I also spoke of the energy lines through the planet (ley lines) and how they are reflected in our own energy or meridian lines. I explained how the Chinese had been aware of these meridian lines for centuries: acupuncturists stick pins into them at various pressure points. Well! Shiver me timbers! Next day in the press I was almost burnt as a witch. 'Sarah Miles claims we should stick pins into our flesh to heal our aches and pains.' We have come a long way over the past sixteen years, but back then I was put firmly (again!) in the 'potty' box.

Ever since that candle had gone out I had felt severely tested – driven to push at the boundaries of awareness. This is hard to comprehend, I know, but it was a fact. The voice's pressure, along with the inevitable strangling whenever I was reprimanded, frequently became an unbearable burden. Oddly, though, the respites of peace were blindingly light, but they only happened when I was writing, singing, praying, doing yoga, meditating and walking – none of which bought home the bacon! Times were tricky.

As the days went by I found myself less and less able to bear the voice's interference in my life – I had been manipulated by it for nearly seven years – especially now that Robert had brought me back across the Atlantic for no reason, I couldn't see Olivier, I had no money and no proper home for Tomcat, who was unhappy at his school.

One morning, I awoke to the appalling realisation that my career had taken a definite tumble – and convinced that every piece of advice the voice had given me had been worthless. For the first time, I knew I needed help, which shamed me, but my loyal pals, the voice and the strangling, had well exceeded their sell-by date. With those facts firmly established I decided to see a medium – something I'd never have dreamt of doing under normal circumstances.

That was how Gladys and I found ourselves walking up Park Street, through Hyde Park and onward to the well known Spiritual Centre in Belgrave Square. I didn't know anyone to help me find a medium, or of anywhere but Belgrave Square to go. When I say *we* went for a walk, the truth was that I carried Gladys most of the way – not that I had much option by then, she being fifteen years old with her malignant tumour an' all – bloody heavy she was too.

We were taken into this small room where a mousy elderly lady told me that Arthur sent his love. The next fifteen minutes were taken up with me remaining adamant that I'd never known a single Arthur in my whole life but each time I contradicted her, the medium laughed herself into a woodlouse-like roly-poly, explaining all the while that Arthur found it hilarious that I had forgotten him. She repeatedly prodded my memory with Arthur's characteristics – his gregariousness, his naval origins, his being a real Jack the Lad, one of the boys down at the pub, propping up the bar with a pint, until I became impatient and realised I'd made a huge mistake in coming in the first place.

'I'm sorry – explain to Arthur it's a case of mistaken identity – I really must go now.' I put Gladys down, stood up and collected my jacket.

'He wants to say sorry for his bottom trouble.' This was getting more bizarre by the minute.

'Bottom trouble?'

'All the operations he cost you.'

The penny dropped. When I left for America Robert had kept our boisterous, friendly, sociable, easy-going Old English sheepdog and I had taken Gladys. Robert had brought them home on the same day as a surprise for me – they were two months old. The separation had caused them to pine for each other, hence Gladys's tumour on her thigh and Arthur's tumour on his bum. The endless operations had cost Robert a fortune – poor Arthur and his bum! He was the epitome of Jack the Lad! I wonder if that medium's message would have come through if I'd left Gladys at the flat and gone alone?

As a last resort I went to Chalk Farm to talk things through with R.

D. Laing, a friend of Robert and the only psychiatrist I knew of – but *I* didn't know him, so how could he could help me? Once there, I was unable to open my mouth. I'd never shared my experiences with anyone, except Warren and Harris; jumping in at the deep end with an actual psychiatrist, no less, brought with it the fear of mockery, disbelief or, even worse, being diagnosed as mentally ill.

'Well, spit it out. Spit it out.' He sat in his leather swivel chair, twirling around, gazing thoughtfully out of the window, flexing his fingers until my tale was told. It was early evening and the occasional whiff of whisky on his breath suited him no end. When I'd finished, I expected him to laugh, disbelieve me, or send me packing. He didn't turn a hair, but made me write down the name of a priest. The Reverend Neil Smith of St Saviour's Church, Chalk Farm. 'I'll tell him you're coming. He may appear a little eccentric, but don't let that fool you – merely camouflage. He's just up the road here. There are many priests still exorcising unwanted spirits from haunted places – but very few from people.'

'Why?'

'Probably because modern society chooses to suppress these things.'

'Why?'

He shrugged half-heartedly. 'Incompatible with market forces. Trusting in something so ephemeral is unrewarding, unfashionable – takes courage.'

'Will the priest be able to do his stuff even though I'm not religious?'

'Should make no difference. Good luck. If he fails, we'll think again.'

'Eccentric' put it mildly. The Reverend Neil Smith turned out a fearsomely frenetic old bird. As I knelt there in the church with his rantings and boomings behind me, just like a Hammer movie, I developed a fit of the giggles. I attempted to suppress it, but once I'm started, nothing on God's earth can stop me.

'Out! Out! O ye festering spirit!'

The Reverend continued to do his stuff with unwavering sincerity, strutting back and forth, his voice echoing through the empty church. He seemed to be so into his own thing – thank God! – that he failed to hear the grunts and snorts as I tried to stifle the giggles.

What a ludicrous lark! Was R. D. Laing having a good laugh at my expense? Had he set me up? All I wanted was for the pantomime to be over as soon as possible so I could pay the priest and get the hell out of there. Eventually there was silence.

'How do you feel now?' He was strangely reticent after his patriarchal booming. 'Best if you go home and just sleep for as long as you can. Promise to take it easy for the next few days?'

'I promise. How much will that be?'

'Put whatever you want towards the church fund.' He pointed to a wooden letter-box next to the font. 'I must be off. Good day.' I bunged in thirty-six quid, everything I had, and off I went, laughing myself into the best night's sleep I'd had in ages.

R. D. Laing's dying words tickled my fancy. He was playing tennis with an American friend, Bob Firestone, in the South of France, when he suffered a heart-attack. His friend panicked. 'We must get a doctor!'

'Doctor? What fucking doctor?' said Laing, and died.

Oh! The fickle fads of fashion! R. D. Laing was a perfect example: he was as fashionable in his day as he is unfashionable now, nevertheless he gave me good advice. When all the mockery and giggles had subsided I realised that the fingers had not pressed around my throat since that ridiculous exorcism. I see now how easy it is to mock the unknown, and how difficult it is to accept a new awareness once the reason for one's mockery has been found lacking.

Waiting for the Blue

It was wonderful to be living with Tomcat again – and Gladys! Mother, bless her, had galloped up on her white charger, offering to buy (at a good deal for her – natch!) the lease of my Mayfair bolt-hole. So with that, and my LA abode finally sold, I had enough money for a proper home. Tomcat and I chose an area of eighteenth-century perfection, regularly used in period films, as we discovered to our annoyance, Portland Road, Holland Park. The house was inconveniently built flush to the pavement, with uneven floors and steep rickety stairs that creaked something chronic. Yet its unspoilt charm, magnificent wisteria and south-facing garden entranced me – but not Mother! She let me know in no uncertain terms.

'Nothing but an old workman's cottage. You can't live here—'

'It's like a country cottage, Grandma,' interrupted an enthusiastic Tomcat.

In 1982, I decided to have a stab at both Viola, in *Twelfth Night*, and Lady Macbeth at the Shakespeare Company in North London with Philip Madoc as Macbeth. These were two of the three roles in the canon I'd always wanted to play. The third – and one I yearn to play most – is Cleopatra. I chose the Shakespeare Company because I didn't want to be shot down, and North London suited my purposes beautifully because the main critics stayed away. I enjoyed my time up there for it enabled me to regain some lost confidence. What reviews I did get were good to excellent. I'm still waiting to play Cleopatra and I think I'm worthy of her now. (Forgive my moment of cockiness, but I have yet to see a Cleopatra who dulls those feelings of worthiness.)

I had recently completed a film with the romantic adventurer Sterling Hayden. His questing nature and his spiritual dimension were lovingly depicted in his autobiography and gained my everlasting respect. Why is it usually men of the rarest sensibility that feel obliged to anaesthetise that better part of themselves with booze? Those dreary bouts of belligerent, maudlin drinking prevented me from loving everything else he stood for. He was an exact replica of Nicol Williamson, my sixties beau, whose boozing had been the main reason that he and I parted. So it was ironical that Nicol was also in the cast, the only ex-lover with whom I hadn't kept in touch. Looking at him again made me marvel that we had ever been close, for now that we were fully grown-up, he just wasn't my type at all.

Sterling Hayden, Nicol Williamson and Oliver Reed, who was also in the film – all magicians in their own way and all drunks in their day. But neither Sterling nor Nicol were as incorrigible as old Olly Reed.

Klaus Kinski played the lead, which placed a cloak of gloom over what turned out to be a doomed enterprise. The film was appropriately called *Venom* and Klaus seemed determined to live up to its name. From what I was able to glean, the only excuse for his demonic outbursts sprang from his daughter, Nastassja Kinski, being on a roll. After Polanski's *Tess*, she became the new darling of Hollywood, courted, caressed and cast wherever she went. I believe Klaus was actually envious of his own offspring.

What baffled me was the behaviour of Olly and Nicol, those infamous sixties hell-raisers. They crept silently around Klaus's temper, smiling sweetly on tippy-toes. Did they consist of nothing more than hot wind and jelly babies when the chips were really down? One day when Klaus was being particularly obnoxious, I asked Nicol, 'Why don't you give him one?' Nicol looked at me in horror and turned tail.

I asked Olly the same. 'Why do you stand for it?'

'I'm no fool.' Did no one dare to take on Klaus's tirades? Some days he didn't show up for work. The reasons were always flimsy, such as his dresser having hung his jacket on a wire rather than a wooden coat hanger.

One morning I met Klaus on the stairs as I came in to work, so I decided to start the day politely. 'Good morning, Klaus.'

He didn't even acknowledge me, but continued to look straight ahead. Fed up to the gills with his arrogance, I growled and grabbed him by the shirt collar. 'I said good morning, Klaus!' Because I'd backed him up, he lost his balance on the stairs and was forced to sit. He stared up at me, like a child, stunned. 'Next time I say good morning I want a civil response.' With that I stepped over him to get to my dressing room. From then on he smiled, said good morning, and was generally pretty normal around me, at least.

I was still at my most contented when creating songs, but the chances of finding someone to translate my melodies and lyrics on to paper and have patience with my dyslexic inability to read music was nigh on impossible. Therefore meeting Charly Foskett, a tall, blond Geordie musician and composer, was the bit of luck I needed. Charly was a real one-off – but, then, most Geordies are. He was unusually skilful, playing many instruments with ease as well as being a competent artist, carpenter and sempster.

I hadn't been with anyone for a long time, and just as I was beginning to believe everything had rusted up for good, Charly, homeless and on the dole, came to live with us temporarily at Portland Road and in no time had constructed an impressive sound studio down in the basement. Charly and the sound studio were heaven-sent for Tomcat, who was still a rock-a-billy with a blond quiff, for he, too, had grown very keen on music, and had become a great little performer in his own right – or so I was to find out after the event.

While Tomcat had been living with Anne and Robert in their new home on the river at Chiswick, his then wayward step-sister, Alice, had planned a fourteenth birthday treat for him. The two of them snuck out of Tomcat's bedroom window for a night at the Whisky-a-Go-Go in Soho. Tomcat, with his exceptional dancing style, caught the attention of the drummer from the band Jo Boxers, who were performing that night.

'You dance well,' said the drummer.

Quick as a flash, Tom responded 'If you think this is good, you should hear me sing.' Within a week Tomcat was making his first demo disc and shortly afterwards (not having let on about his age), he went on tour fronting the band with the Lady Alice Douglas as his manager. What a team!

Apparently Robert and Anne knew none of this until it was a *fait accompli*. I, too, knew nothing about his nocturnal escapades, which goes to show that, when it comes to secrecy, Tomcat can give even his old ma a good run for her money. He was, as usual, between schools.

145

He had been pushed out of his school in Victoria, as well Ibstock Place, Roehampton, for the second time, and was about to honour Sheen Comprehensive with the pleasure of his company. (Poor Sheen!) His school years had been complete chaos, so any success was bound to be vitally important to his self-worth. So once we did find out, and both of us being aware of how a bit of success had transformed our own school years, we let Tomcat get on with it for the school holidays.

One night Robert and I braved Soho to catch our son in action. Tom dashed on, grabbing centre-stage, then devouring it, tearing the whole joint apart. It would be easy to colour the occasion with maternal pride, but I exaggerate not an iota when I claim that Tomcat was a definite star in the making, a hugely energetic well-coordinated spider with a slightly debauched water-baby beauty topped with a golden quiff. Robert looked at me, aghast. It was an alien sensation for us both to see our only child up there storming the joint with a kind of raunchy, raw but infinitely sweet sexuality.

Should Robert, Anne and I have forbidden Tomcat to perform with the Jo Boxers? That is the question. We were damned if we did and damned if we didn't. I believe Tom would have experimented with drugs anyway. Back in the early eighties, awareness of drug abuse was still in the Dark Ages, and at this point, to my knowledge, Tomcat was only smoking marijuana occasionally. Warren Barigian's warnings echoed in my brain. 'He's a holic, hon, he's the type. The inability to concentrate, hyperactive, a craving for sugar which leads to drugs. What we have to research is how to rectify that initial chemical imbalance within the system combined with hereditary genes.'

It was at this time that someone gave me Susan Hampshire's book on dyslexia. Why hadn't Tom's school in Victoria enlightened us? How could I have been so out of touch not to have gleaned any inkling as to the cause of the so-called stupidity that had dogged Tomcat and me all our lives? How could I have heard of dyslexia only in 1983? Even more shameful was that, unbeknown to me, I had a cousin Tim, a professor at Bangor University in Wales, who had studied dyslexia for decades. Why had my parents failed to put two and two together? I didn't know of cousin Tim's credentials until I'd read Susan's excellent book. Was it too late for Tomcat, just as it had been too late for me?

Without wasting any more time, Tomcat and I set out for the Dyslexia Centre in Slough where we got ourselves tested. I turned out to be 85 per cent dyslexic; poor Tomcat was 87 per cent. The tests also proved that he was colour blind. I was number blind and spatially blind too. Driving home that day, I felt a kind of deliverance.

Tomcat eyed me with those huge blue eyes of his. 'So what does it mean, Ma?'

'It means we aren't stupid.'

'But I already knew that.'

'Well, I didn't.'

'So what do we do now?'

He had me foxed.

After Tom parted company with Sheen Comprehensive I was at my wit's end as where to send him. I recalled my mother's desperation after my various expulsions and that she had chosen to despatch me to the Arts Educational School. I decided to let history repeat itself. In any case, I had no choice: nowhere else would take him. The school was reluctant at first, due to his appalling track record, but after meeting him and seeing him perform, they agreed to give him a try.

Once he had settled into the rhythm of the Arts Educational, my agent heard that they were searching on both sides of the Atlantic for a beautiful sixteen-year-old boy to play the lead, a young monk, in *The Name of the Rose*, opposite Sean Connery. Tomcat went to audition and three weeks later was told it was between him and an American boy. 'I have to go to Paris for a film test, Ma.' He seemed awfully laid back about the whole thing. When I had my first break, the lead opposite Olivier, I was over the moon for weeks. How times change. I offered up my services.

'No, Ma! I want no help from you. I'll do it my way!' He seemed so sure of his way that I hadn't the nerve to argue.

I vividly recall the day that script arrived.

'It's come, Tomcat!'

He came downstairs and took it from me. 'Don't touch it, Ma.' He promptly put it on the window-sill in the hallway and returned to his room. That was five days before he was due in Paris.

Three days later, unable to bear it any longer, I went up into his bedroom. (There was never any smell of marijuana, so I presumed he was just sleepy.) 'Tomcat. You must be word perfect before that Paris flight—'

'For Christ's sake, Ma, leave me alone! I don't want the words to come out too pat – there's never any surprise when actors know their lines *too* well.'

There was an element of truth in what he said. 'Learn the lines first, that's your starting-point. From then on you play with them as you wish.'

'Please, Ma, leave me alone. I know what I'm doing.'

'I don't think you do, Tom. Can we have a talk?'

'There's nothing to talk about.'

He even forbade me to accompany him to the airport, so determined was he to go it alone. That really hurt. I abhor pushy mothers and I had always tried to get the balance right between guiding him, caring for him and giving him his freedom. But this new attitude of Tomcat's had me completely stumped. He wanted to be an actor, or so he said, and here was the plum part of the year juicily ready for plucking.

I understood how hard it could be, for a child of successful parents to step out of the shadow, yet I had had no idea that Tomcat had such fears for he had always been so up-front with his aspirations. I don't believe we had ever been the kind of parents to care about winning and losing: just playing a clean game had always meant more to us than any amount of success. In fact, I had made a conscious effort in that direction, having been subject as a child to my father's incredibly competitive nature. I had just wanted us all to be happy. Perhaps I didn't push Tom hard enough.

I have to admit that my heart went out to me as well as to Tomcat as I waved him off to Paris that day. We could have had such fun learning the lines and experimenting with the scenes together, as mates. He didn't get the part. The director thought he was far more talented, beautiful and exciting than the other guy ... but the other guy knew his lines.

Tom's headmistress called one day to say that, talented though Tom was, she would need a telephone call from me personally to inform her of his asthma attacks. He had been missing school. I went to have it out with him. He was in his room with Jake, his partner in crime and best friend since they were six, lying nonchalantly on my unique six-by-seven-foot Italian sofa-bed – specially designed for my Mayfair flat – dropping ash all over it.

'Answer me, Tomcat.'

He continued to stare at the telly. 'What was the question?'

'Are you missing school?'

Tom shrugged with disinterest. 'Nah! I never give it a thought.'

Jake reprimanded him. 'Don't tease your poor mum, Tom, that ain't cricket – that's *dyslexic*.' Jake made 'dyslexic' sound wet.

'We don't play cricket. That's the point, Ma, we never get to play real games – nothing but soppy tap-dancing.'

Jake gave a poofy gesture.

'Jake. Do you miss school too?'

'Not nearly as much as school misses me!'

'Jake's tap-dancing out on the streets.' They both burst into hoots of laughter. Jake, streets ahead of Tomcat academically, could afford to mess around a bit and still be top in exams. How I wished they'd never met in the first place.

Back in 1962 I had made a film directed by Joe Losey called *The Servant*, with Dirk Bogarde and James Fox, so when Joe telephoned me again in 1983, asking me to be in the film version of Nell Dunn's successful play *Steaming*, with Vanessa Redgrave, nostalgia eclipsed my better judgement and I accepted without having read the final script. I had recently met Nell Dunn because I wanted the rights of another of her stories, had liked her a lot and was most put out that she showed no interest in rewriting the film script of *Steaming* herself, for a rewrite was most urgently needed.

'I know nothing about screen-writing. I simply take my percentage and let them get on with it.'

I found her indifference quite astounding from someone of such obvious—integrity. 'Take the money and run, eh?'

'Just like you.'

'How d'you mean?'

'You've accepted to do the film, haven't you?' Touché. I needed the money. Perhaps Vanessa Redgrave did, too. Patricia Losey, Joe's wife, was a lovely, intelligent woman, but no screen-writer. It was heartbreaking because I saw great possibilities for a sensitive, penetrating and erotic insight into the privacy of the feminine psyche.

'Just grit your teeth and bear it,' said Nell, the wise old sage.

Gritting my teeth and bearing it was pretty much all I did for those eight weeks of shooting. None of it was a good time. I remember Vanessa Redgrave, her evangelical footsteps pacing hither and thither up echoing corridors. I admire her hugely – even love her – but found it hard to separate her from her cause. She tended to loom, forcing her beloved Trotsky pamphlets at me with eyes of such myopic seriousness, that regularly, upon hearing those purposeful steps, I'd turn tail and gallop down the corridor in the opposite direction.

I had always had great affection and respect for Joe Losey, so it was painful to witness him fading a little more each day, along with Diana Dors, who was also fading – not a little, but a lot. Did they both know that *Steaming* was to be their swan-song? I believe they did, for they both told me as much.

Vanessa and I had been daily promised new blue script pages, which never came. Joe bade the whole cast to remain loyal to the stilted dialogue with not an *and* or a *but* out of place. My frustration became unbearable – yet each day, still no blue pages.

'You're too gullible,' teased Vanessa. 'There'll never be any blue pages. We've been conned.'

An unexpected bonus was getting to know Diana Dors. It's a shame we met so late in life because we were instantly struck by an ancient recognition, similar to the experience I had had with Margaret Leighton. What a wise and witty woman she was! Her camouflage was so sumptuously bedazzling that one can hardly blame the media for failing to discover the true worth that lay fizzing underneath – until the twelfth hour, that is. I bet when I move on I'll find her and Maggie the greatest of kin spirits.

Talking of moving on, it was Gladys's turn. She and Tomcat had grown up together. Perhaps it was clashing star signs, or something, for they had never seen eye to eye over anything, not since the very beginning, and if the truth be known they were both as deviously tricky as each other. So life went on, with their antagonism unblunted and unrelenting, until Tomcat's sixteenth birthday on 20 October 1983. Just as Tom stood up to blow out the candles, I bent under the table to pick up Gladys so she could see too, only to find her dead. It took me a great while to fill the void her passing left behind, for she was irreplaceable.

I sometimes went down to see Robert at his new home on the river at

Cuckoo, my Yorkie, with her firstborn Oxton (Robert's second name) and the pups we kept, Oxton and Batty.

Thanks to Peter Hall firing me, we found Chithurst Manor.

(top left) Our first Christmas at Chithurst.

(above) The conservatory Chuzzer designed and built for us.

(above right)Tom – a clean machine - in the conservatory.

(right) Chuzzer himself.

Hope and Glory.

Chithurst: life through the lattice under the apple tree.

My sister Nessie strolls through the garden.

(below) Lovely in all her glory.

The Black Madonna at Jasna Gora.

Jasna Gora: there was no ghost when I took
this photo of the Black Madonna in the chapel.

Sitting in a corn circle.

My last photo of Robert,
with a crook given to him
by Michael Bentine.

Tom with his wife Fifi.

Walking the dogs – as usual.

Tom and Lovely. This photo was the last of a roll where all the other shots came out perfect. When I took it, I was kneeling on Robert's grave by his head. I wanted a picture of Robert's favourite point of view of the house.

A week later I asked Carolyn, our Girl Friday, to take the same view with me and Lovely. I showed both these photos to experts, who ruled out a fault on the film or light coming into the camera.

Chiswick. I never went without being asked first, and Anne never displayed any negative feelings when she saw me at the door. Robert had built on a beautiful conservatory, but then Robert plopped down conservatories wherever he went, like a male dog marking his territory.

One day Anne told me that his study down at the far end of the garden was finally completed and that that was where I'd find him. I crept down the narrow but large garden, peeked through the window and spied on Robert as he worked. I laughed to myself, for I had done the very same thing at Byfleet almost two decades earlier. I'd spied on him then because I was lonely and needed to know what the hell he got up to in his working hours. I spied on him that day in Chiswick, too, with the Thames running past at high speed. He wasn't working this time, simply sitting there, dreaming. Probably dreaming of those same old Byfleet days when his work was so frenetic and prolific. As he looked up and spotted me, the pain lifted and the sun came out. He was positively beaming.

'Why so far away?'

'I need the exercise.'

'No. I mean why were you *dreaming* so far away?'

'Dreaming is better than chatter up at the house.' He was speaking again. Very slowly. The patience required to listen was nothing compared to the patience needed to form those blasted words. Such an irony – Bolt, the great wordsmith. 'How's Charly?'

'Fine, thanks.' There were times when I would fool myself into believing that the whole episode with Charly was a kind of stop-gap because Robert's love for me was just as strong as ever. Even though I had never said a word, Charly believed, too, that Robert and I were far from over. 'We're off to Kathmandu.'

Robert looked up at me with a profound longing. Was it for me or Kathmandu? Undoubtedly the latter, for he wouldn't have changed his mind so soon ... would he?

'How goes things?

'Horridbull!'

'Have you any pain?' He waved his good arm dismissively towards the house. Silence fell. I didn't want to ask any more for I found it all too bewildering. Surely Robert wouldn't have pushed me out of Doneraile Street to become despairing so soon.

What I found particularly painful was the damaging effect all this was having on Tomcat, for I felt his recent deterioration was due mainly to Robert not remarrying me. He knew I had returned from America to start up a new life where we three would be back together again. Charly was a great guy, but he was not Tom's dad. I also maintained that Robert's decision not to see Tomcat during those first crucial weeks after his stroke had caused Tom a lot of suffering. I believe that whatever tragedies befall a family, they must be experienced by the family as a whole, but what am I saying? I wasn't even family at the time – or now. What a mess!

It was not a happy time for Robert's elder daughter, Sally, either. I had always been very fond of fiery, emotional Sally. Out of all the children from his first marriage, Sally suffered most from her *Man For All Seasons* royalties. That regular cushion of comfort prevented her from having to put her talent on the line, for talented she undoubtedly was, both in music and art. I recalled her having been the only native at The Boltons who was genuinely friendly.

'Dad and you should get back together, 'cos it's you he really loves.' Was she aware of their upcoming marriage when she said that? Was there any connection between Robert's marriage to Anne, and the tragedy that befell Sally soon afterwards? Or had it been a combination of life's ordinary challenges plus the failure to access her true potential? Her marriage to a successful stonemason, Neil Simmons, not to mention their beautiful daughter, Rosie, seemed to be fine.

Whatever her motives, Sally drove her car through the balustrade next to Putney Bridge and into the Thames. Whether by accident or design, her death remains a mystery to all who loved her. It was only Robert who remained adamant. 'She committed suicide,' he continued to claim, right up to his dying day.

Shamsha and Sunyata

Early in 1984, full of anticipation, Charly Foskett and I found ourselves flying over the spectacular Himalayas on our way to Kathmandu. My brother Chuzzer had lived there in a palace off and on for years. Then the clean dry air there – now it's the devil's armpit of pollution – was good for his asthma.

Just before we left London I had had a car accident. I was driving up Ladbroke Grove when the driver in front braked violently, leaving me no alternative but to do the same, thus flattening my nose on the steering wheel – the usual punishment for tail-gating. My nose was smashed so crooked that the surgeon had put it in a bizarre splint, which created quite a stir upon our arrival in Kathmandu.

People gawped – not, alas, at my astonishing beauty, but at my esoteric nose shield. Was I some Arabian freak, ancient Egyptian, or some weirdo from out there somewhere? As time went by, the gawping frustrated me as much as my inability to relieve the mad itching, high on my cheekbone, under my splint.

When I had addressed envelopes to Chuzzer over the years, I had conjured up a glorious vision of this palace of his in much the same way that one conjures up a face from a voice down a telephone. Chuzzer's famous palace turned out to be no more than a modest crumbling villa set within a dilapidated walled garden. Chuzzer explained, 'Palaces are two a penny out here – in fact, everything with a walled garden is called a palace.'

It didn't take long, however, for the palace to weave its own brand of stark well-being around us. Chuzzer was scrupulous in teaching us how to protect ourselves from the lethal Eastern bugs, yet those little buggers always knew better. Charly Foskett was a freckly, reddish-blond and the mosquitoes made mincemeat of him and his mosquito net, all of them aching to get a suck of Charly's sweet,

153

soft, milky skin. Poor Charly! After a week he went missing beneath a swollen, scarlet blanket of lumpy rawness, never to reappear until his return to England.

During the first week Chuzzer, Charly and I, nifty on our Nepalese bikes, pedalled to Bodhnath, a Buddhist *stupa* on the outskirts of Kathmandu. A *stupa* is a Buddhist temple, a solid white dome around which worship takes place rather than inside. Its atmosphere, and indeed that of the surrounding area, as we arrived was most particular: it seemed thick, almost heavy with spiritual potency.

Oriental smells wafted across from the nearby market, mingling perfectly with all the castes, classes, religions, wise men, rich men and hippies gathered there to pray. We joined the general flow encircling the *stupa* and I placed my hand upon the great ancient prayer wheel surrounding it. The wheel consists of hundreds of spinning bronze cylinders, all stamped with prayers as well as containing secret mantras and prayers within. You put your hand on the approaching cylinder and spin it as soon as the person in front removes theirs. That day I was following a hunchbacked dwarf (sorry! a physically challenged, diminutive Nepalese) with the filthiest hands covered in suppurating sores. This was to have dire consequences.

My prayers were always simple, yet quite exhausting because I had to visualise everyone individually. First I'd pray for Tomcat's well-being, then bless each member of my family followed by loved ones, then all animals (it was the only time I had none of my own). I often found myself doing two circles of the prayer wheel praying for Robert's and Olivier's full recovery, then get annoyed with myself for praying so long for the two blokes who had dumped me. I'd pray for dead friends before asking their and God's forgiveness for my endless shortcomings. Finally I'd pray for world peace, asking if we humans could lose our arrogance swiftly enough to heed the balance of nature and the earth's needs – a prayer form pretty similar to most people's, I imagine.

Haggling for a few knick-knacks had never felt so carefree as in the Nepalese market that day. To find myself laughing benevolently while being ripped off was a new one for me. Yet it was true.

Cycling home to the palace, I was chased by a brown mongrel, snarling and snapping at my pedalling feet. As he gained speed he transformed beneath my heel into a black Damien/devil-dog frothing at the mouth. Brother Chuzzer tossed a warning. 'Keep pedalling fast!'

154

I kept pedalling, but no faster than the dog could run. Then a bug flew into my mouth and, without thinking, my hand followed after. That reflex action to catch the bug was my downfall, because the rancid taste on my fingers triggered off the memory of the diseased pauper in front of me at the prayer wheel where we had repeatedly touched the same spot.

Bloody, infested *stupa*, swarming with horrendous grow-your-own-born-again hippies, self-indulgent, me-generation crap, all pretending to be holier than thou with their phoney quasi-religious dogma, oozing self-deceived repentance, the whole place seething with delusion and falsehood, rife with earth's diseases!

O ye of little faith! Yet those dark thoughts had arrived for a reason: I *knew* I'd just caught *something* – but what it was would remain to be seen. The manic hound was still jumping up at me with unrelenting vigour, when a rustic-looking chap with a stick appeared from nowhere and hollered at the dog. Heaven be praised! The dog obeyed.

Within twenty-four hours my tummy went funny so I decided to chicken out of the three-day hike across the hills above Kathmandu. I reluctantly waved off Chuzzer and Charly and my physical decline became rapid. I ended up, utterly humiliated, bleeding from both ends as I stood in the bath all day. Those who have suffered dysentery will know what I'm on about. When the men returned, hunters home from the hill, I was swiftly taken to the Western Hospital, yet the pills prescribed had no effect whatsoever.

Two days later, still in the bath, with my condition deteriorating through weakness, Chuzzer remembered Dr Marna Bajra Bajracharya, a Nepalese doctor. 'I'll be back soon.'

He returned with a brown paper bag. I eagerly opened it to find – 'Rabbit droppings?'

'No! Precious metals taken from the earth and mixed up into a Dr Marna's Delight.' I was reluctant to take them at first, but better a rabbit poo of hope than no hope at all. I had been ill for six days, three of those in the bath.

Three days later I was back on my bike. I saluted Dr Marna, and visited him many times. His practice was in the slums of Kathmandu, with cow-, dog-and goat-shit right up to his waiting-room door – and from there on a thick mass of flies. Yet his reputation as a healer, especially of tetanus, was renowned worldwide. He also had a repu-

tation for solving sexual problems, with his curiously effective aphro-
disiacs (I had thought up till then that there was no such thing).

From that point I began to feel healthier than I could ever remember.
No wonder Chuzzer loved it there! He took us to Pasupatinath on the
Bagmati river where, close to the edge, bodies are burned and the
succulent whiff of human flesh – sweeter than chicken – seems perfectly
in order. The Brahmins are in charge of the burning ceremony, performed according to your pocket. The rich can afford to be thoroughly
burned, ending up in a soft powder which is swept into the Bagmati
river. For the poor the ceremony is short and to the point, with half-
burned limbs later sploshing into the soupy river.

The whole town wandered down to the river at dawn and dusk, as
did all the animals, cows, sheep, dogs, goats, to cool off their fly-ridden
parts and dunk their heads into the thick gruel of excrement and
burned or half-burned human remains. There were many old people
too, most of whom shimmered with health. I couldn't help comparing
their hardy resilience to my pathetically frail immune system. There
had I been, laid low for a whole week for putting my hand in my
mouth, whereas they managed to transform a heavily polluted river
into a life-enhancing holy porridge. That made me think. Perhaps the
river wasn't polluted. Perhaps it was full of precious nutrition and
therefore organically potent. (A few years later I returned and plunged
into that soupy, nutritious gunge. When I got out I felt simultaneously
triumphant and revitalised.)

Going to the loo in the hills of Kathmandu (there's a song there
somewhere) had to be a swift affair. One day Chuzzer was sitting on
his chosen spot, when he flung up his arms thinking that someone
had a gun at his back. It was no gun but a wild boar, who rudely thrust
poor Chuzzer forward, face over tip and then, quick as a flash, stole his
unfinished business – there's efficient recycling for you.

Charly and I had been invited up to the famous Tiger Tops, where
they take you by elephant on jungle safaris. I didn't want to go because
the playing grounds of the rich had never appealed; only my mysterious
passion for elephants swayed me. My mount was a great bull elephant
called Shamsha. There was some strange link between us that streng-
thened daily, so much so that his mahout allowed me to bath him
myself.

'Shamsha never permit strangers near him. Very strange.' Apparently

Shamsha had known I was coming five minutes before I arrived, or so his mahout told me – the flatterer!

Shamsha stood mid-river, steady as a rock, loving every minute as much as I did. When I had him lying down in the water, he rolled over, just like a great old English mastiff asking for his tummy-tickle. His tummy skin was so much softer than the rest. He opened his huge back legs wide, convincing me it wasn't just his tummy he wanted tickling, but I didn't want to come between Shamsha and his mahout.

We all have an earthly environment that suits us best. Up in Tiger Tops, I discovered I belonged in the jungle. My hair went glossy, my skin took on a glow that needed no extra nourishment from a jar. Alas, Charly wasn't to be the beneficiary of this new shimmering Sarah, for Charly had been far from well during the trip.

'You wanna take Shamsha out alone on your last day?' asked the mahout. I wasn't sure about this, but thought, since Charly was ill in bed, I had nothing to lose.

That last ride on Shamsha at Tiger Tops was something I'll take to my grave and keep on smiling about. How delicately he manoeuvred his great hulking mass through the rich vegetation, the kind only found at the jungle's epicentre. Why wasn't I afraid? There must have been thousands of creatures out there ready to pounce, but riding high on Shamsha I felt as snug as a bug in a rug. It was one of those occasions when you know you are experiencing the rarest, sweetest piece of life's cake, and you must savour every crumb.

Out in the open once more, quite suddenly Shamsha stopped dead.

'Come on, Shamsha! Move!' He refused point-blank to budge, simply stood there, quaking.

'What's up?' As far as I could see we were completely alone in the midst of flat bushland. So why were Shamsha's knees knocking? I kicked him as if he were a horse, which must have looked idiotic, but still he refused to budge, merely flipping his trunk as if sniffing the air.

In the farthest distance I heard a rumbling noise like Apache Indians on the warpath. Spewing up dust everywhere, a speck materialised, aiming straight at us in the shape of rhinoceros! Why was Shamsha so terrified? What could a rhino *do* to a massive creature such as Shamsha? Horn him to death, I suppose. How I regretted my lack of knowledge on jungle matters. I had recently read *Elephant Bill*, one of my favourite books of all time, but recalled no tips whatsoever on rhino lore. Are rhinos and elephants deathly enemies?

Just like Omar Sharif's endless entrance in *Lawrence of Arabia*, the rhino thundered into close-up. Then, with hoofs beating time to Shamsha's heart, he suddenly stopped dead – the rhino, I mean. If he could have, he would have scratched his head for he looked from left to right as if to say, 'What *was* I doing?' I wasn't about to tell him that he had been mid-stampede. What was he looking *for*? Then he turned round regretfully and wandered back whence he had come, nibbling some dry brush rather forlornly as he went.

My departure from Tiger Tops and back to Kathmandu was a soul-wrenching experience. All packed up, astride Shamsha, we approached the riverbank where a tiny rowing boat waited to ferry us across. Shamsha and I were both a little hang-dog and down in the dumps. At the river's edge Shamsha lay down for me to alight. Before departing we looked at each other, and I found a love much higher than his elephant's eye.

When I was half-way across the river, Shamsha roared his final farewell. Its awesome power gave Heathcliff's 'Cathy! Cathy!' a bloody good run for its money. One of the pieces of music I asked for on *Desert Island Discs* was that of a Shamsha roaring. *My noise.* A mixture of Robert's Doneraile farewell, Heathcliff's 'Cathy! Cathy!' and Shamsha's biblical cry ricocheting across the river and down centuries.

Shortly before returning home Chuzzer, Charly and I took one last bike ride to another irresistible Buddhist temple known as Swayambhunath. To reach this timeless *stupa* you are faced with hundreds of steps to climb, an effort markedly lessened by an escort of mostly cheeky, sometimes vicious monkeys who guide you up.

From the temple, in addition to the most incredible view that blasts you out to pastures unknown, we could just make out some of the streets we had pedalled through to get there. Charly loved 'Freak Street' best (or worst, I could never quite work out which). One day with his recorder hidden, he taped a Freak Street drug hustler who accosted him.

'What you want?' he asked Charly. 'You want woman?' With me right beside him. 'Hash? Pot? Uppers? Downers? Coke? Crack? Smack – heroin?' Charly used his Freak Street tape under a song on an anti-drug album he made a year later.

After I had twirled around the prayer wheel for about half an hour, the sound of a far-away flute began to pull my attention from it, until I abandoned my prayers and almost sleepwalked towards the culprit.

I sat down and breathed it all in, transfixed by the flute player's long, strong Nepalese fingers, flickering over his instrument like a sun-kissed shoal of herring. And I found myself totally hooked by the shocking pink ring sparkling on his wedding finger. Jewellery doesn't interest me. You could flash Elizabeth Taylor's diamond at me and I wouldn't look twice, but this shocking pink babe was mesmerising.

That night I dreamt I had come into possession of the ring. The moment, still in the dream, that its brilliant pink splendour was secure on my wedding finger I had an almost orgasmic high on which I danced, on and on.

I woke early and sat bolt upright, knowing what I must do. I took my bike and returned to Swayambhunath. There he was, the Nepalese flautist in the same place – his patch, I presumed. He clocked my eyes, transfixed by his ring.

'I no speak.' He called another Nepalese over. They spoke together.

'He no speak English.' Every day a new surprise. 'He say you like his ring.'

'Yes. I like his ring.'

'This ring he get from a yogi in the high Himalayas.' I wanted to believe him, so I did. 'Like yogi, he must pass on when right person come along.' I'd never heard such a canny sales pitch. 'He think you come.' I was then instructed that if I were to have it I was never to find out what stone it was, or to have it valued. Although I suspected he was about to hand over a socking great clump of glass in exchange for millions of rupees, I didn't care a fart. I had to have the ring at any price: its street value wasn't the issue, its magic was.

'Tell him I will return with my brother later on.'

Chuzzer was dubious, suspicious, even, at first, but once he held up the ring to the light and bit it he knew it wasn't glass. It was surrounded with fourteen ancient pearls, inset in a heavily worn silver setting. He had no idea what stone it was, but had to concede that the light that shone from its fathomless shocking-pink depths was astoundingly bright. The flautist was keener on the rituals involving the ring's safe custody than the money side of things. We struck a fair bargain, for I had

159

paid more for a two-foot-by-one piece of old carpet in the Bodhnath market.

Once home, I decided it was my turn to do the shopping. As soon as I was back out biking the streets, the rain came down. The Nepalese welcome the monsoon with great celebrations, but for me it heralded my last week. I was going to miss Kathmandu, and I wasn't sure why since my magic ring would be accompanying me.

Back in the palace kitchen, drenched, Chuzzer helped me unload my basket full of goodies.

'Where did you put your ring?'

He was looking at my bare finger. Oh, no! Surely I hadn't lost it out there on the muddy streets of Kathmandu? I stood there for a moment unable to take the joke. Why is my bad luck so relentless? I put down the shopping, and turned my bike round. 'I'm going back over my tracks.'

Chuzzer shouted after me, 'Don't be stupid! You don't stand a hope in hell of finding it!' But I was in no mood for logic. If there was any justice I'd find it out there somewhere.

The rain was in competition with my tears. The Nepalese keep their eyes glued to the earth in case they luck upon some rich person's droppings. I found Nepalese men mostly lazy and plain, but the women, with their inherited capacity for hard physical work, stunning bone structure, perfectly proportioned bodies and long necks were a joy to behold. But that night they were all in the way. Bleak with despair, I loomed up various unlit streets, trying desperately to cover my earlier tracks. Chuzzer was right, of course. Not a hope in hell of finding it in all this humanity, mud and crap.

Crossing one street without even bothering to look left or right, I was knocked over by a motorbike that skidded in the mud and landed with a bang against my right thigh. I couldn't have cared less – thigh pain was nothing compared to ring loss. (But the dent in my thigh cost plenty of time and money to fix over the next five years.)

That night I dreamt of my ring, dancing somewhere near, as I hovered on the borders of wake and sleep. I could almost touch it. The belief that it *was* near continued to haunt me all through the next day, and the next.

'You only set foot in the kitchen when we returned from Sway-ambhunath, so stop mooning round the house like Lady Macbeth.

What's done cannot be undone.' (Charly had seen my Lady Macbeth.)

'I know it's here somewhere.' I had only my dreams to rely on and Charly and I were now on our last full day in Nepal. First thing in the morning we'd be soaring high above the Himalayas.

That last night the ring gave me no respite. After tossing and turning for hours I rose at five thirty and pedalled off. I wanted to say one last prayer at the Hindu shrine up the lane, where the energy was particularly benevolent. While I was praying I felt something telling me to back-track carefully to the palace. It was the first time I had experienced the voice sensation since the exorcism and it was so gentle.

As I approached it on that crisp last morning in Kathmandu, with all night noises, alas, gone for good, I got off my bike to open the big wooden gates. In so doing I noticed how much I had to stretch my fingers to lift the heavy latch and haul open the hefty gate. For some reason I peeked round, and there, behind it, in probably the only unburned grass left in Nepal, nestling up against the palace wall, was my magic ring, twinkling cockily at me in the early-morning dew. How its startling pinkness clashed with the emerald patch of grass! Did it speak?

Mission accomplished. Intuition improving slowly. You deserve me for a while longer. Let's go.

Family Back in Order?

Back in Portland Road, Charly, his mate Andy and I had just put the finishing touches to our conservatory – my contribution was to paint it with glorious clashing Tibetan colours – when in waddles Robert, the veritable King of Conservatories.

'What a difference that makes!' He loved it. 'Congratulations, Charly!'

I hadn't been sure about having one, but Charly and Andy had insisted that my treasured wisteria would be safe, its roots embraced within it, so I acquiesced. Charly, always quick to observe Robert's needs, took Andy out to the local pub.

As I handed Robert his tea, I knew, by the gravity with which he took his mug, that he had something heavy to impart.

'I'm through with Anne.' I decided not to ask why but to wait until he told me. (He never did.) 'I'm getting a divorce.' He looked up from his tea. I wasn't sure what was in his mind that day. Sitting in silence, just sipping our tea, he noticed my magic ring. 'What a beautiful stone that is. What is it?'

'I don't know.' Silence. 'It belonged to a flute player in Nepal.'

'Too pink for a ruby.' Robert looked haunted, as if his life was splitting apart. 'Could we get back together again?'

For some reason I didn't answer, but went for a breath of air in my garden. Was he crying wolf a second time? Was I to pack up my pleasant life with Charly only to be driven out on the London streets to tread water all over again? It would certainly be best for Tomcat. I laughed to myself. Dreams *do* come true, I know they do, especially if you happen to be in possession of a magic ring. I kissed it surreptitiously. Yet even as I kissed it I was convinced that those old familiar forces – whatever they were – had been orchestrating this reunion all those years between, and were continuing to do so on a more subtle level.

Back in the clashing conservatory, I stood behind Robert and quietly inhaled that sweet smell from the top of his head. It was like breathing in some ancient and familiar intimacy. 'Don't stand there sniffing me. Can we both forgive enough to try again?'

Charly, like Robert, put all his energy into his work and, because our split took place while he was in the midst of his *Smack* album, he was uncharacteristically philosophical. Robert couldn't climb the rickety stairs of Portland Road, so while we hunted for a suitable house, he lived in a horrid modern, yet ever so posh, flat in Battersea overlooking his beloved Thames.

Eventually we found the house we wanted: Sussex House, Upper Mall, Hammersmith. It was Georgian, of classical perfection and situated in its own romantic walled garden. Robert and I found it a most appropriate setting in which to bring our two shattered halves together once again. Was it smiling at us because it knew dreams had finally come true and that Tomcat had both his parents under one roof once more?

We had made a pact to go halves on everything so, to find my half of Sussex House, I had no choice but to sell my *Charlemagne* painting, my only good investment. I was loath to part with him, especially since he and I had never actually lived together. If *Charlemagne* had managed to make it to Sussex House, he would have snorted proudly, 'I've come home!' So had all our other worldly chattels. How unexpectedly correct it felt to have them reunited, with no clues as to the pain suffered in the interim across our great divide. It was astounding how everything, great or small, fitted just so, as if Sussex House had been waiting for the pleasure of our furniture's company. In many ways it felt as though time had stood still since the Old Mill days, for both houses were similar in style. The spacious, two-room basement proved a perfect hideaway for Tomcat and his outrageously precocious gang, led by his friend Jake.

Originally Sussex House had been built on the river for the Duke of Sussex when he laid the foundation stone for Hammersmith Bridge. Next door was the picturesque pub, the Dove; to the back the M4; to the left Hammersmith Bridge and the Furnival Public Gardens; to the right, Upper Mall. Was the heady energy in Sussex House due to its colourful history or to its being sandwiched between the M4 and the mighty Thames? It must have been superb in the olden days, when it was a shooting lodge to the forests of Hammersmith. Later the Prince Regent used it as his drug den. He would sail down the Thames to Sussex House, which in those days was plumb in the middle of the red-light district, pick up his broads and have himself a field day with opium, laudanum and God knows what else in our bedroom/drawing room. This exquisitely proportioned almost-ballroom, with its original panelling, took up the width and length of the house, boasting a magnificent westerly view across the river from six floor-to-ceiling sash windows. Sitting up in bed we could see Hammersmith Bridge, which seemed to be indulging in a fresh face-lift daily.

The house's history goes on and on. C. S. Forrester wrote *Captain Hornblower* in my study at the top. At the turn of the century some of Emily Brontë's personal belongings were mysteriously discovered downstairs at the back of one of the parlour cupboards. Sussex House gave birth to the first printing of *Through the Looking Glass*.

Robert trundled around London in a specially designed Range Rover. The roof went up a couple of feet at the back to allow space for an ultra-modern wheelchair and to get in Robert had only to press a button for the back to open, allowing the wheelchair to be mechanically lowered. The whole contraption looked like something from James Bond in the year 3000.

Robert insisted we remove the ancient side wall of the garden near where the dustbins were kept to enable him to negotiate his wheelchair around the side of the house and up a ramp which took him directly into his study. It all made terrific sense, but I kicked up a hell of a fuss because there was nowhere else to keep the dustbins. Yet the wall and the dustbin holders *were* removed, which made a fine mess of the initial tidiness; Robert's study door was also altered for wheelchair purposes. I suspected he'd probably never be seen dead in the wheelchair and I was proved right. I never saw him negotiate the new side entrance. He was a stubborn man all right, Tomcat's dad! Yet that same stubbornness was one of the qualities that had floored medical science.

Once Sussex House was vaguely in order, Robert began to improve miraculously, both mentally and physically, as we slumped back into our old familiar pattern of organised chaos. I found the new Robert heaps more seductive than the pre-stroke version. He had discovered a way into his feminine energy, the anima, which altered his character for the better: the once almost chauvinistic, brutal common sense became more tender, understanding and more all-seeing.

The highlight of our day together, apart from Robert's regular trips to expensive restaurants, was our evening dunk in the magnificent Jacuzzi that Hugh Hudson, of *Chariots of Fire* fame, the house's previous owner, had installed in a basement room, lined with cedarwood, and no expense spared. It was hugely beneficial for Robert's rehabilitation. There he'd sit like a Sumo wrestler (with wine beside him!), sweating off some of the excess food and drink his poor old body had been forced to digest during the day. I'd give him his daily massage and watch him benefit from my old, lost healing techniques, the same I had abandoned in LA after Father's death. It was good for me to re-establish them and regain some confidence. So, in our Jacuzzi hour, we were both on to a good thing.

The only downside was having to pass Tomcat's basement flat. It would have taken a stronger woman than I not to take the occasional peek inside. 'Don't!' Robert would warn. 'Let him live like a pig. He's too old now.' Would he were a pig, for pigs are fiendishly fastidious. I yearned to see life in Robert's simple black-and-white terms, as equally as I yearned for him to refrain from comparing Tomcat's filth with that of pigs. Yet Tomcat was as stubborn as a mule in his refusal to toe the line – even down to basic plugpulling.

In I'd peek. What a mistake! But, then, it's human nature to be drawn towards the ghoulish. Robert was right as usual.

'But if I don't do something—' Robert would wave me aside.'

One morning I could bear the stench no longer and took seven dirty coffee cups, swilling with half-smoked fags, dirty plates caked with dry food, underwear, knives, forks, spoons back up to the kitchen. I tried to comfort myself that all this was perfectly normal for a teenager's den, but the comfort dwindled sharply when I came across more coffee stains, cigarette burns plus a couple of burned spoons down the side of that once fantabulous Italian bed.

After a good bout of meditation to calm me and give me courage, I went down next evening to find Tom and Jake lying watching the telly as usual.

'What are these?' They looked at each other.

'They look like burned spoons to me,' shrugged Tom, without removing his eyes from the screen.

I tried again. 'Why are these spoons burned?'

'OK, Ma. You win. We sneak out for a bit of hash once in a while.'

'Since when have you been smoking hash?' Silence. 'And since when does hash need a burned spoon?'

Tom cleared his throat and looked at me for the first time. 'Thanks to my mingy allowance, I'm forced to buy cheap hard stuff and heating the spoon is the quickest way to soften it up.' Did I believe him? I was still completely ignorant of hard drugs, and had little experience of hash (resin), preferring marijuana (leaves), so their story sounded reasonably plausible. Or was I automatically slipping into the comfort of denial?

'If I catch either of you smoking dope again . . .'

'We're listening.'

'I'm going to the police—'

Tom turned on me. 'You didn't go to the police in LA, did you? Oh, no! You condoned us smoking at home.'

In LA I once talked over Tom's behaviour with Warren. 'He's stealing dope from people's homes, stuffing potatoes up exhausts, throwing raw eggs at stucco homes, never coming home when I tell him.'

'He's gonna smoke anyway, and smoking dope out late at night spells more danger than smoking weak stuff at home, hon.' So I had allowed them to smoke an occasional weak spliff at home.

Leaving the room I heard their crass guffaws. Never threaten that which you can't deliver. They both knew I wouldn't go to the police, for what would I tell them? That my son was smoking hash? Big deal. What was I going to do?

Robert was convinced that Tom would grow out of this stage soon. 'He's just like I was – becoming a man, marking his territory, showing us all he can piss against his first tree. He'll snap out of it in no time.'

'How long a time? You didn't get an allowance. You *had* to earn a living.' Was my beloved family back in order? Back under the same roof, maybe, but further out of order than ever.

Yet more family troubles were brewing. Mother's birthday fell on 12 January. Like me, she was a Capricorn – one of the reasons, no doubt, why we occasionally butted horns. I decided to give her a full treatment of aromatherapy as a present. She had been looking a bit peaky lately, so I thought it would soothe her troubled limbs if not her soul. On the appointed day I took her up to St Johns Wood.

'Will I have to undress?'

'Why is that so awful?'

'I don't want to undress. It embarrasses me.'

'I doubt it'll embarrass her.'

I dropped her off and promised to telephone later to see how it was going.

When I rang, the aromatherapist told me to come immediately. Mother was unable to finish the treatment due to a bad migraine. When I arrived the therapist took me aside. 'She hated every minute of it. How appalling for your mother on her birthday. She's so out of touch with her body.'

'Aren't all those in mourning out of touch with their body?'

'Not in that way!'

Back at Sussex House I tried another tack. 'Come and relax with me in the Jacuzzi.'

'No. I'm off to bed.' I refused to take no for an answer and, after relentless persuasion, I got her in. Then I couldn't get her out. I stood there with a towel because the cedar sides and floors could get a bit slippery, but Mother wasn't budging. She had placed her abnormally swollen stomach against the most powerful jet and nothing in God's kingdom was going to get her off it.

'You go and prepare dinner. I'll just stay here a while longer.'

When I returned she was undoubtedly in a trance beneath her pink, flushed exterior. Something was up but, knowing Mother, she wasn't about to share it with anyone. Reluctantly she climbed out of the Jacuzzi. 'Just look at my stomach!'

By waving it away flippantly she hoped I would pass on to other things. 'How long have you been bloated like that?'

'Oh, quite a while,' she said vaguely.

'I think it's time to have a check-up, Ma.'

'What for, for God's sake? To be told I'm dying of cancer? I know that already.' Her ironic laughter echoed Maggie Leighton's upon hearing she had MS. 'I never had that same extraordinary will to live. I prayed every night for God to pass your father's stomach cancer on to me.'

'Seems he heard you.'

167

'And how! I was happy to die *for* him, but not as well as him!'

I became uncharacteristically bossy and insisted that Mother make an appointment with Dr Mary Adams, a close friend of the family, who had brought all four of us children into the world. Mother was promptly sent into hospital for tests, only to be proved right, for her stomach cancer was already fairly well advanced. The news didn't seem to bother her – in fact, I'd even say she seemed relieved.

On a purely selfish level this angered me. Why would it not? Our relationship had been slow to show its depths, yet recently we had grown into the comfort of putting aside mere titles such as mother and daughter and had begun to appreciate our true partnership. She had been made to suffer my growing years of rebelliousness (something for which I now had tremendous compassion), and party to my secret Olivier *amour* since I had been a teenager. We are always closest to those who know us best and Mother knew me better than anyone. She had become my closest friend during my treading-water years. More important still: I respected her greatly.

Withdrawals

In May 1985 I took Mother to the Cannes Film Festival. When I opened my case at the Carlton, I recognised none of the clothes. I had picked up an exact replica of my suitcase at the airport. Gordon Bennett! It was the first night, and I was to be on the grand jury headed by Milos Forman.

'Just look at this woman's taste, Sarah!' Mother exclaimed, delving into the suitcase. At any moment I was going to have to pose for photos with the rest of the jury for the first night's ceremonies.

'Help!'

'Borrow something of mine if you like,' said Mother with a twinkle, knowing I wouldn't be seen dead in her clothes; in any case they were two sizes too big.

I was left with no alternative but to go as I was. My suitcase never showed up and all my best clothes had been in it. I refused to buy new ones because I hadn't that kind of money to throw around and nothing in Cannes was cheap. By the fourth day one newspaper commented that I had been seen twice in the same dress.

'Thrice,' contradicted Mother Mine.

For me, the best fun of all was not the festival razzmatazz, but observing Mother transform into the movie star she always should have been. I observed her weaving her spell up the Croisette with her natural grace and no murmur of cancer from one day to the next. What a woman! And what a lesson for me when my time comes.

My film, *Steaming*, which I hadn't yet seen, was shown one night in honour of Joe Losey. Dirk Bogarde was there, a real pro, yet it turned out to be the worst moment of the whole two weeks for me. I remember being hugely disappointed, which was odd because I already knew that the film was no good.

The highlight of the festival was undoubtedly the last day when all the jurors were taken by police escort to a destination unknown. We remained holed up in the hills above Cannes until we had finalised the voting. There was plenty of juicy hostility and conflicting choices. Milos Forman kept a tight hold of the reins, naturally getting his own way in the end. I disagreed totally with the final choice for the Palme d'Or and since that film sank without trace, you will forgive me for not remembering its name.

Back in London the phone rang. 'Hi. I'm Robert de Niro, and I'd very much like to take you and Robert out for dinner while I'm in town.' He was to star in Robert's film *The Mission*, shortly to begin shooting for Puttnam and directed by Roland Joffe in South America.

It was fascinating to observe different people's attitudes towards Robert's stroke disability. Some sat and shouted at him as if he was either a loony or deaf. To give de Niro his due he didn't shout once and I presumed he did all the talking out of compassion for Robert's difficulties. He talked actor-talk, obviously keen to get his character right.

While I was eating my asparagus I became mesmerised by a large dollop of sleepy-dust on de Niro's top lash. Why wasn't he aware of it, since it was hanging over his eye? How could he see us without seeing it? Or did he only see the role he was about to play? Surely force of gravity alone would play some part in the puzzle. He turned and smiled at me. I was staggered he could see me at all.

During pudding he went to the loo. I was relieved, having been worried stiff that his sleepy-dust might fall into his main course.

After his return from the loo I noticed that the sleepy-dust was loyally hanging in there. This won him a Brownie point for it proved he hadn't bothered to look in the mirror. After coffee, conversation dried up, presumably because de Niro knew there were no more useful character hints to be squeezed out of Robert. I was unable to prevent time from dragging that evening, nothing sufficiently showbizzy came to mind, so we just sat there like lemons. Robert was disguising his pain with his usual brilliance, throwing me secret signs that his paralysed side was needing movement. I gave it a rub. Enough of a hint, surely.

'Must keep the blood flowing.' Yet we all still sat there. Just as I began fervently to wish I had brought some money with me, Robert (Bolt) forked into his pocket to pay for the meal. I'm sure de Niro would find some valid reason for failing to put *his* hand in his pocket, but for the life of me I can't think what it would be. Wasn't it he who had asked us to dinner? How often do rich people fail to put the hand in the pocket? Yet whenever their meanness is pointed out to them they respond with the same old cliché, 'I never carry money on me.' But no villain was Mr de Niro; merely a victim of a system that allows one to become nonchalant with privilege.

Perhaps three times a week Robert would toddle off to his favourite watering-hole, eat good food, drink good drink and enjoy good company. Why not? He hadn't too many pleasures left. I never begrudged him his flashy lifestyle, but I *did* begrudge the way he always ended up paying. It was as if everyone who went to eat with him felt he should pay for their willingness to eat out with a stroke victim. I rarely accompanied him because I don't like eating money. Besides, we might have gone halves on everything, but my half wouldn't run to luxuries because I wasn't earning much at that time (any time!).

To keep up my financial end, it became imperative that I earn some money – fast. Although the timing was appalling, I had to grab what was on offer, and an American TV special, *Harem*, turned up, to be shot in Seville. Leaving home at this moment was bad timing for life was hard. Mother was visibly declining and playing her dying role with almost too much dignity. She had decided to die in a public ward on the National Health. No offers to better her circumstances were accepted. 'No. I want to leave the four of you as much money as possible.' How much more stupid can humans get?

Robert was too frail to take on Tom's troubles and I, too, had failed in my attempts to find a way through to him. It was as heartbreaking for me to have us all back under one roof as it must have been for those who watched to comprehend my lack of effect and parental guidance on Tom's behaviour. Only those who have experienced wayward children know the difficulties, frustration and pain of continual failure. Robert hid all feelings and concentrated on his work.

Michael Cimino made a quaint entrance into our lives in tight trousers and high-heeled cowboy boots. He was to be Robert's latest taskmaster, hot-foot from directing the greatest flop in cinema history, *Heaven's Gate*. Cimino's project with Columbia was a film about Michael Collins and the Irish Troubles. Robert had put a great deal of research and sweat into creating an exciting screenplay, but all to no avail. The Coca-Cola plant in Southern Ireland was mysteriously threatened in protest at the film being made at that time (Columbia Pictures was financed by Coca-Cola), so Columbia and Cimino, high-heeled cowboy boots and all, wisely retreated.

It was in Seville that I met Ava Gardner properly. Almost twenty years earlier I had come across her briefly in Madrid under very different circumstances – read *Serves Me Right*! We remained good friends till her death. She took a great liking to me because I was a fellow Capricorn. I'm not at all convinced star signs are a reliable bedrock for friendship, but Ava had no doubts. Underneath the archetypal elderly movie star with a drink problem, there dwelt a truly fascinating woman. For twenty years she had revelled in being the belle of the bull-fighting ball. The stories she had to tell of Frank Sinatra and Mickey Rooney, if true, were beyond belief, and if not, I'd be up for libel if I were to repeat them.

When I arrived home for a weekend before trekking back to Spain for my final two weeks' shooting, I held Robert tight. I had been missing him dreadfully. 'You prefer your computer to me,' I told him.

'What nonsense!'

'Then we'll pack it up. I'll get it set up in the Seville hotel and Tomcat can come too.'

He looked at me regretfully. 'We'll see.'

'Not good enough.'

He sighed and complied.

Next day we received a letter in the most immature handwriting. It said that our son was on heroin, and how shameful it was that we had chosen to close our eyes to it. It came from an ex-girlfriend of his, apparently, who couldn't bear to witness him going to the dogs any longer. Perhaps I had been in denial, but I sure as hell snapped out of it right then. How could I go back to Spain and leave Robert to cope with it? How could I drag Robert and his computer back to Spain, leaving Tomcat here alone? How could I take them both back with me and put Robert through hell?

'I'll take Tom back to Spain with me. I have no choice.'

I managed to pay Mother a quick visit in her chosen public ward.

'I'll only be away another two weeks.' She smiled, resigned and peaceful. I chose to keep the latest bombshell to myself. As I kissed her goodbye I knew she had been aware of dark secrets in the air, but had decided to leave well alone. I was grateful for that.

The interesting thing about that whole ghastly period was how I managed to remain strong and centred all the way through. Did I have the voice, which had forced me to lean only on silence, to thank for that?

The doctor prescribed some pills to help with Tom's withdrawal symptoms and a huge bottle of methadone, a heroine substitute. Later I discovered that the substitute was just as addictive and dangerous as the real thing. 'Don't let him take more than the prescribed amount. He'll want to.' I bought a new soft leather briefcase that locked with a code in which to keep the pills. Before leaving Sussex House for the airport, I realised I hadn't put the pills in the briefcase and, cursed with number blindness, I had forgotten the bloody code. A detour back to the shop was imperative.

I was perplexed at Tomcat's ability to be simultaneously perfectly sweet and perfectly repellent. He was certainly more approachable after he'd had a couple of his pills. He wanted me to dish them out like Smarties. 'Ma. It's ten o'clock, time for my pills.' His eyes glazed with greed. Sitting down to open the briefcase I realised I'd forgotten the damn coding yet again. The shop assistant had written it down some-where – but where?

'Here, Ma. Allow me.' Tomcat took the briefcase and opened it.

I was astonished. 'No wonder they've nearly all gone. How the hell did you find the code?'

'You kindly mouth the numbers while you open it.'

During one scene, my film entrance, I had to walk up a train corridor, enter a railway carriage with hefty baggage, divinely outrageous hat, a mass of jewellery, three pet monkeys and sit down. On the first take the monkeys, which were obviously untrained, tore me to ribbons, yet I was determined to complete the scene. By the end of the take I was bleeding considerably. I asked the cameraman if I could keep the out-take because it must have been hilarious. At the time he said I could, but he never followed through.

Back in my caravan the film doctor kept shaking his head while bathing my wounds. 'Your son is a heroin addict, eh?' I feigned surprise and he gave me a wry look. 'We need to keep him quiet for the next ten days, don't you think?'

173

'I don't know what to think, Doctor.'

He was most supportive. 'You must concentrate on your many scenes,' he said gently, wiping more overlooked blood from my earhole.

One morning I was awoken by the hotel manager, asking me to step this way. Apparently Tomcat had fallen asleep with a fag in his hand which had set fire to the bed and charred a section of the room. Of course I offered to pay for the damages and quite considerable they were. What was I going to do with him? Where were we going to go from here? A shiver went through me.

I refused to think further ahead than each day's filming. In these TV specials they get rid of the expensive actors as quickly as they can. I was already on overtime and, due to the chaos on this particular production, was being heavily overworked at the eleventh hour. The director, Billy Hale, had come straight off his blockbuster, *Lace*, which had attracted the biggest audience in American TV history. It's hard for success like that not to go to one's head, and Billy Hale's head was no exception. He went from Billy Hale to Billy Inhale in one fell swoop – scoop!

Once filming was over I decided to take Tomcat skiing in the Sierra Nevada, just a spit and a promise away. He had promised to stay clean once we returned to England if I delivered these ten days' skiing.

'I want you home!' cried Robert.

I told him I needed a skiing trip like a hole in the head. The timing was all wrong: Robert needed me and Mother was fading fast. My sister, Vanessa, was kindly carrying out all daughterly duties, and I felt bad about that – not out of guilt but out of a need to be with Mother, caring for her, loving her. But, at the same time, I felt the skiing trip might be just the tonic Tom needed.

Thus began ten days of hell. If only I had been able to keep Tom on a chain! He was outrageous with his deceit, lies, manipulation and cruelty. But he knew no better as he switched daily from his bunk bed of cold-turkey shivers to Snow God on his skis, swooshing down the slopes with great style and ease. Once, without my noticing, he took me in the lift to the highest run of the resort and left me to ski down on my own. Skiing is no problem for me but heights are. Tom knew this and took great delight in terrorising me.

Humping down inelegantly on my bum, a stranger spun up beside me in a neat half-Christie, and, digging in his ski-poles, handed me a joint of marijuana with great aplomb. 'Here. Take this, it'll ease the fear.' I was so scared of looking down that I took a puff or two out of desperation even though I'd packed it in. The interesting thing was that the fear began to disperse almost immediately, allowing me to concentrate on my stance and my skis rather than the sheer precipice beneath. With those few puffs I was able to visualise how I *should* be skiing rather than the terrifying drop. That sounds like a pot commercial.

'There. You'll be fine now. Just stay cool.' He took the joint and off he swished in a cloud of snow. What a special fellow!

I was utterly exhausted when *my* special fellow and I arrived home at good old Sussex House and those welcoming Dutch-barge arms of Robert's. I felt the whole ten days had been a waste of time and money. These addicts become aliens. You have to learn to find compassion for them, for they don't mean it: it's just that they are controlled by a force so much stronger than them. But then I wasn't wholly aware of the devastating hold heroin has over its addict. Poor old Tomcat was just a leaf blowing in the wind against it.

I never once thought I'd lose him, for *something* told me I wouldn't. Once he had hit rock bottom and faced the devil head on, I *knew* (because I'd been told) that he would find the monumental strength required to pull away. My son might be many things but a victim he ain't and I was waiting for the moment when he would give the devil the two fingers. Little did I know what a long wait it would be.

We put Tom into Clouds, the best rehabilitation centre available. It's an expensive process and you have to pay in advance in case the patient makes a run for it. During the first eight weeks he spent there Tomcat showed remarkable signs of that strength mentioned above. Robert and I felt he might just make it through. I went down for weekends, when family members were given help too. We were educated in the whole business of drug abuse in the family. It was there that I learnt about tough love – and horrendously tough it was too: if Tom were to have a relapse, we would pay for his rehabilitation but not for his habit. In other words, we must show him no mercy, no hot cocoa, no warm hugs, no roof over his head, no nothing until he committed to coming clean. We had to push him out onto the streets until he hit rock bottom.

Thousands of pounds later, Tom completed his course and received

175

his flying colours from Clouds. Immediately he came out he joined up with Jake and began using all over again. This time I went to Jake's parents' home to find out if there was anything to be learnt from their method of coping with their son's habit. It was a far from pleasant visit for they weren't hearing what I was saying.

'There's no heroin in our home. No drugs of any kind. You're mistaken,' they said, while showing me the door.

After Tomcat had been living on the streets for maybe two months, the phone rang one day. I didn't recognise the voice. 'Get your son off the streets and back home where he belongs.' I had had many similar anonymous phone calls, and I didn't like them one bit. Didn't they understand that I wanted to open my arms to Tomcat more than anything in the world? Imagine what it's like knowing your son is out there somewhere, astride some fearsome motorbike, a dispatch rider on smack! Life! But perhaps we all get what we deserve. Serves me right? Perhaps. But was this brutal tough love right?

Since Mother felt the end was near, I needed to be down at Lewes Crescent to stay there with her to the end. Mother and I had made a pact that I should hold her hand and pass her through into the next dimension – she had become a half-believer by then. Robert urged me to get the hell down there and bloody well get on with it. Vanessa had done a brilliant job, but needed and, indeed, deserved some respite as well as some time with her own children, Luke and Ned. I pleaded with Robert to accompany me, *with* his blessed computer, naturally, but he wouldn't hear of it, so leaving him alone once again didn't riddle me with too much guilt.

'It's a time for a woman to be alone to do those mysterious womanly things,' he said, winking wildly. What a bugger he was!

Mother and I had about ten days of pure bliss. She was so peaceful lying there in her great bed overlooking Brighton seafront. Her natural beauty had taken on an incandescent quality. She ordered me to bring out all the contents of her drawers so I could choose any of her scarves, gloves, jewellery, stockings, handbags, scent, makeup that took my fancy. Unfortunately her feet were bigger than mine and Vanessa's so her hundreds of pairs of expensive shoes were redundant.

At last I was allowed into her bed. Typical that I had to wait till she was dying before permission was granted to creep between those forbidden sheets for a cuddle. Her bed had always been out of bounds when we were little, so I had never experienced those necessary minutes of intimacy so imperative for stable growth. (But looking at Tomcat's 'stable growth', maybe she had a point!)

After I'd been there nearly two weeks I returned from shopping to hear Mother calling down to me in a stern tone of voice, 'Sarah! Leave all that and come up here a moment.' It sounded most ominous. 'Robert just rang. You must return home immediately.'

'Whatever for?'

'Tom barged in as soon as you left.' Why hadn't Robert mentioned that Tom had returned home? 'He's firmly ensconced back in his basement and there's nothing Robert can do about it. He really did seem quite upset, darling.' I went to the telephone, but Mother stopped me. 'Come and sit on my bed a moment.' She patted it as she always had done, firm yet wooing. 'Listen carefully before you jump to your own conclusions.' She indicated for me to rearrange her pillows before she delivered her speech. 'I haven't got long. This is a fact. Robert has a little longer, if Tomcat doesn't finish him off sooner. This is a fact. Tomcat has no time at all unless something is done pronto. This is a fact.'

'Great speech, but—'

'Pack up your belongings. Drive straight home, and call the police—'

'*What?*'

'Put him in jail where you can keep an eye on him.' Apparently Mother was unaware that jail was the British drug centre, but I let it go.

'And when he's safely behind bars can I come back to bed with you?'

'Yes. Now hurry.' I complied, even though I had my doubts, because her eyes so wanted a little peace.

At Sussex House I found a fairly wobbly Robert, but he wouldn't talk about what had transpired the day before. I called the police, as Mother had suggested, and they arrived the following morning while Tom and Jake were out.

'My son is a heroin addict. I'm frightened for his and my husband's life.'

'I see, Miss Miles – I mean, Mrs Bolt. We'll need proof, you know that?' I took them down to the basement and let them get on with it.

They had sufficient evidence – needles, or the smack paraphernalia –

when they returned upstairs. One of them held up a burned spoon and told me they had probably been using as recently as last night. It was then that I learned that a burned spoon is for chasing the dragon – inhaling the smoke from melted-down heroin. 'This might interest you too.' He held up various pieces of paper with Robert's signature practised all over them. 'You should try for a more complicated signature, sir.'

'I have had a stroke. Only use my left hand.' This embarrassed him, I could tell.

'Your son knows that, sir. I suggest you phone Coutts and see if he has been successful.' It transpired that Tom *had* been successful – almost fifteen thousand pounds' worth of forged cheques successful.

'My fault, I forgot,' confessed a cowed Robert. Unbeknown to me, to save himself the bother of trundling in, Robert had given Coutts written permission for Tom to cash cheques on his behalf. This news was as unbelievable to me as it must be to you. But I was becoming resigned to hearing flabbergasting news resulting from Robert's impaired sense of logic. During that same ten days Tom had taken a video camera and an old TV. He had wanted to whip Robert's Oscars, until he discovered they weren't pure gold. I was a little less lucky, for he took my favourite award which was solid silver.

The two policemen couldn't have been more sympathetic. 'Being under age he won't go to prison, as such, but to a remand centre.'

'On what charge?' asked Robert.

'Forgery'll keep him in and safe for a while.'

'Will it have bars so he can't escape?'

'Oh, yes, ma'am. Believe you me, he won't be able to escape.' I breathed again for a moment. Mother had been right. I needed the luxury of knowing, for a few weeks at least, that my only child wouldn't be found dead.

When I visited Tomcat at the remand centre, there were bars all right. If this was only a remand centre, what would a real jail be like? Wherever I looked, there was nothing but bars and the whole place was gruesome, in both structure and stench. Waiting for visiting hour with all the other mums was another experience I'll never forget. The sadness! The painful incomprehensibility of their present plight on top of mine was all I needed. But I got a lot more when we were all herded into the visiting room like discontented cattle.

I spotted Tomcat sitting behind a table with his beautiful aristocratic nose halfway across his face. He shrugged his shoulders with what might have been embarrassment – or was it shame?

'How did that happen?'

'I got too cocky with the warder.' That was the first time I'd ever known Tom take responsibility for his own actions. Were things looking up? 'I'll soon be out of here, Ma, and I've certainly learnt my lesson.'

'How's that?' Sadly, I didn't believe anything he said any more.

'I'm in an isolation cell. Cold turkeying in an isolation cell ain't pretty.'

'Survive that and you can survive anything.'

He looked at me, guiltily. 'How's Grandma?'

I had to remain hard as granite otherwise I might cry. 'Still alive.' Tomcat had always loved Grandma, yet not enough, it seemed, to have allowed me my time of peace with her. I pinched myself, for I had already been told that heroin addicts, like severe stroke victims, have no logic, no love, loyalty, consideration, no feelings for others, only the need for their next fix. 'But not for long.'

'Come on, Grandma'll outlive all of us.' Did I detect fear in his eyes?

The phone rang early next morning on 22 January 1986. I woke up alone because I had taken Robert into Princess Grace Hospital for more tests the previous afternoon. While I had been in Kathmandu he'd had a gallstone removed, and since then he occasionally had gippy pains.

'Hello. Mrs Bolt?' Had Tomcat escaped? Had I left it too late before insisting Robert have the tests? Had he died under the anaesthetic? 'Mrs Bolt, this is Sister speaking. Your mother passed away at two thirty this morning, most peaceful it was.' Ten days after her seventieth birthday.

'But that's impossible. I'm coming down to see her today.' The shock was so immense that I collapsed, slid down the radiator and, as fate would have it, the pointed heat-adjuster nozzle rammed its way into my coccyx. That physical shock was as powerful as the first had been emotional. The two together made a bumper New Year present.

Driving down to Hove to behold a dead mother rather than a live one made the journey excruciating, even with a swansdown pillow to pad my throbbing coccyx. But seeing her was more bearable than I could ever have imagined. She was lying there so peaceful and serene

179

that I experienced a new and quite unexpected joy. What was she trying to tell me? Certainly to fear nothing. How translucent she was – ethereal bordering on the sacred. She had transformed into a young girl again. Yes. My mother had finally come into her own. She had returned to Father, and they were reunited, as they had been on their wedding day. That's what Mother reminded me of. A virgin bride waiting to be blessed.

Practising Forgiveness

In May 1986 I was back in Cannes with Mother – but this time she was eyeing me from above as I walked up the Croisette with Robert on my arm.

We were there with David Puttnam and his wife, Patsy, to help with the promotion of their recently completed film *The Mission*. During our stay I bumped into John Boorman. Although we'd never met and nothing was said, I vividly recall him giving me the once-over, not in a sexual fashion but professionally, as if I were a horse at a bloodstock sale. Little did I know that he was viewing me as potential 'mother' material. I ended up playing just that – his mother in his next film that same summer, called *Hope and Glory*, an autobiographical study of his childhood years during the Second World War.

It was an ensemble piece, and as such was most refreshing. If I had a gripe it would be that the film's agenda changed when the money-men pulled out in the third week of shooting, leaving John with nowhere to go. Columbia picked up the tab, on condition that it all be shot from the boy's point of view. I thought that the film concentrated too much on the final river sequence and the boy, rather than on London, the Blitz and the interrelationships. But, then, I wasn't John Boorman, and it was his boyhood memories we were interpreting, not my interest in the families of the Blitz. But, having said that, a great many people felt as I did.

While shooting on location in Henley, a pearl fell out of my magic ring – I had been allowed to wear it in the film, so reluctant am I to take it off. As it was needed for continuity, an assistant took it assuring me that a first-class antique jewellery shop in Henley would repair it. Reluctantly I handed it over and John told me I was free for the rest of the day. This relieved me as I was very tired.

Robert was away that day, collecting his new boat. He yearned to nourish the seaman part of his nature and had designed a very smart, streamlined motor-boat, with all mod cons plus radar especially designed for his one left arm. He'd reminded me of Just William as I waved him off early that morning – a wicked spring in his step and those big blue eyes sparkling with the excitement of new toys. 'Champagne on my return!' he shouted.

When I got home I locked up the house and went straight to bed. It was so hot that I undressed completely and got under the duvet. Within seconds I had nodded off. I awoke slowly as one does after a deep sleep, to find a huge black man standing in the doorway. Horrifying though it was, I'd been hijacked between sleep and waking and my reactions were far from sprightly. My vulnerability made him smile a slow, knowing smile.

He came over, pulled off the duvet to expose my nakedness and, after placing a towel over my head, put a knife at my stomach. I must have passed through the fear barrier because only three thoughts ran through my mind: (1) Why a pink towel when I'd put a white one in the bathroom only yesterday? (2) What would guts look like spilling out all over the bed? Soft and gungy, trailing blood across the bedroom, or more stiff and formed like oozing bloody body snakes? (3) I do hope Robert won't find too much mess. Everything else was blank.

I could tell that his mate had arrived from the appearance of a second pair of grimy sneakers. They tied my hands behind my back.

'Hand over the Tom!' they kept repeating. Had Tom failed to pay his dealer? Tom was back on the streets again, on probation, avoiding his probation officer, forever ringing up demanding money. I still had Mother's jewellery in the house. That together with my own made an excellent hoard, but I was damned if I'd let them know where I'd hidden it. Only later I discovered that 'Tom' is rhyming slang for tom-foolery jewellery.

'I've been cleaned out already by my son's heroin habit—'

'Lying bitch!' Their shouting and potential for real violence spiralled as they hauled me around the house, bundling me from room to room, yet I still remained protected in a surreal slow-motion zone.

'Where, bitch? C'mon! Where?' Their desperation was escalating to a pitch of frantic, uncontrollable panic, from which a climb-down would be hard without the reward of jewellery or bloodshed.

Once they'd thrown me into the top-floor kitchen of Sussex House, where the jewellery was hidden, something familiar triggered off an alarm in my head, ordering me to surrender and hand over the jewellery. They snatched the three bags from me without checking the contents. I made a mental note: always have an old bag hidden away somewhere filled with crap jewellery, 'cos most of them don't know sugar from shit.

Finally they threw me back on the bed, tied my legs, gagged me with a scarf, placed the duvet back over me, plus several pillows and then sat on my face. At the same moment they must have switched on the television, very loud. Why?

Only two thoughts entered my head this time. How fortunate it was I hadn't been raped – so far. How grateful I was that they had decided to suffocate me instead of knifing me, because this way it would leave less mess for Robert to find. I decided not to struggle. Slowly the countdown to death became comfortably apparent. On establishing the close proximity of my last breath, I still felt only gratitude that they'd chosen this clean suffocation method ... so thoughtful they were ... so thoughtful...

Then a great weight lifted off my face. I waited for a few minutes feigning death in case they were still there. Certain they had gone, I butted back the duvet. I wriggled free of my wrist rope, undid my gag and ankle straps before getting dressed quicker than a jack rabbit. My heart awoke with a thump when I saw the cut telephone wire. As I crawled over to turn down the blaring TV the adrenaline kicked in for that first rush of fear. Christ! Once the sluice gates were opened, it pumped through my roaring heart, almost splitting it in two. Catching sight of my quivering fingers, I realised they would have stripped me of my magic ring had I been wearing it. Would the whole thing have happened at all if I had been wearing it, or would its magic have protected me?

On reaching the hall I saw that the front door was still locked. How had they got in? Too scared to investigate, I ran out through the walled garden to the house next to the Dove pub. The owner had many foreign students living there. Just my luck to get one answering the door.

'I – I co-co-co – I – I – I ring! Ple-ple-please—!!' Obviously not familiar with the avalanche of fear and shock being belched up on the doorstep, he decided that what I needed was a hard slap across the face. I got it – and how! Someone else came to the door and reckoned I needed a quick brandy from next door. In the meantime, to stop my gibberings, the first guy had drawn a bucket of cold water which he upturned all over my head. I wasn't having a good day.

When Robert returned, all perky from Toyland, he found his precious home swarming with forensic guys plus hordes of police. The intruders had shimmied up the side of the house and through a slightly open bathroom window. It transpired that Honor Blackman, directly across the river, had been done over recently in the same fashion. When I rang her she was still reeling from the shock. I asked her to describe the knife for it had been most particular, turning inwards in a Morrocan fashion. She described it perfectly.

'Kiss your jewellery goodbye – you can whistle for it. The police are incompetent idiots!' As it turned out she was right. How lucky I was that she described that knife so accurately because otherwise I might have gone through life thinking it had been Tomcat's dealer wanting his dues.

At the time of the mugging my Burmese cat, named Wren after my mother, had been on my bed. She always slept with me, but afterwards never set foot in that room again.

I say the Lord's Prayer every night. I don't just mouth it, I live each line of it, and if I can't say it, then I must wait until I can. 'As we forgive those who trespass against us.' Not for the life of me could I say that line. To hell with forgiveness, I wanted a gun – badly! Revenge is a killer! I suppose that's what puts me off a great deal of the Bible. I didn't want to forgive them, just shoot their bleedin' balls off!

I am far from racist, but it took roughly six weeks for the violent desire to shoot all black men to subside, but 'As we forgive those who trespass against us' still got stuck in my gullet. Three months later, having worked mighty hard, I was again able to say and mean that particular line.

Returning home another day I found a lager lout from the Dove pissing up against my wooden front gate. This in itself was quite a common occurrence, but not what followed. I gave him my usual line.

'What's wrong with using the river?'

Whereupon he turned to face me, too pissed to remember he was still pissing, and continued pissing all over me.

A couple of weeks later I came into my front garden to find a stranger standing on the steps to the front porch. 'Good evening, Miss Miles. I'm a reporter.'

'Who let you in?'

'Your husband, I think it was.' Since Robert opened the door to any Tom, Dick or Harry who rang the entryphone, I wondered why he wanted the wretched thing installed in the first place. The reporter insisted on escorting me round the side of the garden that joins the Furnival Public Gardens.

'Do you know the gentleman hanging from your tree?' Well! Hang on the bell, Nelly! A man in a dirty raincoat was being unhooked by the police from a branch of my tree that hung over the public gardens. 'What d'you say about that?'

'I don't know him and he isn't in *our* garden he's in the *public* gardens.'

'Ah! But it's your tree!' Hard to believe we were heartlessly negotiating the final resting place of some poor, forgotten down-and-out. But that's what the media does, turns us all into barbarians.

'If you print that he's in *our* garden—'

Next day, headline news in the paper: 'Aids victim hangs himself in Sarah Miles' garden.'

Roughly ten days later, with *Hope and Glory* almost in the can and Tomcat still loose on the London streets, having just run away from his latest rehabilitation centre at Weston-Super-Mare, Robert decided to take his new motor-boat on its maiden voyage up to Richmond. We invited my old school chum S. P. J. with her two teenage sons, Dickon and Danny, my sister Vanessa with Luke and Ned, and Paul, the young man who helped Robert with all matters nautical.

As we left Sussex House to walk down to where we had moored the boat, there seemed no separation between raindrops.

'D'you want to fight on in this deluge, Robert?' He looked seriously nautical in his wicked new navy blue outfit and cheeky captain's cap.

'Fight on!' he replied with gusto. Did I see S. P. J. and Nessie give a slight sigh of resignation?

On board it was tricky to distinguish land from river. I hoped Robert was familiar with his new toy's radar equipment in case we got stuck or capsized somewhere.

'I know what I'm doing!' said Robert masterfully. He had always said that in his pre-stroke days. I had capsized with Robert three times out of six, but at least we were in a motor-boat now, which would be much more resilient to Robert's endless mishaps than a precarious sailing dingy.

Once under Barnes Bridge, Robert's imperviousness to the deluge became catching. I spotted a man waving at us from the river.

'Stop! Robert, look over there!' I pointed excitedly in the direction of the poor chap. 'I think he's drowning!'

'Nonsense!' replied Robert. 'He's just waving.'

'Look! He has his clothes on!' shouted Dickon, excited now too.

'Quickly! Let's throw him a life-saver!' yelled Danny.

'Don't you dare!' reprimanded Robert. 'They cost a fortune!' Unlike Robert to worry over such trivialities.

'I think Robert wants to ignore him,' put in a wise old Nessie.

'But Robert ignored Nona, Johnnie Windeatt—' The suicides in our lives.

'Should've ignored David Whiting too!' The drowning man was splashing frantically as we approached. Robert looked like thunder as Paul threw over a life-saver. The drowning chap let it sail right past him.

'You see!' observed a triumphant Robert. 'He wants to be left alone!' But this remark went unheeded by the rest of the gang as we all hauled the drowning man aboard.

'Christ! He's heavy!' Once aboard it was hard to keep him down, for he wriggled like an eel. It was amazing the strength he managed to muster up with soaking clothes, to squirm himself straight back into the water.

Robert turned round ruefully. 'I told you so!'

'Come – one last try!' This time we pinned him securely to the deck and fetched him some coffee and a fag. He turned out to be a well-to-do Cypriot called George Cosmatos, with a large family and no money problems. He simply needed for everything to stop. I knew that one myself.

'I just want to die.'

Robert, still playing with his blessed radar toys, heard this remark. 'You see?' he said snubbingly, before turning back to his complicated equipment. He must have worked it pretty efficiently, because once we arrived at Richmond Bridge the police and ambulance were already there. 'My radar works!' shouted the victorious schoolboy.

George shivered as he saw that they had come to take him away. Before disappearing into the ambulance he made them put him down a moment. He turned and pleaded with me to visit him one Wednesday afternoon at the Roehampton psychiatric hospital. As he climbed into the ambulance, he called back to me, like a virgin, 'You will keep your promise?'

'I will.' Off the ambulance sped.

The following Wednesday when I arrived at the front desk of the hospital, I was told that George Cosmatos had drowned up at Putney two days earlier.

When I returned home, Robert took it calmly. 'I told you so.' He had been proved right every step of the way. What a humdinger of a maiden voyage!

At about this time, while I was finishing shooting *Hope and Glory*, Tom was found in Hampstead with blue lips, almost at death's door. He had escaped from five rehabilitation centres. It seemed he just wasn't ready to face the devil head on. I was stuck on the set, so Robert took advice from a heavyweight drug psychiatrist, who told us that deliverance for Tom was only available in the USA, where knowledge of drug rehabilitation was streets ahead of what was available in Britain.

Tom made the decision to fly over to New York with the psychiatrist for assessment.

He was sent on to the highly regarded Minnesota drug centre, Twin Towns. Running away in America wouldn't be the same piece of cake it had been in England, so Robert and I felt he might stand a better chance of making it through this time. All we could do was pray.

Trapped on set, I found myself pulverised not only by the suddenness of his departure, but also by my obvious failure with the tough love philosophy.

Testing Trevor

Professionally I was suddenly on a roll. *Hope and Glory* had received great reviews and Michael Radford, thanks to a dinner with my old friend, Sally Mates, had asked me to play Alice de Trafford in his next film, *White Mischief*. Kenya was a place I'd never been, but on arriving in Nairobi, I didn't feel that sense of coming home I had felt when arriving in India or Nepal. No doubt a great part of me belonged in the East if it belonged anywhere, but unlike the Happy Valley set, my soul didn't belong in Kenya, wickedly atmospheric and exhilarating though it was.

Before I left England the producers were keen to employ Trevor Howard and asked me if, in my opinion, Trevor was still able to learn his lines and behave himself. I thought it was a bit of cheek, asking me, because it put me in an impossible situation. 'What if I say yes and Trevor fouls up?'

'We won't blame you, we promise. You know him well, that's all.'

'If Helen is with him, no problem, but I honestly believe that without her it could be dodgy.' (Helen Cherry was his wife.)

Once we arrived in Nairobi the cast and crew were given a week to readjust to the altitude, which we all managed with ease. Then Trevor arrived for his two-week schedule, but no Helen. 'Where's Helen, Trevs?'

He looked a bit hang-dog. 'Working. She was offered too good a part to turn it down.'

'Will you manage without her?'

'I'll have to, won't I?'

Later that day I caught him pissed as a newt. 'Too damn hot, I can't breathe.'

In the hotel the following evening one of the producers came up to me. (I won't give his name because he's a nice chap, really!)

'Sarah, Trevor's not only drunk but decrepit. He's not going to make it.'

I had to restrain myself from twisting his nose. 'Be fair. I told you not to employ him without Helen.'

'He's way past it – completely out of his skull this afternoon.'

'We were all given a week out here to acclimatise, yet you put Trevor to work straight off the plane with no Helen to fight his corner. I cannot be held responsible.'

'We're not holding you responsible. We're just telling you why we have to fire him.' I knew only too well that if Trevor was fired, it would end his career. Besides, what a bum note for such a splendid career to go out on. No, I couldn't have that happen.

'If Trevor goes, I go too.'

'Don't be stupid, Sarah.'

'If you fire Trevor, I'll make sure, publicly, that you not only look stupid but downright cruel.'

'Is that a threat?'

'That's up to you.' I got up and went to find Trevor.

He was in his room, pretty far gone. What could I do to prove that he was capable of performing his special brand of magic, if given time to adjust? I looked out of the window to see the money-men, producers and such like sitting round a table at the poolside, their heads together in a rugby scrum, as if plotting secret ways to demolish Trevor. My sense of injustice (my downfall) raged through me as usual, causing me a great hankering for revenge.

An idea hit me.

'Trevor, put on your swimming trunks and meet me in the lobby in five minutes.' I ran upstairs to change into my swimsuit. Trevor was waiting in the lobby in the loudest pair of Bermuda shorts I'd ever seen, clashing with his scarlet face. That open, sparkling innocence of his I found hugely endearing, just perfect for what I had in mind.

'Don't look the least bit drunk. OK?'

'Why? Do they want to fire me?' No flies on Trevor.

'Yes. So let's show them!' Trevor's face puced up with the challenge.

'Lead the way, Smiles!' Off we went down to the pool.

On arrival all the money clones were still pow-wowing and the pool was empty and clear. Perfect timing, I thought. I had been staggered in Belgrade, one time, to find Trevor diving into the hotel pool like

Nijinsky. He had been just as pissed in Belgrade as he was right then, so why not?

'Trevor, do your *pièce de résistance.*'

'Which one? I have so many.'

'Your superb swallow dive. I'll go up the other end and you dive in – make it flashy – then swim under water, straight through my legs.'

'How will these antics stop them firing me?'

'They claim you're not only a drunkard, but decrepit—'

'Decrepit, am I? Bastards!'

Good. I'd hoped he'd rise to the bait.

He was in complete control bouncing upon the diving board. The pow-wow slowly loosened up as heads began to turn in his direction. The plan was going swimmingly. Trevor twisted round to them. 'Decrepit, am I?' After delivering a Robert Newton roar, he flew in the air and gave the kind of dive that would have made a swallow proud.

Once he had swum a length under water and gone right through my legs – his dazzling Bermuda shorts lighting the way – the pow-wow had become an appreciative audience. The plan worked out triumphantly. Trevor was reinstated, provided I would be prepared to stand in for Helen when required. Little did I know what I had let myself in for.

Trevor hated learning lines. Whenever I brought the script into his eyeline it was like a red rag to a bull. If I so much as opened it at the day's scene, he would become cantankerous and impossibly bolshie. At the time it was a nightmare yet with hindsight I see it as having been a privilege. They just don't make Trevor Howards anymore, and for me, that's what life's all about, meeting great characters, gathering memories to help one grow a little, and to act as an antidote to mediocrity.

The whole company went down to Lake Naivasha where we camped in tents. It was spellbinding, the light, the smells, the birdsong, the barbaric night noises of howling wild beasts laced with the rhino ablutions – a very serious business. It was down there that I got to know Iain and Oria Douglas Hamilton. What a great job they were doing in raising our awareness of the approaching extinction of the African elephant. Back then, in the 1980s, their work was still in its infancy. Iain invited me to go up in his private plane and flew me low over the last herds of Kenya.

How many times did I hear him exclaim as we came across another fine matriarch slaughtered for her ivory? I couldn't bear any of it. I know these creatures are doomed, therefore cannot bring myself to look forward, only back with regret at what we have failed to do. When will the realisation dawn on us that once the balance of nature has been lost, humanity will also perish? *We are all one.* The guilty party is *us*, the sixties generation. We should take most of the blame for decimating the planet, for we knew what was coming, but did too little too late.

At a 1930s Happy Valley race meeting in Nairobi, my character, Alice de Trafford, swans around with a little bush baby and we became great friends. However rehearsals are not the real thing, so when, 'Action', was called on the first take, my bush baby, unaccustomed to galloping hooves, nipped me through my glove, drawing a pinprick of blood. One of the assistants saw it and without my knowledge called the nurse. I told her I was perfectly fine, sent her on her way and forgot all about the incident.

A few days later I was shown an English tabloid. The headline read as follows: 'Sarah Miles, savaged by nocturnal wild beast, is rushed to hospital for life-saving jabs.' Unquote. The article went on to claim that I was suing the film company. I was outraged: if this fantasy had actually taken place, suing would never have entered my head (I'm against suing anyway) because I vehemently believe that the oceans belong to the fish just as the jungle, into which we humans trespass at our peril, belongs to the wild beasts. I'm an old hand at seeing lies about me in the press, but this pinprick exaggerated to Hammer horror took the biscuit.

On my return to England I requested that the reporter come in person to Pinewood Studios and apologise for a story of pure invention. He sent along his second eleven who, naturally, couldn't be held responsible. I tried many times to contact him personally for I wanted an explanation, but all to no avail. He was soon promoted to be the paper's top showbiz columnist – just my luck!

Two months later, Oria and Iain Douglas Hamilton rang, for they had come to town and were longing to meet Robert, having heard so much about him. I told them to come right over. When they appeared, I escorted them upstairs to our bedroom – the ballroom, as we called it – where we found the bed empty. Robert was enthroned, at the far end, a regal Humpty-Dumpty, in a high-backed brocade William and Mary chair, all clean and sparkly pink in a red-and-white-striped night-shirt. He looked magnificent, displaying mighty fine legs in shiny black boots. 'Robert, meet Oria and Iain.'

'Champagne or whisky?' Bringing them forward to shake Robert's regal hand, I couldn't help but notice a gap between the top of his knee-length socks and the rim of his night-shirt. There, sweetly on display in the gap, was the jauntiest set of cock 'n' balls in the kingdom. Had Oria and Iain glimpsed this rogue cluster escaping from the loose leg of his white pants, I mused.

In the kitchen later, Oria remarked, 'Now that was a vision I won't forget – worth coming all the way from Kenya for! His presence is so massive it can give even exposed genitalia the dignity of the Crown Jewels.'

Athenian Interlude

I decided I wanted to meet the old lady in her nineties who lived three doors down from us, in the grace-and-favour coachhouse adjoining Kelmscott House, and rarely went out. She was the main character in a wonderful theatrical story that I had been told while still at RADA and I was eager to find out if the story was true. Her name was Athene Seyler, and she was not only a great old dame of the English theatre but the author of a surprisingly enlightening book called *The Art of Comedy*.

I knocked at her door. It was open, but no 'Come in' bellowed forth, so I plucked up courage and crept up the Miss Havisham wooden spiral staircase. It was like being in a time capsule and I was thrown back into the nineteenth century, cushioned by portraits of Athene everywhere, one with her late husband Nicholas (Beau) Hannen, and another that amused me somewhat. It was a self-portrait of George Bernard Shaw. 'This is what Athene thinks I look like.' signed G. B. S. On entering the long main room, I could just make her out, sitting at the far end in an armchair looking over the Thames. The autumn sun sparkling on the water rebounded back across her snow-white hair. Being loath to interrupt her obviously deep and intimate relationship with her river, I stood there, similarly bewitched, taking it all in. Watching the Thames's massive power tumbling by reminded me of my swim the previous month. I would dive in from a friend's garden further up Chiswick Mall but on that day I failed to get my timing right, which didn't often happen because I have a huge respect for the river's fickle, merciless undercurrents. One must plunge in right on the turn of the tide. A single minute can make a hell of a difference, and that day, diving in a fraction late, I had paid a heavy price.

Within half a minute I was transformed into the flimsiest piece of flotsam, utterly powerless, propelled by a force stronger than anything I'd ever experienced (except the force that put out the candle). I tried my utmost to grab onto something but the Thames hauled me back to its centre. I attempted to do what I always do in my moments of alarm – surrender! – but it's damned hard when you're being hurtled at great speed towards Hammersmith Bridge.

Approximately half a mile from Putney Bridge (too ghastly for Robert if he were to lose both his daughter *and* his lady in the same stretch of river), the current lost its ferocity, which enabled me to grab a clump of weeds that didn't give way. If they had, I might not have been here to tell the tale.

Athene turned and saw me. 'Oh! You made me jump!'

'Sorry.'

'Who are you?' She possessed much the same magic chin-wobble glorified by my old chum Margaret Rutherford. No doubt at all: we were going to be friends. She must have cottoned on to similar possibilities, because she pointed to the sofa in front of her. 'Do sit down.' She looked at me some more. 'Did you say who you were ... just now?'

'No, I didn't. How d'you do? I'm a neighbour. It's taken me six months to pluck up the courage to barge in, as I did so rudely just now.'

'Would you like a martini?' She waved her stick towards a drinks cupboard.

'No, thank you.' Judging by the sigh of relief that followed, I thought the filthy lucre might have been in short supply. 'What will you have, then?'

'Nothing thank you—'

'Orange juice?' It popped out like Dame Edith Evans' *hand-bag*.

'Thank you – I'll fetch it. Can I give you a refill?' I believe the great beam that followed clinched our friendship. She handed over her glass as if shuffling into a better position to view the next race. With my confidence swelling up nicely, I continued, 'You know it's famous, don't you – your hat story at the Ivy?'

She was chuffed to bits. 'Alas, I've heard it told by so many people, I've rather lost sight of the true version.'

'Was it at the Ivy?'

'That's it. The Ivy. I was off to a garden party and I'd just bought this

194

lively hat, breathtaking, it was, with a tiny bird hidden among the flowery feathers – a real Simpson's special.'

'I gathered it was Fortnum's and *two* birds in a bird's nest.'

She flipped away the exaggeration with her cane, like Moses parting the Red Sea. 'A whole flock, why not, with a couple of eggs thrown in? It could have been Fortnum's, of course.'

I felt the need to plough on. 'You sat having your lunch when you—'

'Spied a woman opposite in *exactly* the same hat—'

'What did you do?'

'It wouldn't have been so embarrassing had we'd been in *ordinary* hats. How well I remember her eyes piercing through me like an arrow. Trying to make light of it, I pointed to my hat and shrugged, 'C'est la vie!' but she just kept staring right through me. Unable to take the discomfort any longer, I pointed to my hat a second time and laughed with a nonchalant shrug – but the vexed Valkyrie was having none of it.' Athene's chin gave some more delicious wobblings.

I couldn't over-estimate the thrill of having Athene act out her very own, almost mythic tale right before my eyes – and to think that most of showbiz thought she was dead. I was so delighted they hadn't bothered to find out, for this way I had her hilarious jewels of wisdom all to myself. Her timing never failed her, with beautifully rich speech patterns delivered with an immaculate silky style. On she glided. 'Her lack of humour was plain to see. Finally after two more abortive attempts to get her to see the funny side of our ridiculous predicament, she rose, tossed one last ghastly glare in my direction and strode out haughtily without paying. I remember that very clearly, and presumed she must be someone fearfully important.'

'Oh. I thought *you* strode out haughtily?'

'No, *she* did. *I* had nothing to be haughty about. I paid my bill, collected my hat box and went to the ladies' room where I had an almighty shock. Catching myself in the mirror I discovered my hat was *not* on my head.'

'You'd forgotten to take it out of the Fortnum's box—'

'Simpson's! There it was, all wrapped up neatly in tissue paper. Poor woman! How rude I must have seemed … you may be right about Fortnum's …'

Over the next three years, Cuckoo, my new Yorkshire terrier, and I visited Athene most days. I would sometimes bring over soup and snacks and always the day's gossip. Just as I came second to Robert's computer, so I came second to Cuckoo in Athene's affection. No self-pity, simple fact.

During those first few weeks Athene simply knew me as that 'strange little creature' up the Mall. For some reason I never told her who I was, not out of false modesty but because she never asked, and there never seemed to be a right time. Besides, I like it when people don't know who I am, and since she'd been stuck up in that room for the past fifteen years, she probably wouldn't have known me from Adam.

One lunch-time I came round and Athene looked at me strangely before wiping away the remains of her Meals on Wheels.

'Judge Tumim tells me you're *forty*!' The judge was our neighbour.

'Oh, Athene, and some!' She looked aghast.

'*And some?*'

I knew I looked younger than my years, but surely Athene was overdoing it.

With breath recovered and chops wiped clean, she put down her napkin on the tray. 'My, my! You *do* put up a bluff!' Her immaculate delivery and timing of that last line remains stuck to me, limpet-like. I continually try to repeat it, and always get it wrong.

Athene was tickled pink to find me the wife of *A Man For All Seasons*. 'Great, great play that – as good as Shaw.' How the time shot by when she was relating her theatrical tales of Shaw, Max Beerbohm Tree, Terence Rattigan, Noël Coward, Helen Terry, Sarah Bernhardt and Mrs Patrick Campbell. She continually spoke of Beau Hannen, her only real love, who triggered off softer, more intimate memories. How nimbly Athene could scuttle between moods. Beau usually heralded a burst into tears. 'Why have I been trapped here so long when I want only one thing, to go to my beloved?' The martini had differing effects. That day it made her maudlin. 'All my friends gone ... nobody left any more ... I wonder how Larry is?'

'Larry who?'

'Olivier, my child, Olivier ... or are you too young to have heard of him?'

Athene went on and on about Larry, of how she had discovered him at the Central School, and the desire to confess all became hard to quell. Perhaps it was fortunate that I did quell it, for I doubt that Athene would have approved of my having been Olivier's mistress. Her greatest wish, she said, was to see Olivier once more before she died.

With immense difficulty I managed to arrange for him to visit her. He was rarely in London then, spending more and more time down at his Malt House in Sussex. But that day I was determined. Athene's face was all lit up like a child's when a buttercup is placed under its chin.

'He's coming tomorrow? Or is it the next day?'

'No, Athene, he comes on Thursday. The day after tomorrow.' Thursday came and I helped to get her looking her absolute best. Mind you, this wasn't a difficult task since Athene always looked her best. They had high standards, those Edwardians. I bought a mass of flowers, and made the coach-house look as welcoming as possible – but Olivier never showed. The agonising memory of that interminable afternoon of waiting remains, punctuated by the clock's half-hourly chimes.

The next day Olivier telephoned: he had been unexpectedly rushed into hospital.

'Please make Athene understand.'

'You shouldn't have accepted. She's too old to be let down.'

'Where is that famous forgiveness?'

He was right. Disappointment on Athene's behalf had eclipsed proper concern for him. I cheered up. 'No face-lift this time, promise?'

'I love you so – always with you in spirit.'

Yet though he meant it, my heart still aches from being cast aside towards the end. Had he grown too old to deceive any more? Or did his shame keep him at bay? Mother thought it was Joanie, but I'm not so sure. I knew it was going to be tricky: dying gracefully for one's wife and family is bad enough, but dying well for your mistress too? Whatever caused the severing is finally neither here nor there, but my heart is broken and the reason is that I believe my love could have made his dying beautiful.

By way of compensation for Athene Robert and I gave a dinner party at home for her ninety-ninth birthday. Sir John Gielgud, also an old favourite of hers, kindly agreed to come, as well as Jeremy Irons and his wife, Sinéad Cusack. I hoped this second-eleven group made up for the Olivier débâcle. It was splendid to see Gielgud again, after so long, and in such fine fettle too.

I proudly took Tom along as my escort when I won the British Variety Club award for *Hope and Glory*. We found ourselves at the same table as Terry Wogan. He was sincere, honest and open with Tom, who had just returned from Minnesota, a new, clean machine. Terry turned and saw me eyeing the two of them with interest. 'He's a good fellow this one. Hey, Sarah, why have you never been on my show?' I had been asked a few times but had declined, finding the whole format too overwhelmingly geared towards fear. But because of his genuine, unconsidered amiability towards Tom, I reconsidered.

'I promise to come on with Athene Seyler on her hundredth birthday.'

'She's dead, isn't she?' Why did *everyone* think Athene was dead?

Terry was delighted at the prospect of this occasion. 'Make sure you keep that promise, now.'

It wasn't a difficult promise to keep because Athene still had over a year and a half to go, so the whole occasion was comfortably far off in the land of misty maybes.

Tom made an excellent escort and behaved beautifully. I was both thrilled and relieved to have him home again. He had been at Twin Towns rehabilitation centre for eight weeks and then for almost another year in a half-way house, Way 11. Robert and I had travelled out to Minnesota for Family Week, to which parents of addicts come to talk through all the pain, resentments, revenge, hatred, love, jealousy and neglect. It was a real heavy time for the three of us. We were certainly put through our paces, and I worried that it would be too much for Robert. But my 'age bluffing', as Athene called it, had nothing on Robert's ability to bluff his frailty.

The specialist had told me that Robert was simply enjoying the extra icing on life's cake, and admitted to being baffled as to how he was functioning at all. 'A walking miracle,' he once said to me and twice a day in Minnesota, this 'walking miracle' had to integrate, either one-to-one with a counsellor or in a group with other parents and their addict offspring. This was tough on everyone but more so, in a way, for Robert and me because of our wretched showbiz profiles. Being forced to toss intimate, sore, sordid and bedraggled memories with your son in a group situation isn't an ideal scenario for confidence-boosting. It was there we were to learn that drug addiction is a disease from birth, a chemical imbalance, just as Warren had told me over a decade earlier.

The monumental gravitas of the experience paid off a thousand-fold, though, and hoovered up a great deal of dirt from our grimy consciences. The fragmentation of our lives, the voice demanding I be alone, the divorce and the failure to come together again during those dark treading-water years, Robert's stroke, of which Tomcat had been forbidden at first to be a part, all had played their part. We hoped that by exchanging blame for love – I had taken a great slice of that blame, but not all of it – we could create a strong foundation of richer understanding from which family values could blossom anew.

No Family Week can replace the momentous willpower each individual has to muster up to come clean, but I was so impressed with it that I tried hard to get the idea off the ground in England. I failed because the clinics thought that a weekend was long enough, although I tried to persuade them that a weekend was too short a time for the parents to relax enough to accept or question resentments, and then be given time to mend. It had been so effective in America. But I was told that there weren't sufficient funds to introduce Family Week in England, so eventually I gave up. But with or without Family Week, it is the addict's decision to muster up the mighty strength needed to withdraw from the devil's mesmeric pull. Tomcat did it!

I knew that a safety net was essential if Tom was to stay clean and I found him a perfect house in Chiswick. From then on he was beholden to no one, for he had two spare rooms to let out if need be. It worked because he has never asked for a penny since. Robert went halves, but my half cleaned out my *White Mischief* money – my only savings.

During Athene's ninety-ninth year she asked me over to watch her one evening in one of her films, *Doctor at Large*. I sat on the floor, half watching her entrancing profile and half eagerly awaiting her first entrance on the screen. During the film she turned to me. 'Have I appeared yet?'

'No, Athene, not yet.'

'I must have got the wrong film. Would you get me another martini?'

'Athene, you've already had two.'

'I know. And one more makes three.' She was just like Robert. I gave in and fetched her one.

'Here I come! Oh! Look at my hat! Isn't it divine?' Divine it was, but not a patch on Athene, who was displaying a curious Oriental slant to her saucy eyes. Her timing was as easy as licking honey off a spoon and in striking contrast to the stiff, wooden performances around her.

When the end titles came up I had to go home for Robert was cheesed off with my endless visits to her.

'I'm off now, Athene.'

She grabbed her forgotten martini. 'When will Cuckoo be having puppies?' That was her main desire, to own a tiny Yorkshire terrier just like Cuckoo.

'Soon, I promise.'

Back at Sussex House after I'd given Robert his dinner, the phone rang. It was Andy, one of Athene's relations who lived in the back room. She had fallen over, broken her hip, and had been taken to hospital. I knew she shouldn't have had that final martini. Why hadn't I been stronger?

I found her in a public ward where the old lady in the next bed was suffering from senile dementia. This would have been bearable had she not begun to scream at roughly five thirty through till ten at night. Her shrieks were profoundly alarming because she was convinced everyone was her mother – especially me.

Athene bent towards my ear. 'I want you to do me a favour and talk to Matron.'

'Of course, Athene. What about?'

She leant in even closer. 'I don't mind being washed all over by *black* strangers, but do they have to be *male* strangers? I may be an old fuddy-duddy but that's how it is.'

Athene's hundredth birthday party was a corker! To have recovered from her new hip operation at ninety-nine years old was a feat in itself, but her triumph on *Wogan* was masterful. She broke the whole of England's heart in one fell swoop. She recited her first ever audition piece, Rosalind from *As You Like It*. Andy and I alternately rehearsed it with her over and over, but being an inborn trooper, never at any time was her dazzling wit as apparent as on the night itself.

We were given the tricky task of following Placido Domingo a task made doubly difficult due to Athene's insistence that I carry Cuckoo on. 'Once I'm seated, place her on my lap – my portable Dutch courage.'

Unlike Gladys, Cuckoo was still green, with only one performance under her belt in *White Mischief*, so it was completely understandable that, while waiting in the wings, she indulged in a freak-out, the cause of which was, simply, Placido Domingo. It was plain to see from the way her hair stood right up on end that the frequency of his famous vibrato was out of harmony with Cuckoo's. I knew she'd be off before the end of the aria.

'Hang on to her! Don't let her go!' cried Athene, as our entrance music struck up. Her face depicted utter hopelessness as she watched her Dutch courage (not that she needed any) scampering off. It would have been hard to follow Athene's Rosalind had I not been given the Queen's telegram to read out. James Fox, my old beau from RADA days, participated too, but Athene was the star and the evening her triumph.

Reuniting and Severing

Peter Hall, director of the National Theatre, asked me to join his swan-song at a luncheon given by Duncan Weldon, a theatrical impresario. I remember going into the loo and coming out to find Robert sitting at a table with Peter, his opera-star wife, Maria Ewing, and their daughter, Rebecca. I noticed that Peter rarely turned to direct any of his conversation to Robert and this threw me because he and Robert had been good friends in Robert's pre-stroke days. But, then, I've noticed lots of people feel ill at ease around severe stroke victims, for they pose too much of a threat. This is quite understandable.

I hadn't met Peter before, and felt uneasy because he kept staring at me. Had I, like Robert de Niro, got some sleepy-dust in my eye, or a bogey in my nose?

'You are my Imogen,' he kept saying. I wasn't familiar with Shakespeare's *Cymbeline*, but Robert insisted I read it when we got home. The thought of his lady at the National Theatre clearly tickled Robert.

I had heard that Peter was a stickler for verse style, so when he rang two days later asking if I'd read the play, and wooing me to play his Imogen, I found myself holding back. My last experience at the National, with Olivier, had ended in disaster. Here I was, on a roll for the first time in ten years, with two good new movies under my belt and with another classy film offer in the pipeline. Did I want to risk it? Wasn't joining Peter Hall asking for trouble? He would be directing *Cymbeline*, two other plays *and* his wife in *Salome* at the Royal Opera House all at the same time. My intuition (my, by now, softer voice) told me it wasn't the right career move.

Whatever anyone thinks of Peter Hall, the fact remains that he gives great phone. Yet I refused to be swayed, for I'd done some further homework and discovered that Peter was a stickler for *his* kind of verse style.

'I won't accept to be *your* Imogen without an audition.'

'So be it.'

I went on the appointed day and auditioned. Peter, pleasantly surprised, expounded unchequered sighs of relief. 'Thank God! You have
a natural talent for verse. I can see no problems whatsoever.' I believed
him. Why ever not? My verse *was* good. And so it was that I joined the
National.

The cast included Robert Eddison, a great Shakespearian actor of rare
integrity, Eileen Atkins, Tim Piggot-Smith and Michael Bryant.

Peter had asked me up to his office one evening, after rehearsals.
During our talk a call severed him mid-sentence, demanding that he
go into the next room. While he was away my eyes fell on a masculine-
looking leather *chaise-longue*. Robert's doctor had advised him repeatedly to keep his feet as high as possible and I had been trying – and
failing – to find a piece of furniture attractive enough to do the job and
assuage Robert's pride. There, in Peter's office, was exactly what I had
been searching for. Mighty handsome it was!

I went over to try it out and make sure that it was sufficiently sturdy
for Robert's nigh-on twenty stone. When Peter returned, I said, 'This'll
be perfect for Robert. Where can I buy one?'

As he came towards the *chaise-longue* it dawned on me that he
might think I had consciously chosen the casting-couch scenario, so
as he put his arm up against the back of the *chaise-longue* I ducked
out under it and went over to collect my bag. 'I'm serious about the
chaise-longue being perfect for Robert. It's for his feet – they swell
up.'

'I'll find the address for you.' He avoided my eyes as he showed me
the door.

The handsome vicar of St Peters, our local church in Hammersmith
whom I often saw returning from Athene's coach-house, having
given her communion, stood at the front gate one day wanting to
talk to me. Once settled with a cup of tea he asked, 'Are you and
Robert married?'

'No.'

'You should be.'

'Why?'

'The way you look at each other – what a love story!' This I found most flattering – that he'd noticed, I mean.

He winkled out of me pretty much the whole of our history. 'Being atheists we were married in a register office.'

'All the more reason to do it properly this time.'

Back in the bowels of the National Theatre lay the rehearsal hall. (They had been forced to put scarlet tape on all the doors leading to it because I kept getting lost, due to my spatial dyslexia problem and the appalling design of the theatre's bowels). It was the first rehearsal off books for the final scene of *Cymbeline*. Robert was convinced that it had been Shakespeare's favourite bit, orchestrating the finale, deftly pulling all plots and relationship threads together and tying the final happy-ever-after bow.

During this scene the whole cast is present on stage. When it came to one of Cymbeline's speeches, Peter Hall decided to interrupt Robert Eddison, who was doing a magnificent job as the regal King Cymbeline.

'Robert. Either address the audience or the other characters, but don't address thin air.' The style with which Robert occasionally addressed mid-air left the rest of us standing. His performance was truly the beacon around which we all merely stumbled.

'I've been acting Shakespeare for sixty years, so if you—'

'Just do as I say.'

'But I always address thin air at certain times – Shakespeare knows when those times are.'

'Only *I* say when – and when is never.' Although we went back over that section again, things quickly disintegrated until, 'Sorry, Robert, but you don't hear me. Stop addressing thin air!'

'If you don't like my acting style, why cast me?'

Peter didn't like that. 'My mistake, so now I'm left with no choice but to fire you.' An eerie, shocked silence descended on the rehearsal hall. Robert stared, suspended in disbelief.

'Are you firing me in public?' Incomprehension sat naked on his features.

'Come outside and I'll fire you in private.'

Watching Robert Eddison's tall, slumped back disappearing through the door behind Peter was too much for me. If I couldn't bear it, how could he? Robert was in his late seventies, having served Shakespeare with all his might for more than half a century. After a firing like this, he might never work again. Had Peter thought of that? He might even go to his death-bed with that firing the last event of his hugely eventful and triumphant life. (As it turned out, he did.)

God blast Peter Hall, is all I could think. I turned to my fellow actors, still standing there in shock.

'Well? Are we going to allow him to get away with it?' What happened next was normal. The whole cast retreated into the woodwork, conveniently becoming both anonymous and transparent.

'Is no one going to come outside with me and comfort him?'

Apparently no one was, so out I went and waited in the corridor alone.

Five minutes later Peter reappeared.

'Peter, surely you're going to reinstate Robert? You can't be serious? He's brilliant—'

'Out of my way.' He pushed past me. 'All right everyone, we'll continue with Act Three Scene Two.'

A week later he asked us to work the following Saturday. 'Hands up anyone who can't.' I put up my hand. 'Oh? And why can't you work this Saturday?' Was I being super-sensitive, or had his attitude towards me changed since the Robert Eddison episode?

'I just can't.'

'And what's so special about this Saturday that you can't make yourself available?'

I had *never* been unwilling to work before, not in this production or any other. Since Robert and I were determined to keep our wedding out of the media, I took him to one side to explain. 'Please respect my desire to keep it secret. I'm getting married this Saturday.'

What happened next was astounding. Perhaps it was the tone of voice more than the words that threw me. 'What do you want to do a thing like that for?' (His exact words, for I'll never forget that moment.) He then turned back to the ensemble and replaced his director's hat as if nothing had happened.

And so, that following Saturday, while the rest of the team sweated their guts out in an ugly rehearsal hall, Robert and I, in the blazing sunshine, got ourselves to the church on time. By some fluke I had managed to gauge the event just right, for it turned out a dreamy, almost fairy-tale occasion. Only family and our closest friends were present, plus animals, music, candles, daffodils and children.

I wore pale rose pink, subtly flattering Robert's sage green, and not a single child cried, candle dripped, daffodil died or dog crapped. We both had to admit that the vicar had been right, for we both felt *very* right being wed that second time. Why? Because the whole ritual of 'getting married' and the ceremony itself weren't based on a youthful rush of hope or lust, but on the knowledge of a benevolent continuity.

The peace that came over me was completely new – so almost multi-dimensional that I was certain those treading-water years and all the pain I'd suffered through the mental, physical and psychic manipulation had been worth it. No peace is ever as profound as that experienced by the culmination of heavy trials and tribulations. I believe the voice had finally triumphed, mending the marriage that had been wrongly smashed asunder. Surely now Robert and I would be given a period where this feeling of timely deliverance could first reline and then refill our depleted well?

Back at the National things were different. Suddenly Peter began to give me conflicting notes, which undermined my confidence. Yet when I asked him to sit down and talk through any elements of my performance that conflicted with how he saw Imogen, he impatiently twisted his body away before looking at his watch and rushing off. 'I haven't time.' What with directing three plays all at once, and his wife opening at the Royal Opera House, he was right, he didn't.

The actor trains like an athlete. His performance is timed and geared to be at its peak on the first night. Timing that sacred process of getting the part as comfortable and true as possible differs from one actor to another. However, I didn't feel too panicked after my exchange with Peter because we still had six weeks in which to get it right. Nevertheless it didn't prevent me from wanting and needing to sit down to try to comprehend what it was he wanted from my performance that he wasn't getting – which, after all, was his job.

Naturally, though, I became jittery. I'm fine as long as I know what's required of me, but Peter had somehow taken the rehearsal-room floor from beneath my feet. Had I been paranoid, I would have suspected a conspiracy, but we were artists, not politicians, so that could never be.

Instead I fought on, hoping that after *Salome* had opened, he might find time to help me get my Imogen into shape.

During our run-throughs I had noticed many a stranger in the audience. This flummoxed me for I had thought rehearsals were closed. One day I asked the stage manager who the strangers were and what they were doing there. 'Rehearsals are open to anyone who wants to come. It's called "work in progress".' I found it particularly nerve-racking to give a performance with which the director wasn't happy in front of strangers.

'Could I bring anyone I wanted to a run-through?'

'Get permission first.' Peter wasn't around and the desire to have Robert see my performance to shed a little light on the proceedings became of paramount importance.

Our next proper run-through was on Saturday, and since Peter wasn't around for the next two days, I asked the stage manager if I could bring Robert.

'I can't see why not. I'll clear it with Peter.' He seemed to have no doubt.

When the Saturday run-through arrived I helped Robert into the rehearsal room and put him into a chair. That afternoon, two other strangers were there I remember. Once we were all seated Peter arrived. He gave the most perfect double-take when he noticed Robert sitting there. He whispered nervously, 'Are you sure I'm allowed to be here?'

'Perfectly sure. I had permission from the stage manager.'

After our run-through I looked over to capture Robert's initial reaction. There he was, beaming like a tabby cat with a bowl of cream. He might have suffered a stroke, but his critical faculties were very much intact. He was able to give out a film's ending soon after it had begun and still walked out of theatres and cinemas when he knew there was no hope of redemption. Though I had impressed him greatly in both *Hope and Glory* and *White Mischief*, when I later chose to do a play called *Asylum* – out of desperation, thanks to Peter Hall – at the Lyric, Hammersmith, Robert so disliked the writing that he couldn't see my performance, but everything he had to say about the play and my performance was right on the button – even though I received some great reviews from the critics.

That fateful evening Robert congratulated those whose performances had impressed him before taking me out to my favourite Japanese restaurant. Once settled with a great mound of raw fish pieces in front of him, Robert whispered in my ear with great solemnity, 'You're going to be a sensational Imogen.'

'You're being kind because you love me.'

'No. All great acting's finally down to intelligence, charisma and daring.' He pulled away, making a gesture as if to push the statement into thin air in order to keep me humble. 'You'll end up giving a performance of all three.'

'Not if I don't get some help, I won't . . . What do I do?' He shrugged, while popping in succulent yellow-tail.

'Just play her as you did tonight and once you've earthed her in confidence—'

'Hard to earth her when Peter isn't around to give me any soil.'

'How many weeks left?'

'Almost six.'

'A piece of cake. You'll be ready to break everyone's heart in one.'

I slept like a baby that night.

Next morning was particularly glorious, not only because I was feeling on top of the world but because the sky was that crisp and cloudless March blue, the brand of blue that reminds you that spring *does* eventually follow winter. I spent a beautiful day studying the play, walking Cuckoo, dropping in on Athene and cuddling Robert.

At four o'clock the phone rang.

'Hello, it's Peter here.' Why did his whisper fill me with gloom? I was determined to keep it light.

'What a stunning day it's been, Peter.'

'For those lucky enough to enjoy it.' He mumbled on before stating, 'You are not my Imogen.'

This hit me hard. 'If I am not your Imogen, Peter, you have only yourself to blame.'

'Why's that?'

'Because you rarely show up and when you do you refuse to give me even the slightest clue as to how you want *your* Imogen played. I can't do it by osmosis.'

He trickled on about how I wasn't his Imogen until his voice trailed back into a dark whisper. 'I have no alternative but to fire you.'

I was numb with incomprehension. 'Say that again, Peter.'

'I'm firing you. You are not my Imogen.'

'But *why*?'

He mumbled on weakly in a half-hearted manner, saying nothing, before putting down the phone.

I sleep-walked into Robert's room.

'Seen a ghost?'

It all came tumbling out and as it did so Robert joined me in turning ashen white. He put his head in his one hand. 'Haah!' An unbearable roaring followed, the same painful elephant roar he had given when I was asked to leave Doneraile Street.

I put that to him. 'Why did you make me leave when you'd ask me to come home to you?'

'Because I couldn't be the man you deserved.' (Every word came out slow and deliberate.)

'What kind of man is that?'

'The kind of man who, right this minute, would go and blow Peter Hall's brains out.' I was touched by how hard Robert had been hit by the news. 'The injustice of it!' He began to roar again. I was fearful lest he have another heart-attack. '*I – can – do – nothing – because – I – can't – speak!*' I tried to calm him down. Robert never got over his hatred of Peter Hall.

Next day the tabloid headlines were full of it. Our castle walls were a mass of black and silver *paparazzi*. So hot was the news that some reporters actually climbed over our wall, shouting up through the windows, begging for my side of the story, willing to pay heavy money for it, too. Robert and I found ourselves marooned. Tom came round and protected us beautifully. Fearless, worldly-wise and completely able to defend his parents from the injustices that followed. How I blessed him for coming clean!

The Peter Hall episode left me so lacking in confidence that I could have ended up in the loony bin, just like the mentally handicapped creature I portrayed in my next play, *Asylum*. My Imogen in *Cymbeline* would have put me firmly back on the map as the stage actress I was. To have had that chance ripped from its creative womb, before it was properly formed and birthed, left a raw scar seeping with incomprehension. Later, I discovered that for two weeks he had been secretly rehearsing another Imogen, Geraldine James, down the corridor. I pity him if he has a conscience and I pity him if he hasn't. Thank God for all those years with the voice demanding me to stay strong in silence, for without them I never would have come through.

Whenever I sit and list both my fortunes and misfortunes I am constantly staggered at how equal the curses and blessings turn out to be. Yet I had to put many hard hours of discipline into forgiveness. To forgive Peter Hall took about ten weeks – four weeks longer than my mugging! Robert found my desire to forgive baffling.

'Stop working on forgiveness and sue!' I'd never witnessed such hatred in Robert before or since. I laughed as I reminded him of what Gore Vidal had once said to us at a party: 'When you get to middle age you stop fucking and start suing.'

'So! Start suing!'

'I'd rather stay young and continue forgiving.'

'You're mad. Quite mad!'

I was hugely touched by the number of fellow National players who wrote praising my performance, all deeply shocked at what Peter had done. It seemed his enemies were numerous: Jonathan Miller had plenty of damaging tales to tell; Olivier wanted his scrotum on a platter.

After a piece in the *Mail* by Lynda Lee Potter giving my side of the story John Osborne invited Robert and me to stay at his peaceful home in Clunton, Herefordshire, where he lived with his wife Helen. There it became clear that Osborne too had some meaty bones to pick. It was delightful to witness Robert and John, two great English gentlemen of the theatre, neither knighted, exchanging memories. Sad, too, on another level, because Osborne was weak in body, and financially ruined. Yet he still insisted on champagne daily.

This daily champagne was an important touch, because it brought back memories of the extravagant parties he had given in the sixties each year down in his beautiful Kent home. Parties in the old style, the kind that only he gave, the kind we are all, except David Frost, too mean to give any more. It was important for me to thank him for his continual generosity, made even more poignant in his last years due to his impoverished lifestyle.

Robert and John had their memorial services within two days of each other. I bet they were both looking down, slapping their thighs and hooting! Osborne's had a sign outside the church stating that 'Fu Manchu' (Peter Hall) was forbidden entry. Robert would have liked that.

Is there a theme running through my life that I should be looking at? During my school years and professional life, most of the trouble I have found myself in has been due to the fact that I will not stand by and witness the abuse of power. Likewise, if there is any opportunity to become powerful myself, I run, cowardly, in the opposite direction. Is it cowardly, or have I see too many decent people corrupted before my eyes? Power is only useful according to the love it can manifest. Nothing else. I have no talent for manipulation, either of myself or others. I come straight out from the heart, never stopping to think first! This certainly makes me my own worst enemy.

Yet am I? It is imperative for me to follow my lodestar. To stand up with a clear conscience and say I strive towards integrity and to that end place my life and the daily living of it *before* my career. It will always be two steps forward and one step back, but is it a harmful aspiration to follow such a lodestar? All this must seem pretty nutty in these materialistic times in which we live, but I'm nutty enough to believe I'll have the last laugh because I am free.

Coming Home

If Peter Hall hadn't fired me, we never would have found Chithurst. I have this to thank him for.

It was autumn 1987 and my childhood vision – the one I'd seen when I was seven years old in the palm of my hand – was all around me. Robert and I were sitting under a gnarled apple tree on a back lawn overlooking the ancient stones and lattice windows of eleventh-century Chithurst Manor.

'We need hunt no more. We've come home!' I swore I saw a tear of relief trickling down Robert's cheek. 'I feel Thomas More all around us.' It was certainly a 'Moreish' house.

The previous weekend I had attended a healing seminar held in a Tudor house, Stanley Hall in Essex. During the final meditation, helped no doubt by my surroundings, I saw my childhood vision return: the lattice-framed windows transformed into silver healing diamonds of cosmic blue, pulling me into a luxuriant loving safety. I interpreted it as Stanley Hall becoming my home, but I knew that could never be. I remained puzzled on the return journey to Sussex House, yet the powerful sense of that childhood vision looming closer refused to fade. I construed it as an auspicious symbol of things to come, so when I returned home I asked Robert if any possible houses had come through the post. 'Nothing.'

I rummaged through the bin and found one of interest.

'I must have missed it,' said an excited Robert, flipping through the particulars.

Next morning I rang to make an appointment and was told by the estate agent that there was no hope of seeing the property until Friday.

'But this is Monday.'

'Sorry, but there's a queue of people wanting to see the property.'

'But what if you sell between now and then?'

'If someone puts in a fair bid, that's that, I'm afraid.'

When I repeated all this to Robert he put on his coat. 'Come on! We're off!' He piled me and Lisa Anderson, a friend from LA, into his Range Rover and off we went to Sussex. He found the house with no problem. We parked right at the bottom of the drive and a woman came to meet us.

'You must be the Clin—' She stopped mid-word. 'You're not the Clinton Smiths, you're Sarah Miles!'

I got out of the car. 'We would very much like to look over—'

'But I'm expecting the Clinton Smiths in five minutes.'

'Five minutes is all I need!' replied Robert, climbing determinedly out of his Range Rover and hobbling at speed across the lawn to the front door.

We had been house-hunting on and off for three years and didn't care where we lived as long as the combination of genuine countryside, old, unspoilt house, church, river and woodland were present, as in my vision. Here they were, as destined, yet there was nothing grand about the place, for that was the whole point.

Everything we had seen up till then had been done up like a dog's dinner and ruined, but Chithurst Manor had been spared. It was apparently the smallest manor in England, more of a cottage, really, an estate in miniature, with formal gardens, fruit trees, topiary, stableyard, lawns and croquet lawn. It was surrounded by pastures and wild areas of woodland and it had a unique sand-based spring that bubbles up eternal (it's in the Domesday Book).

'Your vision exactly.' Robert was thrilled to bits and made no bones about sharing his glee with the owners (*not* the way to strike a good deal!).

As it turned out, that same morning a Le Mans racing driver had offered almost double the asking price without even stepping out of his racy motor to mosey around inside and it wasn't even raining – just our luck. Again it was Robert who remained fearless all through the negotiations and phone calls that followed between lawyers. Me? I just sat there, dumbfounded at the prospect of such an expensive vision about to come true. A vision that never would have been realised without Robert Bolt's unwavering determination. Oh, to have his tenacity!

Wonders will never cease! I was offered a job in the theatre again! I had been convinced that Peter Hall had finished off my career for good, so I grabbed at the opportunity to appear in Pirandello's *Henry IV* with Richard Harris; I'd never met him.

This turned out another appalling career move, for I was unaware that Richard Harris had his own agenda, not to mention his own money in the production, enabling him to insult, even fire whom he pleased, causing chaos left, right and centre. He reminded me of a bedraggled old fox, still cunning enough to get into the pen and run amok, and with us poor chickens too terrified to notice he'd lost all his teeth. The whole episode was silly to a degree. With hindsight he was probably more scared than we were, having been away from the theatre for many years and in need of a hit – but, then, so were we all. The team work was non-existent, the team itself permeating fear and misery. Was my dream of being one of a group of artists determined to work together with trust, respect and loving kindness with the sole purpose of creating something truly worthwhile ever to be realised? Or was I to continue fighting on with a theatrical curse upon my head?

Ian Maxwell (son of Robert) and Paul Hamlyn were both keen to buy Sussex House, but unfortunately neither would raise their bid so I was left to choose between them. I chose Hamlyn because he seemed more keen to preserve its beauty – a better caretaker for posterity. Attended by the usual hiccups, our house move into Chithurst Manor slid into the pre-London tour of *Henry IV*.

The Yvonne Arnaud Theatre in Guildford was our second to last stop before the West End. It was here that Richard Harris decided to fire our director, David Thacker. All during the run he had been abusing power, insulting or firing – or both various backstage members of the team who had no come-back. I bit my tongue while turning the other cheek (having learnt a recent lesson!). But David Thacker was the last straw. He had been doing a magnificent job under impossible conditions and the events that led up to his dismissal were so ludicrously childish that I felt I could no longer arse-lick and fence straddle just to keep the peace. I gathered up my strength and knocked calmly on Richard's dressing-room door.

'Richard, either you reinstate David Thacker or I'm walking.'

He laughed uproariously. 'You can't fuckin' walk, you're under fuckin' contract!'

'Just watch me!' I went back to my dressing room packed my bags and told both the stage manager and my understudy I was off. The latter, naturally, was thrilled to bits as she took her first whiff of 'big break'.

Richard got a whiff too and came to the stage door. 'You'll never work again!' He could be vindictive when it suited him.

'Old news, old chap.'

I got a doctor's certificate to say I was heading for a nervous break-down and that was that. My conscience was clear, so once more I was free as a bird.

At last I was able to inhale the essence of Chithurst Manor, my new home. A fine mature walnut tree was lying flat on its side. The previous owners apologised for they had not found time to take it away. I had various tree surgeons look at it, and they agreed there was no hope because the tap root had snapped. As usual, I refused to agree with the general consensus.

One day a local chap, who was putting in some cold frames for us, claimed that with a winch, pulley and patience all was possible. Over a period of seven days, slowly and surely he gave that walnut back its dignity. Just like Robert after his stroke, the walnut stood proud and straight again. A miracle! It came into my daily meditation as a two-fold symbol: first it was the sign for us being at Chithurst at all, but more importantly it became the symbol for Robert's personal miracle, his determination, strength and endurance.

Chithurst Manor sits in a valley next to a Theravadian Buddhist monastery. Shortly after discovering this I spied a wonderfully fat Buddha in Portobello market sitting in the lotus position. His stomach reminded me so much of Robert's that I had no choice but to buy him as a Christmas present. Three days later Robert received a fax from a Ronnie Colson in Tokyo, inquiring into his availability. It transpired that he wanted him to write the life story of Buddha.

Soon after we arrived at Chithurst Manor, Cuckoo gave birth to six puppies, purely so that I could keep my promise to Athene Seyler and deliver her a Yorkshire terrier just like Cuckoo. Mission accomplished and Athene was ecstatic. I named the boy pup Peewit, and he turned out a real winner, giving Athene hours and hours of fun and games –

215

just what the doctor and loneliness had ordered. I'm sure Athene lived those extra fifteen months because of Peewit, but finally her dream came true and she was reunited with her husband at the grand old age of almost 102. She died in peace in her own bed.

I had prayed for one Yorkshire pup to have a floppy ear and for the other to be tiny. Unexpectedly both these prayers were granted, so we had to keep them both. Robert wanted the boy so we called him Oxton (Robert's second name). The little bitch I christened Batty because of her acutely pointed ears, her love of high places and because she was as batty as a fruit cake. As time went by, however, Robert showed little interest in his poor little Oxton. 'I want a *big* dog!' he kept repeating, and after witnessing poor Oxton hunched up with the mother of all inferiority complexes, I decided that something had to be done.

In the early sixties when Robert and I were courting, we paid a visit to Crufts. Walking up one of the aisles we observed a gigantic, solid ripple of muscle shimmering along a conker-coloured back.

'He's massive! What kind of dog is that?' I had never seen Robert, a Staffordshire-bull-terrier man, so impressed. Just at that moment a woman's booming upper-class voice ran out from behind us: 'Henry!' Henry proceeded to turn his Goliath head slowly in our direction and that did it for of us.

'We'll buy us a Henry one day – eh?' said Robert, giving me a kiss.

I swear Cuckoo understood my telephone call because from the moment I agreed to drive up to Bedfordshire to choose an old English mastiff from a litter of seven, she put her head to the wall and never recovered. It was difficult to choose the right pup because the one my heart went out to was a seductive Jersey cow creamy colour with black tips and two Margaret Lockwood beauty spots on her cheeks. I knew that mere colour mustn't be a factor, so I studied the litter of seven for several hours. I believe Beauty Spots knew she was the chosen one because she sat there staring at me. When the food appeared, all the other puppies ran to guzzle, but Beauty Spots continued to moon over me.

She seemed to know about cars, even though she was only two months old and had never set foot in one. There she lay, like Cleopatra, all the way back to Sussex, as if she had been waiting for this very ride since birth. Cuckoo's nose was severely out of joint and she refused to acknowledge the mastiff's presence in the car. I had timed this escapade around one of Robert's trips to Bibendum, his favourite London watering-hole so on returning home I furtively introduced Beauty Spots, who at two months old was the size of a Labrador, to Batty and Oxton, who immediately wanted to mount her, before taking her for a wee walk across the fields to meet Bob and Margaret who have more dogs than we have mole hills on our lawns.

Bob and Margaret Collins are my closest friends in the neighbourhood and over the years at Chithurst I've watched their small-holding, the gift of a large field and some derelict out-buildings from the local land-owner, flourish in the way farms were always meant to. Beauty Spots went potty meeting all the pigs, goats, ponies, sheep, dogs, cats, chickens, cockerels, geese, rabbits, guinea pigs, turkeys, even a fox at one time, all living together as one large harmonious family. Bob kills his chickens with consideration and schoolchildren come to see where their meat and milk come from returning home more enlightened for most of them haven't a clue before their trip to the countryside.

The only black cloud hanging over their paradise is that the local council has told them they can no longer sleep on the premises at night. Obviously this they need to do because of the danger of foxes and the like. The irony is, they don't *want* to build, they simply want to remain living in the glorified chicken hutch that has been their home for the past five years. Do we have to witness all smallholdings being swallowed up by the brutal anti-nature methods of the agricultural industrialist? Chithurst without Bob and Margaret just wouldn't be the same.

When Robert finally entered his bedroom and saw Beauty Spots lying on the pillow, all soft and squashy, I realised how much a big dog really mattered to him. His eyes welled up with devotion and their relationship was one of the most bonded, loyal and loving that I have ever witnessed.

'What shall we call her?' Because Robert found speaking so hard it came down to one of the two words he could say off pat with no hassle. Fuckinghell or Lovely. For obvious reasons we plumped for the latter.

I am convinced of one thing in this vastly complex business called living: finding Lovely for Robert was the best move I ever made. It's good to know I did something right. One thing is all you need.

Religions with no Divisions

The first time I met the local parish was at the yearly carol-singing that first Christmas. They seemed a friendly lot and the ritual ended up, as it did every year, at the Manor for punch, garlic bread and goodwill. What puzzled me was why our little band of carol-singers didn't go and sing to my neighbours, the Buddhist monks and nuns up at the monastery, who were also part of the community. They had made it perfectly clear how welcome the carol-singers would be, if they cared to come.

Over punch that first Christmas I asked the vicar why the parish was unwilling to share some Christmas joy with the monastery. He eyed me suspiciously, then stiffly replied, 'We never thought it would be appropriate.' It was obvious that he found my inquiry indelicate, so I dropped it – but not before saying, 'It isn't normal procedure to knock on every door before carol-singing to enquire whether the occupants be Church of England, Jewish or Muslim, is it?' Someone offered him some more garlic bread and he grabbed at his escape hatch. And that was that – for the moment!

I see all religions as different colours of the same rainbow beaming down from one original truth. Putting my money where my mouth is, I made it my mission to bring the parish and the monastery together in some kind of harmony – or if not that, then at least an understanding. It was essential for us at the Manor: St Mary's church is in our garden and the monastery is right next door. If these two faiths were not on good terms with each other, it's we at the Manor who would suffer. My fondness for the parish equalled my fondness for the monastery folk, so living sandwiched between suspicious, fractious, sometimes negative energies was not going to be acceptable over the long haul. I saw it as the world's troubles in microcosm. If harmony between faiths is not possible in one's own community, what hope in hell is there for the world to find any?

My mission entailed spending the next year wooing the parish and giving myself a higher profile locally than I would have wished in order for them to trust me sufficiently to bring about this new understanding. When members of the parish asked my feelings about having the monastery on my doorstep, I would suggest that Buddhism is not against Christianity, nor is it a religion as such, but more a 'way', a philosophy for living life. I am not a Buddhist, for I believe in capturing the 'sameness' of every religion rather than dwelling endlessly on the rather old-fashioned – to my mind – differences.

Yippee! I had made some inroads! By the next Christmas it had been arranged: the parish was prepared to sing to the monks and nuns. Needless to say, they were delighted. On the night everything went swimmingly. I hadn't dared hope for such an abundance of goodwill. There we stood, the parish, monks and nuns in their ideal hall, with the acoustics manipulating our voices into sounding angelic, even professional – apart from the tell-tale excess of emotion that occasionally leaked forth. Indeed, a few stray tears were shed. As the parish walked back across the meadow to the Manor that night they were high as a kite on cloud nine, even before the punch! But, then, there's nothing like cloud nine for those who know they have just accomplished a good deed.

The following Christmas I rang a few days before carol-singing to ask the approximate numbers to cater for. The vicar was most pleasant and just as I was about to hang up, he added, 'Oh, and by the way, we won't be singing to the monks this year.'

'Why is that?' I was as nonplussed as he was embarrassed, for he spluttered and went many times around the mulberry bush.

'But it was such a fine uplifting occasion.'

'No doubt, no doubt. But it ricocheted around the country.'

'Good news tends to.'

'But it reached the Bishop's ears.'

'Oh! The Bishop heard about it, too, did he? Good!'

There was silence at the other end.

' 'Fraid not.'

Between the lines I gathered that a talk with the Bishop was in order. 'Can I have the Bishop's number, please?'

'What?' He didn't want to give it to me.

'The Bishop's number, please.' With a sigh of resignation he went and got it.

When I telephoned the Bishop, his fair lady wife answered.

'I am a member of the flock who has a conundrum and needs urgently to talk it through with the Bishop.'

'If the Bishop was to talk through all the flock's conundrums he'd have no time for serious matters.' I could tell I wasn't going to get anywhere with this formidable woman. 'I suggest you talk it through with your local vicar. That's what he's there for.'

'It was he who gave me your number.' However many different approaches I made, she squashed them all very neatly until she won – game, set and match.

I went into Robert's study to share my failure with him. He was in the midst of juggling two projects at once, one film on the life of the Buddha and another on Scott and Amundsen and their race to the North Pole. The producer was our old friend John Heyman, who had produced *The Servant* and *Steaming*. Recently John had spoiled us rotten by inviting us to share his splendid home in the Bahamas.

'I couldn't get past the Bishop's wife.'

'Did you tell her who you were?' I had a problem with using my name to get special treatment but Robert had never shared my diffidence – like an arrow he was, straight for the jugular when he wanted something.

'It won't make any difference.'

'Make a bet?'

His bet was easily won. I spilled out both our names and the Bishop's lady wife turned into oozing putty in my hand.

'Of course! What about Thursday at four?'

At the appointed hour, Robert, dapper as usual, Margaret, my friend up the road at the farm, and I, dressed up all posh for a change, knocked on the Bishop's door. His wife was, indeed, as I had visualised her, huge and formidable – celebrities her only weakness obviously.

'Please wait here a moment,' she simpered sweetly while backing out.

The house was old, musty and tired. 'The Bishop will see you now.' The house wasn't a patch on the Bishop: a tall, spidery gentleman, sitting cross-legged in the far corner of his Edwardian sitting room, twitching his crossed foot like there was no tomorrow.

'Please sit down.' We obeyed while his lady wife brought in tea and biscuits on a trolley. 'What can I do for you?' I had assumed that the vicar had briefed him. Not at all – or had he? I told him the story anyway.

'It has nothing to do with me.'

Then Robert piped up, 'You mean they can sing to the Buddhists this Christmas, after all?'

'It isn't for me to give you permission. It is a local matter between you and your vicar.'

'But the vicar said that you got to hear of last year's carol-singing and—'

'Did he?'

'Did you?' asked Robert gently.

'I didn't.'

Robert went on slowly and thoughtfully, 'If you had, how would you have reacted?'

'I've already said, it's a local matter.'

Margaret, ponging of sheep and cockerels, piped up, 'Do you dislike Buddhists?'

'I don't make judgements. We are all God's children.'

Margaret held on like a terrier. 'In that case could we have a letter from you, sir, stating that as far as you are concerned it is OK to sing to the monks?'

'I'm in no position to write such a letter...'

As I watched his twitching foot speed off to Timbuktu and back, I realised that fence-straddling was an exhausting occupation. I gave him my best last shot. 'Our request isn't harmful in any way, is it? Please help us.'

'I never interfere with local parish matters.'

The journey home was a sad affair.

'Good God!' Robert shook his head. 'No wonder the world's gone mad!'

P.S. Eight years have passed and I'm still in there, fighting. By Christmas ... who knows?

In 1989, on 11 July – my brother Chuzzer's birthday – Laurence Olivier moved on. I read about it in the newspapers.

'You must attend his memorial service,' said Robert.

'It wouldn't be right.' I went and sat at my shrine. I needed to quieten my tumultuous emotions, but first I gave them full permission to go haywire for a while. Later, analysing them with detachment (Yes! There are *some* pluses for putting years into this ludicrous meditation lark!), I was astonished to discover that most of the inner turmoil was down to 'if onlys'. Lionel and I had given each other glimpses of great happiness over three decades, but my timing, as usual, had been up the spout: we met a year too late. Yet love him and honour him I always will. Maybe one day, while I'm sitting at my shrine, he will poke through those other realms and dazzle me once more while I'm reflecting upon his wicked and relentless daring. Quite dazzling.

Robert was still working on the film of the Buddha and had started the second draft of the Scott and Amundsen project, now called *The Tortoise and the Hare*, as well as secretly writing the first draft of *Galileo* for Joey Fury, who is married to my old American friend Lee Grant. How brilliant he was at juggling his various deadlines! No one ever suspected he was playing off all three against the middle. Within his light-hearted openness there sat a devious dark horse.

He struggled for three years with the Buddha script while we attended seminar after seminar with Tibetan lamas and experts from all over the world. When it came to script-writing, Robert's humility and patience with so many experts, who all thought they knew best, was a real eye-opener for me. The lamas were keen to turn Buddha into something of the order of a saint but Robert was hell bent on finding the man. Saints are difficult for us mere mortals to relate to – and especially cinema-going mortals.

While we were attending a seminar in the Tibetan colony in the French Dordogne, a Tibetan lama called Tulka Pema Wangyal Rinpoche, who was the chief, showed me his sacred scrapbook full of great Tibetan spiritual leaders of the last century. Most of them were dead, but then a photograph jumped off the page at me.

'Who's that?'

'Kense Rinpoche.' Until then – thanks perhaps to the voice – I had never been interested in gurus, but this Rinpoche was different. Besides, he wasn't a guru at all. What got me was the formidable sparkle in his wise old eyes, a refusal to take himself or the world too seriously. How they beckoned!

'Is he dead or alive?'

'Alive in Kathmandu. He's the Dalai Lama's teacher.' The lama, Tulka Pema, then showed me a picture of the Dalai Lama lying prostrate on the floor at the feet of Kense Rinpoche.

A week later I was back at Bodhnath, at the very same *stupa* where I'd caught dysentery from the prayer wheel five years earlier. I caught myself touching my magic ring: how my life had changed over the past five years! Robert was fit and pretty much firing on all cylinders once more; Tomcat was still clean, earning his own living and loving every minute of it. There had been no recent theatre work to get chucked out of! Chithurst Manor, my childhood vision, was growing into my very soul. Wow! Peace at last! Steady, Sarah. In times of abundance always remember the famine.

Kense Rinpoche's monastery was right there beside the *stupa*. Living accommodation was both bleak and tough: one small cement room with a mattress on the floor, a tiny table with mosquito coils to keep the majority at bay, a candle and nothing else.

I sat in the temple all day, from eight till six, leaving only to relieve myself. Kense Rinpoche was exceptional for a Tibetan: he was over six and a half feet tall and hugely muscular. This irresistible great bear would sit silently in temple, his face changing all the time. I thought I was imagining the extraordinary phenomenon taking place before my eyes until I received confirmation that it was actually happening. He manifested into other beings. Was he sliding through his many lives as he transformed into a Red Indian, into a French prostitute, a Chinese mandarin and a Zulu warrior?

By candlelight each morning before temple I made a list of questions I wanted answered in Kense's private chamber after temple in the evening, but each day every question was answered in the silence, the prayers and the chanting of temple. I stayed there for three weeks. They were tough, fiercely disciplined days, but I wouldn't have missed them for the world.

I flew home having learnt a few sacred tips on a spiritual level, and realised that sharing them with Robert would be a tremendous challenge. Spiritual experiences brought down to the level of talk sound horribly clichéd, scuffed up and New Age. Even the word 'spiritual' grimes up the purity of essence to be found in the power of silence. Perhaps that is what God intended. No talk of these matters, just daily action, discipline and awareness. I needed to leave my experiences untampered with.

But Robert was curious. 'Give me some clue as to *something* you learnt.'

I tried hard: 'He enabled me to touch upon the limitless capacity for inner contentment found in reverence and devotion.'

Robert cocked me a wry look. 'He was worth all that, was he?'

'That and much more.' I went on to describe Kense Rinpoche. 'He was the jolly, gentle giant. An over eighty-year-old Sumo wrestler, with hands and feet as young, unworn and untouched as a newborn baby's.'

'Obviously never had to do the washing up.'

I couldn't recall Robert ever washing up before his stroke. Was he jealous?

'He simply sat in service for those who happened to need him.'

Kense died in 1991. I had been lucky to catch him. The Tibetan lamas and Buddhists in India, Nepal and Bhutan revere him as one of the most evolved beings of all. It's easy to see why the Dalai Lama chose Kense Rinpoche as his teacher, for he was truly the Master of Masters, the Holiest of Holies.

Charlemagne and the Black Madonna

My first play, *Charlemagne*, a three-hander, had its initiation at the Fire Station, Oxford. The plot I took from life: it had happened to Sally, one of my oldest and closest friends. She married while I was in LA and only on my return did I meet her husband and three-year-old son, Matthew. On the surface they seemed a happy family and I liked my old friend's new husband, the actor Barry Warren, a lot.

Gradually, though, the plot thickened and clues began to appear, suggesting that something was rotten in the state of Denmark. For example: Sally discovered that bits of her underwear were missing. Barry, so he claimed, was a transvestite. Sally loved him greatly and was able to embrace this as long as Barry kept it in the bedroom and away from Matthew, for what harm could dressing up as a woman do? He wasn't being unfaithful, was he?

Then, one evening after supper while we were still at Sussex House, I went down to join Barry and Matthew in the Jacuzzi. Even though the lighting was subdued, I couldn't help but notice Barry's breasts bobbing above the waterline. I realised he was perhaps hoodwinking Sally with his transvestite tale. Later, he explained his predicament and I became the go-between.

Barry's life had been lived in the wrong body. His first memories were of a deep yearning to wear his elder sister's Brownie uniform. It seemed that his whole tragic life had been spent agonising. Could he pluck up the courage to become his true identity – a woman? No. He continued to suppress the truth by marrying twice and producing three boys, praying that the yearning to be a woman would go into remission or disappear altogether.

Barry's only sin had been to keep secret his true desire to become a woman.

'What choice did I have? Sally wouldn't have married me if she had known my true needs. Besides, I was convinced our love could overcome all things – even that.' It seemed he loved Sally so much he wanted to *be* her. Gender realignment is a soul matter *and* a gender matter; the sexual part is peripheral to the more urgent need simply to *be* a woman, and to be accepted as such.

After Barry had finally mustered the courage to make the change (on the NHS there is a two-year wait), he went to live in Menorca for a while: his mother, Lilian, now in her nineties, took it all in her stride, her love never faltering. It was when Sally went out with Matthew to meet 'Clare' for the first time that Matthew, aged six, tossed his classic line at her: 'Don't forget to call Daddy Clare, will you, Mummy?' Both parents were wonderful with Matthew, for they were as open and understanding as it was possible to be, turning Matthew into a lovely man, centred and strong.

Eventually Clare came to live fairly close to Chithurst on a houseboat in Chichester harbour. She was forced to invent a whole new past life because the majority in England would never have accepted Barry Warren as the women he now was. I mentioned to Robert that he – she – was living close by. 'Barry is now Clare, Robert, and she's coming round this afternoon.'

'Oh no she isn't!' exclaimed a somewhat threatened Robert.

'Why?'

'I'm not having him – *her* – whatever – in my house!'

'But you liked her as Barry. She's coming for tea anyway.'

'Over my dead body!'

Robert's reaction resembled that of the typical chauvinistic British male, who through ignorance rather than prejudice considered Barry's journey to be sexual kinkiness. He remained adamant therefore that Clare be denied her visit to Chithurst. So I planned it for when Robert was already in bed and unable to make a run for it. In I barged with Clare.

'Robert, meet Clare.' Robert went puce in the face and refused to look her in the eye, so embarrassed was he at finding himself trapped.

'Hello, Robert,' said a happy, golden Clare. How she suited her newly acquired femininity! What had once been angular, strained and anxious was now peaceful, integrated and wholesome. The best part of Robert's blinkered vision was his ability to change his mind, which stems from an innate humility and lack of ego. Within no time he and Clare were inseparable. Clare came to work at Chithurst as Robert's secretary and a finer team you couldn't have hoped to find but, then, anyone of sound mind would have felt the same.

During my research I found out that many who make 'the change' return to their original spouse, not out of compromise but out of a sense of familiarity, continuity and belonging, oblivious of how the sexual bits and bobs have altered. Jan Morris was a typical example of this, an exceptionally talented travel writer with a great following as James Morris. After the change she returned to Wales, her wife and family. She still writes, better than ever, because she has the freedom now to be who she always was. Also, the family unit is back together again.

Transsexuals, having been to hell and back, acquire an infectious openness, a non-judgemental attitude towards life that should be a lesson to us all. In this respect they are, perhaps, similar to ex-junkies: both have had to face their own devils head-on – and how many of us have the guts to do that? Sally remained as loyal to Clare as she was capable of being under infinitely difficult circumstances and it was a relief to witness them draw gradually closer again. If Clare hadn't died of cancer, after five years of feminine bliss, I believe she and Sally would have come back together again.

Why – apart from my *Charlemagne* painting – did I call my first play *Charlemagne*? There was, indeed, a valuable racehorse in the play called Charlemagne but I also thought King Charlemagne, having been a great and just ruler, conquering and uniting Europe, those realms *without*, resonated perfectly with what Harry, my play's hero, was striving for in his attempts at uniting and conquering the darker realms *within*.

For me, Sally and Barry's tale is the perfect peg on which to hang a play, the theme of unconditional love. Because I had witnessed the whole painful business at such close quarters, I felt the need to undo in my own way some of the harmful PR these folk are up against. Plays and films based on transvestites or transsexuals have been shallow and exploitive, with writers using their predicament as a platform for cheap laughs. In mocking them they spread ignorance, whereas the true drama lies in finding compassion for the hell they have to go through to acknowledge their true identity.

The lead was played brilliantly by Greg Hicks, I played his wife, Clara, and Lilibet, Clara's best friend, was played by Lindy Alexander. Lisa Forrel directed and I produced.

Lesson number one: never act in a play you've written yourself. Direct it, by all means, but don't act in it. Why? Because as a fellow actor you cannot assist with guiding the other actors towards the playwright's intentions, for it would be crassly insensitive to splinter up the team spirit to demonstrate the play's rhythms, humour or interpretation. If I had worn only the writer's cap I could have done all that and much more.

Lesson number two: never, ever open a new play in the same week as the general election! We opened on 7 April 1992 and of course, were eclipsed. When I had booked the Fire Station, which you have to do months in advance, the general election had been predicted for a different week altogether.

Some believe everything in life is luck and timing. I would agree with that – except what *is* 'luck'? Is it God's blessing? Is it karma? Are they one and the same? Or is it fluke? Judging by those who have good luck in abundance, the latter seems the most credible. But, then, our ability to see the whole picture while we are still alive is sublimely limited.

Timing is something else altogether. In April 1992 England wasn't sufficiently aware or, indeed, open-hearted to accept transsexuals. It was fascinating to read the reviews for from them one could deduce which critics were straight, gay or closet gays – the latter were unable to respond with any detachment.

Driving home on Good Friday after the first night I looked up and saw the full moon. It told me quite clearly that I was about to be crucified. It was as plain as the nose on my face. I said as much to Robert.

'Nonsense!' Robert had seen the Saturday night preview and had been overjoyed, not only by the play's construction but by the audience's response – they had even laughed in the right places. 'There's no way you can be hurt this time.'

How wrong he was! There was a way, all right. It was the critic of the *Daily Telegraph* who found a way and crucified me. The play works, even though I say so myself, so he could attack only the subject matter or yours truly. With the latter he had a field day. He pissed all over me, even down to dredging up my tired-out old pee-drinking yet again.

Neither Robert nor I had ever read a review like it. It obviously made him feel so good that he referred back to it for months, and finally crowned it the worst play of the year.

It amused me to discover that homosexuals are another biased group. I know this because I've seen their bigotry in action, often making the poor transsexual's life a complete misery. They feel hugely threatened by anyone wanting to chop off that 'thing' of worship. Why, oh, why does lack of understanding create so much hatred? In parts of India and Eastern Asia the eunuch is worshipped in temples as a god/goddess, and placed way above mere mortals.

The other reviews were good to excellent and the audience's word-of-mouth grew like Jack's beanstalk, once the election was over. The play demands that you take note of your own sexual hang-ups and audiences were dead keen to talk them over in the bar afterwards – I could have taken counselling sessions every night! I didn't push for a West End venue because with a three-hander it's imperative that the chemistry of the cast gels immaculately, which in this case it didn't. No one was to blame: it was just the wrong chemistry.

The word-of-mouth was such that I was asked to put *Charlemagne* on in LA last year, where it received some terrific reviews, and because California's level of transsexual awareness is streets ahead of our own, it was a much less tense affair, with the audiences far more hip to the wit and the play's message.

I hadn't been back to LA for fifteen years, and I was only there for three weeks. As it turned out, the O. J. Simpson saga unfolded before my eyes. Wouldn't it just! Because he failed to appear at the courthouse that first morning, LA's streets were deserted as we all remained transfixed to our TVs. When we were informed that he was a fugitive from justice, I prayed he had either had plastic surgery and fled to South America or had found the dignity to blow his brains out. A kinder scenario, surely, for the children and surely preferable to the grotesque circus that followed.

Later, when he was discovered cruising along the freeway in his white Bronco, I found it difficult to comprehend that the man I had had dinner with at Alice's Restaurant, albeit over twenty years previously, had been capable of murder. Drivers actually stopped their cars on the freeway to cheer him on. The city was putting its hero above good and evil.

Why had I had dinner with O. J.? My agent asked me if O. J. could take me out to dinner because he was a great fan of *Ryan's Daughter*. I said I wasn't into blind dates but Tomcat was most certainly into O. J., 'The Juice', and – I have already established Tomcat's enormous talent for getting what he wants – I was made to telephone back and acquiesce. The Juice behaved like a real gentleman all evening, and was particularly attentive to his smaller fan. After an easy evening, he saw me to the door, said goodnight elegantly and that was that.

Four nights after the white Bronco fiasco I was at a dinner party where, naturally enough, the table was abuzz with the latest O. J. gossip. That is, until the chap sitting on my right boomed a great velvety bellowing, the kind that only comes from years of being comfortable with authority. 'Hush, all of you, he hasn't been proven guilty!' Hush is what we did, for the velvety booming came from Sidney Poitier, renowned for his patient, gentle nature. The intensity of his passion at that moment made me understand just how significant the whole saga would turn out to be: a parable of almost mythic proportions.

Later that evening, Sidney told me he had just returned from visiting Burt Lancaster, who had suffered a stroke similar to Robert's, but in Burt's case he had to be carried everywhere and was unable to talk at all – yet nobody knew. Are strokes considered *that* shameful?

Just before we left Sussex House I answered the phone to David Lean. He hadn't been in touch once since Robert's stroke. But, then, Robert hadn't been expecting any compassion from him because he knew damn well that David's friendships were based on *use*, and Robert hadn't been any *use* to David of late.

'Come on, Sarah – is he physically capable of working with me again?'

'Ask Puttnam, not me.' Robert had done a screenplay for the loyal David Puttnam. It was called *The Brady Story* and told of how Reagan's aide-de-camp, James Brady, had had a severe stroke after a bullet wound in the head that had been meant for Reagan. Robert was up for an Emmy award.

'But I'm asking you, Sarah.'

It's a useless occupation listening to the wife waxing lyrical. 'Ask him.' Robert delivered such a look of hope when I told him David was on the phone.

So it was that, after a gap of twelve years, they began working together in earnest. The project was David's beloved *Nostromo* and Robert's whole body language began to glow with a new *raison d'être*. All that patience, hard work and sweat was about to reap well-deserved dividends. How satisfying it was to witness their great collaboration back in business again. Things were looking up for the Bolts!

David had bought two warehouses in Narrow Street near Tower Bridge, knocked one down and turned the site into a beautiful river garden. The other warehouse he transformed into one of the most splendid houses I'd ever been in. That was because he had finally split up from Sandy Holtz, the almost child he abducted from Agra over twenty years before, and was now married to another Sandy. This new Sandy, whom he met in Harrods, was a clever interior designer. Each room faced the river, creating a haven of silence, maintained even with the endless din of traffic from Narrow Street by the mammoth thickness of the streetside walls.

Robert and I became regular visitors. With Robert positively thriving on his new companionship and workload, I felt able to nip off to Poland and make a little money of my own. The film was *The Touch* with Max von Sydow. I knew it wasn't going to move mountains, but its simple tale of creativity fighting for the light in the dying embers of genius reminded me in some ways of Robert.

I remember walking the streets of Warsaw on one historic day: It was the first time for over fifty years that the Poles had been allowed to vote. The rain was falling in a deluge, but even so I hadn't expected the turnout to be so mingy. Why no Poles to the polls? Upon enquiring I was told that the Poles weren't fools and no one could pull the wool over their eyes. They knew that politics is all a con, even though they had only just started on the road to democratic reform.

Though it suffers from the worst pollution in Europe, Krakow is a truly stunning ancient city in the central European tradition. On my arrival by train I was struck by the yellow complexions of the locals as well as a yellow smog above the town itself. I found them a wise and benevolent Catholic people, obsessed with nicotine, cakes and coffee.

On another relentlessly rainy day in Krakow, I took my umbrella to

Auschwitz. As the guide spoke on, detailing the horrors, the stench of torture welled up beneath my sodden footsteps and the silent screams of the dead jolted me into recognising the potential for evil within my own psyche. It was most shocking indeed. Just as I believe that all young teenagers, in order to make an informed choice regarding meat-eating should be taken to an abattoir, so too should they be taken to Auschwitz for completely different reasons. That way they would be able to identify with, feel compassion for, then mourn the victims of anti-Semitism – racism. Just as important, too, is to recognise, then access that same potential for evil within themselves. For only by acknowledging the nasty little Nazi sitting, albeit temporarily dormant, within each and every one of us, can we ever move on to a more enlightened, even humane state.

This was made even more apparent when I arrived back at my hotel in Warsaw. I was sitting in the lobby waiting for a friend to arrive when a bunch of German students strolled in with knapsacks. Was it any wonder that their glossy skins, rude with dazzling health, took my eye, when set against the chain-smoking Poles all grey by comparison? I asked the prettiest German in the group (now treading on my toes), 'Are you all off to Auschwitz?'

Her unashamed vacancy impressed me. 'Where?'

'Auschwitz,' I repeated slowly. She gazed at me a while longer before turning to a somewhat overly muscular young man. 'What is Auschwitz?'

He shrugged.

I thought I'd press home. 'Has anyone among you heard of Auschwitz?'

One tall, studious young woman peered at me over her specs. 'I know something of that. It isn't in our history books because it is all propaganda—'

'It *is* in our history books!' topped another.

'Briefly!' argued a third. Auschwitz tickled their imagination sufficiently for one young man to ask what I had encountered there. When I got to describing the mountains of soft golden baby curls still lying there ready to be made into Nazis' mistresses' mattresses, the studious girl in the specs began the first steps towards the dispersion that followed. The tail end of knapsacks turned back, eyeing me with disbelief. You can't win 'em all.

On my way back to Warsaw from Krakow I stopped off half-way to pay homage to the famous icon of the Black Madonna of Jasna Gora. She always has a piece of my heart because her so sad eyes seem to mirror the suffering of the world. Her remembrance day is the same as Robert's birthday, 15 August, when literally thousands of people make pilgrimage to her chapel, which is lined with fishermen's netting in which those who experience miracles have left offerings. This is a brilliant idea because the whole chapel glistens with rosaries, crutches and a mass of sparkling jewels of gratitude.

I was driven the five-hour journey by Jatzec, my driver. In the back sat my hairdresser and makeup artist, Greschna, and my interpreter, Anna. Just my luck! We went all the way to the chapel in a rainstorm to find the Madonna covered up! I took a half-hearted snapshot of the empty aisle before deciding to wait the two hours before the icon was to be uncovered. Later, when I had the roll of film developed, it was to see a ghost kneeling at the altar, a tiny bride in lace waiting to be blessed.

The long vigil was worth it: sitting in the aisle of the Black Madonna's chapel, staring up into those eyes of ultimate sadness, was an experience unlike any other I'd had. It must have been unique because I was astonished when Jatzec whispered in my ear, 'It's seven o'clock. We must return to Warsaw – you have an early call in the morning.' How could *four hours* have vanished just like that? It was an immensely seductive timelessness.

We were back in the car, speeding along the three-lane motorway towards Warsaw at roughly seventy miles per hour. The downpour was as heavy as the night was black. Do Poles ever dim their headlights? Yet I remained unperturbed, so full of wonder was I at the Black Madonna.

'Why so much traffic tonight, Jatzec?' He turned to look at me as the truck in front of us came out with no warning. By the time he turned back it was too late. He slapped his foot on the brake putting us into a spin and dramatically speeding up the vehicle. The two girls in the back were silent. Strapped in the front seat in the lotus position, I became aware of the inevitable and it didn't frighten me in the least. The car shot diagonally across the central barrier into the oncoming traffic. At that moment Jatzec turned to me as if to say, 'How come you've got hold of the controls?' I had to admit I thought he had them, for sure as hell someone had!

In slow motion the car proceeded to dodge every truck and everything else on our journey across the motorway. We came to a most sedate full stop on the only piece of grass verge between there and Warsaw. Silence – until my Greschna whispered, 'It was the Black Madonna!' Next was Anna's turn. She was related to the Polish royal family and the loss of most of her relations in the war had turned her into an atheist. Her voice was uncommonly low. 'I now believe in God.'

After that the four of us met up in the evening, lit candles and gave thanks to the Black Madonna. We couldn't share our tale because Jatzec would have got the sack. But to meet up and concentrate on our miracle brought us together in a way nothing else could.

Blowing for Joy

R obert had disliked being separated from me on my trip to Poland, although I had asked three ex-Buddhist nuns to live at Chithurst while I was away and take care of him. When I returned they were perplexed: apparently Robert's bright sun had gone and never shone again until I got back. 'He can't function – you are his life-force.' I didn't believe them. But I had second thoughts when I caught sight of my partner looking uncommonly down-hearted.

Since Robert's stroke I had acquired the habit of observing people's sideways, furtive glances towards the disabled, as if wondering what on earth the poor things were capable of getting up to – if anything – between the sheets. Let me tell you: lots!

Another reaction which bothered me is how often people praised me for giving up my life to take care of Robert. Codswallop! It was Robert who gave up his life to take care of me. I might have always been there (unless earning pennies), no more than a shout away, but Robert didn't *need* me. He dressed himself, showered himself, tied his own tie, uncorked his own bottles, put on his own socks and shoes, even cleaned them himself. It puzzled me why he would always look down first to check out a person's shoes when first introduced to them. I discovered it was down to his class and his era: 'You can always judge a person by his shoes.' Hence his desire to keep his spotless, for he *had* to see his face in them at all times. Just think of it – he did all this with only one hand and his teeth. He was once caught doing nearly a hundred miles an hour on a straight section of motorway, while on his mobile phone. Work that one out!

Tomcat was still a mighty clean machine and going from strength to strength. I was enormously grateful to him for becoming his own man, holding his head high while following his bliss. Nothing in life beats following your bliss. My father failed, for he never got to go down his 'Moon River' yet there was Tomcat, sailing down his every day of his new life. He had rekindled his childhood passion for watches and is currently trying to make a business out of it.

Robert's down-heartedness lingered longer than need be, though, because it was all interwoven with David Lean's sudden decline. Melvyn Bragg had recently completed a clever *South Bank Show* on David and Robert's *Nostromo* work-in-progress. It was a rare insight into the complexities of their relationship, most touchingly captured. After its showing, Robert's fan-mail quadrupled, for not only was it a most entertaining programme, winning a BAFTA award, but it also offered inspiration to other stroke victims.

Then, another Bolt from the Blue: David was diagnosed as having throat cancer. What made it more excruciatingly painful was that the cameras for *Nostromo* were ready to turn. The money and cast were there, and the brilliant John Box had even erected the sets at Pinewood Studios. 'Those sets, my best work ever.' He promptly cleared his throat, otherwise he would have cried down the telephone. What a great sorrow it all was.

As David was dying, both Robert and I were able to get closer to him. David regularly wafted off to India and as he wafted his accent transformed, taking a rather quaint Alec-Guinness-type Indian (-ish!) lilt to it. I couldn't help wondering whether the quantity of designer-death cocktails administered to him towards the end protected him from ever coming to terms with his final exit.

Am I wrong in thinking that final exits are of great significance? I cannot help but believe that the first meeting with one's unconscious, face to face as it were, propels one forward to meet the next adventure with a more alert readiness. Why is that important? Because 'out there', from what I have gathered from the dead, they seem almost impatient in their desire to move on to the next level, onwards to reach some unknown – to us – destination. I spoke of this to David, and although his gesture brushed such silliness aside, he said, 'Go on!' I ended up feeling an unexpected love for the man, and it interested me. I wasn't mistaking it for compassion. Why I felt this love, I'm not sure. Perhaps it was knowing that yet another giant oak had been felled.

Robert's desire to poop out conservatories wherever he went showed little sign of abating, and merely a year after moving into the Manor, he was ready for another poop.

'We'll get Chuzzer to build the conservatory to end all conservatories, eh?' he said, kissing me excitedly. So eager was he to have the biggest in the land that Chichester Council turned us down, but Chuzzer had known we were pushing it, so came in with altered drawings of a more modest, realistic proportion. We chose old English oak, for neither Robert nor I wanted the rainforests on our consciences. We were told it would be impossible to bend the oak into the tight curves required, but Chuzzer knew better, for with patience all is possible.

We used it for eating, resting, sleeping, meditating, entertaining, yogaing, chanting, praying, singing, rehearsing. It is a 'Room For All Seasons and Reasons' and would never have been built but for Robert. It was designed to the golden mean measurements creating a harmony, which gives everyone who steps into it feeling of contentment, even peace.

Three years later, my old friend and music-maker Chad Stuart came to visit from America with his wife, Valerie. They fell under the spell of the conservatory's magic space. I lit the candles of my shrine and asked them if they wanted a cup of tea while we waited for Robert to wake.

They were about to park their bums in the kitchen when I suggested we return to the conservatory with our tea. 'I'm loath to leave candles unattended – Chithurst would flame up like a tinder-box.'

Later as evening fell, the wind got up. 'I'll go upstairs and see if Robert's awake.' I was unaware that Chad had followed me out to have a pee, or that Valerie had chosen to go out of the conservatory door into the windy garden.

Robert was awake. Suddenly we both heard a bloodcurdling scream. Running back downstairs I saw at the far end of the passage the conservatory aflame like Manderley. We all stood for a moment, trans-fixed, with Valerie still trying to get back in at the door through which she had gone out. I realised Robert was in danger for at the rate the fire was gathering momentum, the house would soon be enveloped. I returned to his bedside and told him to get out of the house – quick! He, as always, pushed aside any help. 'Get back downstairs – call the Fire Brigade!' He almost fell out of bed.

Downstairs Chad stood rooted by the power of fire. I learned later that fire does that: it mesmerises some of us into a trance. I screamed at him to call the Fire Brigade. I wasn't thinking too constructively either and began to fill the bread bin with water and toss it over the fire. I was barefoot but there was no time to find shoes, even though all the specially made double-glazing inner glass had fallen onto the ancient tiles of the conservatory floor. The plain muslin drapes were ablaze and catching the furniture fast. Chad called Andy, our gardener, and with superb teamwork we managed to keep the fire pretty well under control until the engines arrived.

The fireman looked at the glass scattered everywhere, then at my bare feet. 'You'd better see to those.' He picked up my foot and couldn't find a mark on it – on either of them. But what he found even more spooky was my shrine: the fire had failed to penetrate the objects on its surface. This was possibly because not many of them were wooden, so it wasn't until he glanced at a large cardboard photograph of Kense Rinpoche, the Dalai Lama's teacher, that he was truly astounded. 'He started it,' he muttered, gruff with incomprehension. All the surrounding wood and other photographs had been burnt to cinders, as did three years of Robert's sweat on the life of Buddha. Ronnie Colsen, the producer, gave it to Bertolucci to direct. For almost a year, he held onto the script, refusing to commit to it or turn it down, thus leaving us in limbo. He then made his own film, *Little Buddha* – and a lot of good it did him.

When I first arrived at Chithurst, I was given permission to walk in the monastery woods. They were overgrown and deeply mysterious, before the new Abbot tamed them, and ambling through them I would often see the same painfully skinny monk moving silently along.

We would sometimes pause by the lake and find nourishment from each other's silent presence. I would observe his whole being incandescent, skin translucent and eyes wide open with bliss. Sometimes I wondered how far I still had to travel to reach such a continual state of grace.

His name was Ajhan Kittisaro. Later I was to discover he thought he was dying of Crohn's disease and had chosen to do so alone and silently in the woods. But, like Gladys, he had been wrongly diagnosed. After his year of silent retreat he was able to bring back the gift of that experience and share it. I was bemused, shocked even, upon hearing his voice for the first time, a most definite Tennessee drawl, and even more shocked that his real name was Randy Weinberg – five-time mid-South wrestling champion.

I had made some good friends up at the monastery, some of whom had been coming round regularly for tea over the past three years: the Abbot, Ajhan Anando, Ajhan Kittisaro, Sister Thanissara, Sister Satima and other nuns and monks too. Our tea-time discussions were usually pretty stimulation affairs, yet sometimes I took it upon myself to play devil's advocate, taking Robert's point of view, which was that of a sceptic, cynic and atheist.

I met a wandering hippie Australian called Gary at a charity concert, where I sang a song I'd written specially for it, 'Listen to the Children'. At the last minute I got him to accompany one of my poems on his didgeridoo. We were a great hit that day. Gary played the biggest didgeridoo I'd ever seen and with it he'd grown into a pretty effective healer. I was interested to see how Robert would benefit from Gary's healing 'blows of joy'.

'Over my dead body!' Robert's reaction was identical to when I had first brought Clare into the house. I recalled my success with her and once again timed it for when he was trapped in bed.

'Robert, this is Gary.' Before he squirmed himself silly, I asked Gary to blow. As he blew down Robert's meridian lines on his didge, Robert slumped into a kind of deep trance. How fascinating it was to observe all resistance dripping off him. 'Oh!' he exclaimed ecstatically. 'More! More!'

Because it had such a beneficial effect on Robert, Gary asked if he could go and blow to the monks at the monastery. I explained that their branch of Buddhism was so austere that no music or musical instruments were allowed.

'Bullshit! Let's go!' So off we went.

We entered their shrine room. All the monks and nuns in the monastery, twenty-four at that time, were sitting in meditation, with the Abbot, Ajhan Anando, taking up centre-stage. Anando was a strikingly handsome American, dynamic, chisel-jawed; part of his head had been blown off in Vietnam. His heroism was made even more visible by his shaven skull, which revealed his impressive scarred dents where the bullet had entered and thankfully exited.

Dutiful monks and nuns as they were, their eyes remained lowered during their meditation, so they didn't see us enter. Except for the Abbot, who said, 'No musical instruments allowed in the shrine room.'

'This isn't a musical instrument. It's made by termites, not man.'

'Nevertheless—'

'Gary, play! As he did so they responded like Robert and within seconds every one sank into the same mesmeric trance. Later Gary commented that never had a group of people been so receptive. Perhaps regular meditation was the cause – and the lack of any music for years!

As we were leaving Ajhan Anando approached us. 'Could Gary come down to the nuns' cottage tomorrow evening?'

Six monks and four nuns were at the cottage the next evening and Gary gave five of those individual 'joy blows'. Standing over each of them in turn he blew along their meridian lines and chakras (energy points).

Over tea in the conservatory I found myself once again playing go-between for some of them as they confided their need to leave the monastic life and return to the world. I was closest to Ajhan Kittisaro and Sister Thanissara. They had both been revered in the monastery, and had hung in there for fifteen years. Was it before or after their joy blows that they had begun to see life differently? Certainly after the experience they allowed me to share their mutual falling in love, albeit only on the spiritual plain since no touching was permitted.

They returned to the world, fell in love on every plane, got married and now live in South Africa's Kwazulu Natal where some friend gave them their very own bit of mountain as a hermitage. Nearby they work as spiritual directors of a Buddhist retreat centre. How we missed them. The other nun who received a 'Gary special' also defrocked shortly afterwards, and is now married with two children.

The Abbot himself, Ajhan Anando, shocked everyone the following year by defrocking and marrying a laywoman. Out in the real world he seemed to revert to type, growing taller, sexy and laid-back. Sadly, though, he began getting head pains, and a year later died of a brain tumour, probably caused by his bullet wounds. I wonder if his tumour would have remained dormant in the peace of monastic life. Perhaps his return to *uncivilisation* had stimulated its growth.

Was it the effect of those joy blows that had caused four people out of five to defrock, one after the other? Had the change of energy within their systems been so remarkable that it somehow confused their logical mind? Or was it just time for them to move on? Who knows? One thing I do know is that few of us have any inkling about energy. We cannot *see* it. Rarely do we *feel* it, except on those mornings when we have none. Why, for no reason, do we have none some mornings and others, plenty? We cannot *hear* it or *touch* it and science cannot *monitor* it. Does that mean therefore it doesn't exist? I believe that sometime in the new millennium we will discover the workings and essence of energy.

Circling through Disbelief

Trash them if you wish, but corn circles are not all hoaxes, not by any stretch of the imagination. Other countries have the circles, but only England has the complicated pictograms, as they are called, in such prolific abundance. Wouldn't it be more appropriate to rejoice in them rather than disparage them through ignorance?

Summers in the English countryside from the South West through to Sussex are littered with their awesome, symmetrical skill. *How? Who* or *what* makes them? For me, the only question is *why?* And indeed why England? why so many pictograms in England alone? In esoteric language, we are moving through into the throat chakra of the planet, which is England, probably because the main sound, world-wide, is English. Esoteric or not, no one can deny that we are certainly squeezing through a bottleneck of chaos right now, throat chakra or no – wouldn't you say?

I discovered corn circles back in 1990 and from then on began to spend more time in the virgin ones (those that had just manifested and in which man has yet to tread), because within those, the energies are most powerful. These energies alter mysteriously: a few made me feel sick or gave me a headache while the majority filled me with such a sense of benevolent goodwill that I'd often arrive home high as a kite. Robert, unable to trample in the meadows, felt he was missing something. 'What the hell are you up to out in the fields all day?'

'Corn circles.'

'Rubbish! They're all hoaxers hoaxing.'

Where did Robert's hoaxers hang out? I wanted to kneel down in reverence before such miraculous handiwork! How, in God's name, can they produce such quality, such quantity? Who are they, these godlike hoaxers? And why are they never caught hoaxing? How can they

242

disobey time, space and logic with their purity of line, perfectly balanced symmetrical symbols?

Robert wasn't having any of it. 'It was on telly. It's only hoaxers hoaxing!'

'At least have the grace to *see* one before passing judgement.'

'How *can* I see one?'

Did I note a touch of sarcasm in his voice? 'Come up and see them from above.'

His size made it difficult to get Robert airborne, but the struggle turned out to be well worth while. Robert's so-called hoaxers design their phenomenal masterpieces from the sky's point of view, so it is best to view them from up there. Just as it is impossible to digest the full mastery of the White Horse at Uffington until you view it from above, so it is the same with corn circles.

'My God!' Robert's belief system was well and truly shaken up that day. He made vast transitions. Was he about to break free from the barriers of intellect and surrender with an open heart to the perfection of the shapes below? I certainly was!

Up there, above Avebury, Robert began to differentiate between the hoaxes, of which there are a few and which are crude by comparison with the real thing, the messy circles the wind makes, and the genuine article. By trampling over the fields it is possible to tell the difference more easily – but only if you catch a virgin circle. A natural patina surrounds each stem of corn and the hoaxers damage this delicate milky patina, scuffing and crushing it flat, or bruising it so that it fails to continue growing. The circles made by some other, mysterious intelligence seem to leave the corn caressed, untouched, the patina preserved. This caressing effect begins at right angles about six inches from the ground from which the stalks continue to grow unharmed. When I observe, at close quarters, the way in which the corn is gently laid clockwise and anti-clockwise, it always reminds me of a dextrous ethnic hair-dresser plaiting complicated rows. It's definitely a *caressing* as if by some compassionate force, so much more gently and succinctly able than human hoaxers could ever be.

Another worthwhile test – please be careful and take the farmer with you! – is to burn some stubble up-wind and watch the smoke travelling across towards the newly manifested circle. When it reaches the circle, the smoke cannot go through the transparent wall of the circle (energy),

243

so it wafts upwards, disappearing into the sky. The pictogram is only the tip of the iceberg, for the energy, as shown by the burning stubble, climbs up and up into the cosmos. (This experiment must be carried out on an at least near-virgin circle because the powerful energies gradually disperse or evaporate.)

'Why do they excite you so?' asked Robert.

'They rekindle a bit of reverence for the unknown.'

'Why is that important?'

'Humility is in short supply.' Robert looked down. There below us was a completely symmetrical and utterly majestic corn circle.

'It's immense!' Robert was dumbfounded. It helps so much when we can experience normal or paranormal phenomena with our own eyes – as long as we trust what we *see* rather than smothering it with the safety of what we prefer to *think*. From that day forth Robert never wavered in his belief. He now knew that the Government's and media's hoaxers were not responsible for most of the corn circles.

This year, 1996 midsummer, the corn-circle makers have given us their biggest masterpiece yet: a pictogram of over a thousand yards in diameter has just manifested in Oxfordshire. It's as if they're trying to tell us to look beyond government propaganda and cosy denial, for it would need an exceptionally disciplined army to make an intricate design on that gigantic scale in three and a half hours of midsummer darkness. No Englishman works that hard for nothing!

The good news is that every corn circle that has manifested has been dated and catalogued. This will allow us to re-examine the makers' handiwork in the years to come, once we have expanded our awareness, and from their dates understand the message or story they are trying to tell us. A story of unity and oneness, I'll warrant! – each and every one of us linked not only to each other and all living things but also to every star, planet, galaxy and millions of universes, simply teaming with various life forms, crying out for the preservation of our cosmic village. But when will we have the humility to hear?

Still Nearer to the Unknown

The telephone rang.

'Aid call here. Robert has pressed his beeper.' I came into Robert's study to find him unconscious, a sickly blue colour and sweating profusely. I rang the ambulance and Dr Marien, our local GP. Robert's determined, rallying heart was inevitably winding down, and in 1993 we began our regular ambulance journeys to King Edward VII Hospital in Midhurst, thankfully only a few miles up the road.

Dr Marien and Dr Gabe, the heart specialist, both thought Robert was too frail for a heart transplant. Nobody had expected him to live fourteen years after his stroke. Will-power and hands-on healing can give us many extra years but cannot, alas, deliver immortality so, with these frequent brushes with death, our meetings with that black winged horseman inevitably grew more intimate. So much so that eventually we were both able to laugh, once he was tucked up in hospital all safe and sound.

In 1994 Dr Marien warned me that Robert should no longer climb the stairs. Explaining this to Robert was tricky and he put up great resistance. 'It's not that you can't climb the stairs but the Manor's old staircase can't withstand your weight.' Robert's twice-daily twenty-stone heave-hos had made it seriously rickety. I demonstrated the decrepit wobbliness of the banisters.

One night, shortly after midnight, having tucked Robert in his new bedroom in the drawing room and kissed him goodnight, I went upstairs to bed. (I slept upstairs after I'd been thrown out of Robert's bed by Lovely, but I knew my place: computer, Lovely, then the wife.)

I was naked and just about to get into bed when the phone rang. It was Robert's aid call. My heart thumped because I didn't want to find Robert a ghastly pale purplish green, not breathing and bathed in cold sweat yet again. Those occasions made me feel grossly impotent. Time

245

and time again, I had pleaded with Dr Marien to teach me what to do, but was told, 'Each time it's different, so it's best just to call me.' Admittedly he was always round within five or ten minutes, but how those few minutes could drag!

I hurried downstairs and there was Robert, sitting up, wide-awake and alert. 'There's someone in the house.'

'How d'you know?'

'A great banging at the back door.' We both heard it then. It seemed pretty big and angry, whatever it was.

Robert perused my nakedness. 'You'd better dress first.' On opening the front door on my way upstairs to let Lovely out I was appalled to find a bedraggled Cuckoo, quivering in a pool of blood on the doorstep. I swept her into my arms and ran through to the kitchen to look at her wounds and clean them up as best I could.

I found a great many pointed puncture marks around her throat. I couldn't recall witnessing anything like them before. At that moment the back door rattled again, violently. 'What's the hell's going on?' shouted a bemused Robert, for he was never frightened. Oddly enough, neither am I – except for crowds, heights and performances.

We have a rather primitive, if somewhat camp, cat-flap made out of gold velvet and that particular night I found blood splashed over it, the floor tiles and the kitchen door – positively ghoulish!

I called my friend Bob, and, as usual, he came down immediately.

'It must be a rogue fox.'

'Come on, Bob, what kind of fox attacks cat flaps?'

Next morning the vet was as mystified as we were.

'Funny puncture marks, those.' He wouldn't commit himself as to what might have caused them. Whisperings of big-cat sightings had been around for some time, but I had ignored them, believing them to be pure fantasy. (Please note: just as sceptical as the rest of you!) Great paw marks twice Lovely's size had been seen down at the spring by various people, but not by me – therefore they didn't exist! One of the monks claimed he had been chased by some such creature. Naturally I didn't believe a word of *that*. Coming from the asphalt jungle, as most of my so-called 'forest monk' neighbours do, I presumed he had mistaken whatever it was for a rather large tom cat.

At around midnight, roughly ten days later, Batty, Cuckoo's daughter and the smallest Yorkshire terrier, screamed a bloodcurdling scream from the direction of the woodland. I ran hell for leather, naked as the day I was born. In the dark distance I thought I saw an alien shape take one look at me drop its prey, poor shocked Batty, and slope off into the woods. (Doesn't say much for my nakedness.)

Batty was in a real mess. Returning to the kitchen I wondered why I had been so cavalier as to allow the dogs the freedom to wander where they pleased after Cuckoo's gruesome attack. The answer was that I hadn't believed that wild cats were roaming free in the Home Counties. That was, until I caught sight of the cat-flap. There had been another kitchen-door attack, and that particular night the camp golden velvet had done a magnificent job, for there, plain as can be, was an imprint on the velvet of toothmarks the size of Lovely's jaw. Batty's puncture marks were deeper than Cuckoo's and it seemed as if her innards were seeping out through the holes. I made a bandage out of a ripped pillow case, wrapped her up tight and took her down to the emergency vet, with the velvet catflap as my proof.

Next morning various vets gathered together to study Batty's wounds, all scratching their heads. Then I produced the cat-flap.

'It's not a fox ... It's not a cat ... It's not a dog ... It's not a badger.' they said.

'A werewolf? They looked at me. 'A swooping eagle?'

They were not amused.

'They're the toothmarks of a very large cat,' said one of them. 'But what puzzles me is why, on both occasions, he chose not to go for the kill.' This puzzled me too ... Nah ... It couldn't have been a wild cat.

Next morning I had to go to London for an early appointment with my editor. Driving past Bob and Margaret's farm at seven a.m., I saw a sight that will remain with me for the rest of my days. A large jet-black cat stood high on the bank beside the lane. I stifled a gasp of wonder as the sun beamed its early-morning light across its sleek and glossy back. I stopped the car. How bright-eyed and bushy-tailed he was, positively shimmering with health! Roughly the size of Lovely, I'd say, but with enormous paws, quite out of proportion with the rest of him. His tail was almost twice as long as his body, held straight out with no curl. His face seemed square from my angle, with pointed, erect ears. Without turning once in my direction, this majestic being clambered down and across the lane with hips rolling to an exotic rhythm, before leaping up the bank on the other side and out of sight.

'I saw him! I saw him!' I had returned home that same day to find Robert in the conservatory, now back to its former glory, having a late lunch with a friend, Francis Macnamara.

'Saw what?'

'The wild cat. It's a panther!' Before I had even finished my description of the beast, great clouds of disbelief wafted towards me. Yet how could I blame them when only two days ago I had disbelieved the vets' wild-cat theory? But I was lucky this time because in the *Daily Mail*, the very next day, there was a perfect picture of a wild panther that had been sighted near Watlington in Oxfordshire. When I showed the photo to Robert he had to confess that it looked exactly like what I had described the previous day.

My theory? In the sixties and seventies wealthy rock stars and the like thought it chic to own exotic wild cats. In the late seventies the new animal licensing laws turned off a great percentage of these wild-cat owners, so with a hippie gesture of 'Peace, man, I'll set you free!' many were left to fend for themselves in the English countryside and have been cross-breeding most successfully ever since.

These English wild cats are profoundly canny, nocturnal creatures and, with little reason to trust humanity, have developed an existence of more than effective camouflage. They live mostly in trees and are perfectly happy to dine on rabbit, of which there is no shortage, for Chithurst sits in a sea of it. I presume my panther went to feast on both Batty and Cuckoo only to discover that their smell and response was profoundly unrabbitish. Perhaps it had been the Yorkies' cantankerously fearsome yapping that had delivered them their escape. It could be that my panther had been domesticated to such a degree that dogs were once his mates and, yearning to recapture the good old days, he had tried to befriend both Cuckoo and Batty as they entered their cat-flap, getting short shrift in the process. Perhaps, even, Cuckoo and Batty had attacked *him*. It was Robert who heard him first, and Robert who believed the last!

Deadlines and Lifelines

as Robert intent on death in Venice? In September 1994, even though he had just returned from yet another trip to hospital, he refused to listen to anyone's advice and stubbornly insisted we take a planned trip to Venice with our friends Kate Ganz and Mary Wesley. Venice is fine maybe, for lovers but it's hopeless for wheelchairs. Robert, though, would have none of it and, having no wish to be a party-pooper, I conceded defeat and off we went.

I won the first round as soon as we arrived at Venice airport, for Robert couldn't get on to the water taxi that was to take us across the Giudecca Canal to our apartment. He huffed and puffed, shaking off numerous men who tried to help him, for both he and I knew the impossibility of trying to lift a paralysed man of twenty stone – especially a proud one. We went the long way round by car, which cost an arm and a leg.

Another journey that cost an arm and a leg springs to mind. Robert was driving home from Bibendum one afternoon, after a slap-up feast, when steam started to spew forth from the bonnet of his new Mercedes. Convinced that the problem was easily solved, he parked the car on Putney High Street, outside the station, and waddled round in his old mac to rummage about under the bonnet.

'Can I assist you, sir?' Robert reappeared to find a smartly dressed young man.

'All's well. I'll just start up the engine.'

'I'll do that for you, sir.' In he jumped with another chap and off they sped, leaving Robert, in an old mac with no money or identification, alone in Putney High Street.

He hobbled to the pavement and began to ask passers-by for help.

Every single person walked around him, thinking, perhaps, that he was a down-and-out. For fifteen minutes he tried to get just one person to give him the time of day. Finally his heart lifted as a copper appeared around the corner. 'Excuse me.'

'Go home. You're drunk!'

'No! I'm—'

'I said, go home!' Frightened – frantic, even – by this time, Robert hobbled his paralysed twenty stone into Putney High Street and stood in the midst of the traffic with his one working arm stretched heavenwards. A taxi was left no alternative but to skid to a standstill or drive right over him. The driver must have seen his utter exhaustion.

'Please take me home.'

'Where to?'

'Sussex.'

'Sussex!'

'Yes. How much?'

'Near a hundred quid.'

'Let's go.'

When Robert arrived home he went straight to bed. I peeped round the door later that night to find he had been weeping – an almost unheard-of happening.

'I'm not sorry for myself, just for the whole human race. What will happen to us all?'

The Venice holiday turned out just as I had prophesied, with Robert unable to go anywhere due to the endless bridges and the depth of the boats. It was made almost bearable thanks to one watering-hole that Robert could get to without tremendous effort, and the company of Kate and Mary.

Over the years Mary's devotion to Robert had been stalwart and steadfast and I love her dearly for that. To watch her assist me with the wheelchair as we scaled impossible hurdles, you'd think she was sixteen not eighty-four. We were both determined to get Robert to St Mark's Square on the last day, but little square was to be seen, only the rounded bottoms of overfed tourists. Death in Venice did not materialise, but the gigantic energy and effort expended was soon to take its toll.

The day after our return from Venice, the walnut tree – my two-fold symbol representing Robert's life miracle and us being at Chithurst – was back on its side, having stood straight and strong for seven years. How it happened is a mystery, for there had been no great wind. Robert saw it as he wandered out of the back door to have a pee, lying there all forlorn like a beached whale. I'll never forget the look he gave me. I knew then that his time was running out.

Two days later he was back in hospital. I could tell that he was getting tired. Lying there on his pillow, his vivid blue eyes were dulled now, revealing the lack of will to fight on.

'Are you going to try and winch up the walnut again?'

'It's already been done. I've secured the steel ropes in cement so it can never fall down again.'

'If the walnut can do it, so can I! Get me a cement heart!' He gave me a testing glance. 'Where's my wine?' Robert couldn't go too long without a tipple or two – and why should he? There wasn't much left for him to enjoy.

In October joy came softly. Robert was out of hospital once more and Tomcat was getting wed to a lass called Fifi Mercer. She was the perfect wife for him. Beautiful, sexy, strong, upright, devoted yet her own woman. Fifi is a winner.

The wedding was at Marlborough Register Office on a particularly beautiful, crisp, sunny October day. Only Fifi's mother, Jill Mercer, her sister Yasmin, Robert and I were present. Nothing could have been better. There was no pomp, no show, no bullshit, just a lot of wonder and love. That was the last time Robert went out and about, for he had put every last drop of will-power into attending Tomcat's great day.

In November he was back in hospital. His heart had now gone into failure. The main valve had become so worn it was unable to pump any more. He was given a mass of pills to be taken three times daily.

'If I forget to take them I'm a goner.'

'Shall I administer them for you?'

'No!' I shouldn't have asked. He wanted to be in charge of his exit.

Robert was still determined to have as many projects on the go as possible, He never wanted word of his illness to leak out, because he assumed that the producers would take the projects from him. This made it doubly hard for me: it's cruel enough to witness one's beloved repeatedly in heart failure, but to be forbidden to share the pain with anyone, even to the point of having to make light of it with Tomcat and Robert's elder son, Ben, sapped all my remaining strength. Having to lie endlessly tended to damage my self-respect.

He had his computer brought into the hospital every time. He was still fighting deadlines, was Robert, several at once, right up to his dying day! Why did he do that? Money? Pride? Greed? Or did he take glee in beating the producers at their own game? I believe it was all about hiding from reality. Perhaps, for him, deadlines were lifelines, for living life is so much harder than working hard, and juggling secret deadlines is empowering.

Robert had been writing the life of Richard Nixon for David Frost. He was excited and intrigued by Nixon's complex character and took to the project like a duck to water. There was a time when Robert was working on the Buddha and Nixon simultaneously and I always knew at lunchtime which one he had been sweating over that morning. If he was in a thunderous mood, it was Buddha, and if there was a twinkle in his eye you could bet your bottom dollar it was Nixon. I hope Nixon knows that!

Home Box Office, who were making *Nixon* with Frost's Parradine company, were very enthusiastic about Robert's scripts. At the beginning of 1995 we received a fax from them saying how thrilled they all were with them and how they were going to invite us both over to New York in April of the publicity launch. Did I detect a tiny bit of colour, called 'belief in oneself', return to those once always ruddy cheeks?

A couple of weeks later we received another fax from Home Box Office, telling us that Oliver Stone had read Robert's scripts but had decided to do his own version with Anthony Hopkins playing Nixon. How could I protect Robert from this brutal news? The answer was, I couldn't. I knew it would be his death warrant. When I handed Robert the fax he went a ghastly ashen white, which remained with him to the end.

David Frost galloped off on his white charger to salvage the project, but failed. I don't believe any of them understood that the collapse of *Nixon* had broken Robert's frail and worn-out heart.

Sitting with me at my shrine one evening, Robert suddenly said, 'My *Nixon* is good, you know.' It was, I'd read it. 'Tricky Dicky loved his wife, Pat, more than anything or anyone. For a writer, Nixon is an absorbing beast, for the hero and villain in him are so spectacularly balanced. Yet only Pat really understood him.' He then beckoned me over for a snuggle.

'Not at the shrine, Robert!'

'If not smack in the face of God, then where?'

The End is always a New Beginning

February 20 1995 was a Monday. The night before, something had told me it was to be Robert's last day, but he had yet to mention funeral plans and the like. His reticence in talking of death meant that I left it to him to choose the moment.

At lunchtime on that Monday he was a little grumpy that his granddaughter, Rosie (Sally's daughter), hadn't shown up over the weekend. He shook his head and looked around his beloved conservatory. 'If nothing else, at least we can say we left behind one of the most beautiful rooms on earth. Aren't we lucky?' Praise indeed, considering the trail of conservatories he had scattered in his wake.

Carolyn, our treasured girl Friday who had been with us for six years, appeared with our lunch. My thoughts drifted out towards the woods, and I began to ponder the fact that I hadn't seen a deer for some time. Robert frequently picked up my thoughts, but with an uncanny accuracy during his last month.

'D'you remember when I saw the deer outside this window?' he asked, tucking into his latest fad, a slimy black eel, which Carolyn had set before him. He had once grumbled that he had never seen a single deer during our first four years at Chithurst. I explained how tricky it was, deer-spotting from one's bedroom with the TV blaring. He gave me a look and from then on took his afternoon snooze in the conservatory.

Hey presto! A deer bounded down across the rockery and, once he arrived on the bank beside the conservatory, posed for Robert, beautifully for quite some moments. It had made Robert's week ecstatic.

'I don't think I'll ever see another one.' As he finished his second eel, he regarded me with a look I had never encountered before. 'Do you?' Was he inviting me to challenge his immortality for the first time? I decided to challenge him anyway, invitation or not.

254

'You tell me, Robert.' I'd finally done it. Crudely, perhaps, but I had done it.

He thought a moment. 'No ... I'll never see another one.'

'How do you feel about that?'

'About dying, you mean?'

'Moving on, anyway.' I had him on the hook and I was damned if I was going to let him go. He heaved a might sigh and settled back in his chair, oil from the eel dripping down his chin. I mopped it up.

'Don't take me to that horridbull place to get all made up – horridbull! I want to stay in my bedroom and go straight into the croquet lawn.' As an afterthought, 'Oh! A cardboard coffin.'

We'd once had another conversation, many moons ago, about how he wanted to be put on a pyre on the back lawn beside our favourite apple tree. I thought this would be a mistake because I was most partial to the old apple tree and was concerned that his great bulk might take not only the apple tree but the whole of Chithurst Manor along with it.

'Then put my pyre in the centre of the croquet lawn.' This made me just as nervous because it would interfere with my croquet: whenever I was aiming for the winning post, I'd remember Robert on his bonfire and miss the shot.

As it turned out we weren't allowed to burn him on a pyre, so we were told, but later I discovered we had been misinformed. I was most sad about that. Burial, however, on one's own property is allowed, as long as you inform the water authorities.

'Then put me at the top end of the croquet lawn facing my favourite view of the house.' Chithurst's many ghosts are not due solely to its antiquity, powerful energies and ley lines running through: it is also sandwiched between two graveyards. Robert's chosen resting place had nothing but an old iron fence to separate him from the overflow graveyard of St Mary's Church, built on a pagan hill of dead bodies. If I ever had to leave Chithurst – and pray God that I don't – I could give over that piece of land to the Church so that Robert was in hallowed ground. He must have gathered my thoughts.

'*But I am not a Christian!*' He bellowed this in the direction of the Buddhist monastery, though he was certainly no Buddhist either! That at least we had in common: no religion.

'Do you want a big funeral?'

'No! Tiny. Everyone to get pissed on champagne – you, Bob and Andy to dig the grave.'

'What about a headstone?'

'None!'

'But you must have *something*.'

He shrugged. 'OK, then. Just "Robert Bolt".'

'No Oxton? [his second name] Playwright – date?'

'No, just Robert Bolt – but make it a BIG Robert Bolt!' He was implacably sure about what he wanted. He looked overjoyed that the weight of decision was finally lifted. 'Come here.' I went to sit next to him and he took me in his good arm.

'None of this rubbish really matters, for nothing can ever separate you and me. Nothing.'

'Those don't sound like the words of an atheist.'

'Now don't start!'

I grabbed him by the collar of his striped nightie. '*When you pop off you bloody well give me proof that I'm right and you're wrong*!'

He tossed me another foreign look as if he would if it were so. 'I'm going to lie down. Come to me after you've walked the dogs'. Just as I was going out the back door I heard him shout. 'I hate Peter Hall!' He had continued to vocalise his hatred of Peter Hall ever since the National Theatre incident. I wished he wouldn't because it gave the silly chap too much importance and it was alien to Robert's nature to hate anyone.

'Don't die hating. It's bad for your health!'

I went down for a quiet moment at the spring, for it had the knack of lifting me to the heart. Absorbed in the feminine shapes bubbling up like two eternal nipples and a belly button re-creating themselves through the centuries, I realised that I was at last beginning to recapture glimpses of my childhood. Those all-seeing first five years of childhood that had faded with conditioning and the brutality of the school system. Life is all about loss, gain and occasionally recapture. Was I about to lose that which I loved the most, just as I was at last able to recapture those precious innocent glimmers of childhood once more? All at once I knew through all the pain, past, present and still to come, I must try to remain lifted to the heart.

I popped in to see Bob and Margaret and told them of Robert's wishes to be buried in the garden. Bob said he'd be honoured to be one of the grave diggers. 'And I'll check with the Water Board that it's OK.' Bob knew without my telling him that the end was near.

On returning home, I found Robert still asleep so I crept upstairs to prepare my talk on alternative medicine, which I had to deliver the following evening. I was fearfully intimidated by the idea of speaking at the House of Lords, especially since my knowledge of such matters was limited and I had tried hard without success to wriggle out of it on two occasions.

Robert's downstairs bedroom was painted rich vermilion red with a gold ceiling and my initials painted in gold leaf around the cornice, in true Tudor (and brother Chuzzer) tradition. After working on my talk for an hour or so, I went downstairs to see Robert. His king-size bed and great oak bedhead, with a hand-carved bull at one end, gave me the distinct impression I was entering the throne room of Old King Cole. It wasn't just the wife hallucinating either, for whenever I brought guests into his room they would remark on a rare feeling of a benign contentment.

Robert's eyes challenged mine. 'Have you decided to talk at the House of Lords tomorrow?'

'I can't get out of it.' He patted my *tiny* place beside him next to Lovely on the bed. Bloomin' Lovely! For some reason, and indeed for the very first time in my life, I pushed her right off it. The look she gave me was equalled only by the forlorn, droopy, downcast eyes of Robert.

'Poor Lovely.' His lips went all puckered.

'Come back, Lovely. I'm sorry.' Back she came, pushing her great weight between us.

As usual Robert read my thoughts. 'Come a little closer and then I can cuddle you too.' I had to learn to be grateful for small mercies. There were times when I regretted sneaking off secretly to choose the bulky bitch.

I had been commissioned to write my first novel and had spent the past three months tripping out with my invented characters, an Irish family called the Macnamaras. Whether I was overly absorbed with my characters, or whether I was using them to comfort me and distract me through the dying process I don't know, but whatever the reason, I was hooked.

'You have the muse,' said Robert sagely. He kept repeating it, until I wanted to know more.

'What muse?'

'My muse. You were my muse and now I shall be yours.' He kissed me.

'I still don't understand.'

'I don't want you going to the House of Lords tomorrow.'

'Come with me then.' We listened to some Mozart, but I found it too emotional and went to make a cup of tea. As I put the kettle on the Aga something told me it was the last cup of tea Robert would drink. This was a spooky moment and I ran back to Robert, thrusting Lovely aside. 'Let's talk!'

'What about?' He brought, from the depths of his being, all the wisdom a life fight such as his can throw up. 'I have no fear now. None at all. All is fine.' He paused. 'I love you, and I'll do what you request ... but don't be disappointed if you hear nothing.' He meant giving me proof of life after death.

We watched the news and cuddled until ten thirty when I went up to wash my hair. I left him with Wren, our Burmese cat, asleep on his chest as usual.

'Come back soon.'

'Can I sleep with you tonight?'

'Ask Lovely.'

When I returned, only five minutes later, with a towel around my head, Robert was in exactly the same position, but he had stopped breathing. Wren was still in the same position on his chest as when I had left. All was immersed in total peace. I felt fine because Robert was fine. I went over and cuddled up beside him with Lovely, Wren, Horrible (the tabby), Cuckoo and Oxton. Batty was upstairs on her perch. We all remained there for roughly half an hour, because I found the atmosphere intoxicating and wanted to remain embalmed in that uniquely special *something* for ever.

I'd have to admit to a feeling of loss at having missed his dying moment; greater honesty would doubtless expose feelings of frustration, perhaps even remorse, at being absent. How dare he toddle off without me? He knew what that meant to me, to be able to hold his hand as he passed through those thin veils of reality into other realms more real to him now. But I ticked myself off for being so selfish. I know that many choose to die privately, like cats. They have a strong desire to relieve their loved ones of any responsibility and perform the exit process on their tod . . . I'll probably do the same myself.

I wrenched myself away to telephone Bob. We decided it wouldn't be too selfish of me to keep Robert to myself until morning. Once the doctor had been informed, the family members would rightfully follow and this magic time would be over. I did, however, call my dear friends Kittisaro, Randy Weinberg and his nun, now wife, Mary. I was so fortunate that they were there at that time because they rarely were. They arrived almost immediately and we lit candles, burned incense, prayed to Jesus, Mary, Buddha, Mother Mira, Ganesh, Tara, Kense Rinpoche, Kwan Yin, the Black Madonna and all the powerful light-giving effigies from my shrine in the conservatory. And so it was that we chanted and prayed for the best part of a special night.

In the morning I made a call to a doctor friend to ask him how to preserve the body. He instructed me to put cotton wool up all orifices and keep the windows open. Luckily it was a cold February so I would have no problems with Robert decomposing in the next week or so. The only hiccup was that Dr Marien was away and therefore the doctor who came to pronounce him dead was a bit suspicious that I had waited ten hours before calling her.

'We'll be taking him away to do an autopsy.'

'Over my dead body!' I suggested she get all the necessary information from Robert's specialist, Dr Gabe. As she was leaving, she turned 'I'll be back soon,' she said suspiciously.

'There's no reason. My husband isn't leaving his home.'

It was fascinating to observe the animals steadfastly refusing to leave the bed for those next three days. I couldn't pull Lovely off for love or money, or indeed the others. None of us were fretting, just happy to be hanging loose around the body. I knew the animals wouldn't move while the spirit was still close, and they didn't – until the third day, that is. Perhaps the Bible had that bit right, at least. 'On the third day he rose again from the dead.' It took all those three days for the animals to be weaned and for Robert's buoyant spirit to rise up out of his tired old body. I stroked his leg in wonder. That same leg, like an oak tree, had lugged twenty stone around for fourteen years all on its own. I knelt down to pay it some well-earned homage. How innocent he smelt, how pure – so sweet! Robert's three children, Ben, Jo-Jo and

259

Tomcat arrived, and a great feeling of peace reigned over Chithurst.

It didn't take long for the press to get wind of his death. They were sniffing round, wanting to know at which church the funeral would be held. Because of my need to carry out his death wishes to the letter, I was left no choice but to stop them in their tracks. I pre-empted any crap they might invent by writing my own article. If I had not, as sure as eggs are eggs, they would have destroyed his death just as they had attempted to destroy both our lives.

In my diary, I keep a note of the Chithurst ghosts. To recount all their tales would be another book, but there is one story most appropriate to Robert's burial. Three years previously Rosie, Robert's granddaughter, aged fourteen, had been staying with a Bedales friend in the top room facing the croquet lawn. I had already noted that my ghosts (all very friendly!) became more active when pubescent girls were staying in the house.

At two o'clock one morning Rosie shook me awake urgently. 'Come upstairs, Sarah! Quickly!' She was in a bit of a state, so up I went. From her window facing the croquet lawn with nothing but woodland and fields beyond, we could hear the eerie sound of a grave being dug. Its relentless rhythm was unmistakable. The noise had an out-of-this-world, almost cosmic ring to it. Usually I'd have gone into the night to investigate without a second thought, but on this occasion I wasn't prepared to. We listened to spades crunching against chalky lumps for about a quarter of an hour until the girls lost interest. I returned to bed.

Early next morning I asked Bob to accompany me to the west-facing graveyard. Nothing to be seen. We searched the whole area, but could detect no newly dug earth. It was most strange, for all three of us had certainly heard it. Even while digging Robert's grave I never connected the sounds. Only a week after we buried him did I make the connection. Time isn't linear.

My first year without Robert was up on 20 February 1996. I never went into mourning because I felt nothing but joy at having Robert all around me, free of his wretched body's endless pain. I set out *trying* to make our life together as beautiful as I could the second time around, but once we reached Chithurst, the last seven years simply flopped into harmony, rendering the need to *try* redundant – it simply *was*, the beautiful becoming more so day by day. We were able to grow into almost one being where no words needed to be spoken.

The morning after Robert's death, Bob came up to see me, full of embarrassment, and uncharacteristically he kept clearing his throat. He had taught science at school and had always thought there was a logical explanation for everything – even to the point of corn circles probably being made by badgers mating (well, perhaps not quite!). He stood there, quite flushed, moving from one foot to the other.

'I was lying on the bed harmlessly day-dreaming when suddenly Robert appeared – just like that. I wasn't dreaming for I wasn't asleep ... In fact, I was wide awake. The ... vision ... or whatever was both very ordinary and like nothing I had ever experienced before.' He stopped as if he couldn't continue. 'Don't laugh.'

'Is that what I'm doing?'

With fresh courage he fought on with his tale. 'I was standing by the river, looking up at the bank next to the conservatory, when Robert came bounding down the garden across the rockery towards the bank and stood there, as if briefly poised in time. [Sounded like Robert's deer to me!] He was young again, really strong – not the type I'd want to mess with. He had no beard and was free of his stroke—' Bob caught my eye and cleared his throat again. 'Did he have a beard when you met him?'

'No, he didn't, now I come to think of it.'

'Anyway he was dancing, literally leaping from foot to foot with glee. Around his head was an aura of rainbows – I only say rainbows because I don't know how else to describe the colours around him, because they were colours not of this world. But the top arch of all was close to a shimmering gold. Yes, really. He gave me the impression he felt regret at having wasted so much time, as if slightly impatient at his mistake and with a restless need to get on with things. Then, quite out of the blue, he said, "Sarah's right and I am wrong!"'

THE END is always a new beginning.